Grace
for Effectual Ministry

Grace for Effectual Ministry
ISBN: 978-0-929400-05-1

Copyright © 2011 by Guy Duininck

Published by Master's Touch Publishing Company
Box 35543
Tulsa, OK 74153 USA

Printed in the United States of America

Table of Contents

Preface

In 1983, my interest was drawn to the subject of grace. As I studied the Word of God, I became increasingly aware that many New Testament scriptures about grace did not concern the grace by which sinners are saved. I also realized that many of those scriptures made no sense at all if the word "grace" always meant, "God's unmerited favor." Believing that the Holy Spirit was guiding me, I decided to embark on a more thorough study.

Early in my study, I identified three primary New Testament graces. Most familiar to me was Saving Grace — the mercy of God and the consequent working of His power available to all sinners by which they can be saved. Another grace, somewhat familiar to me, was Strengthening Grace — the mighty help of God and of the Lord Jesus available to all believers by which they can be inwardly fortified, enabled to stand strong in tests and trials, and empowered to run their races and do their work. A third grace, less familiar to me, was Ministry Grace — the diverse supernatural talents, ministry abilities, spiritual giftings that God stewards to different members of the body of Christ by which they are enabled to accomplish the unique ministries they are called to and placed in the body of Christ to do.

Wanting to learn more about Strengthening Grace and Ministry Grace, I began to search for teaching on these subjects. I enquired in Christian book stores, looked through the library at a large Christian university, and perused many Bible commentaries only to discover that there was little written about these less familiar New Testament graces. Because of the lack of teaching available and the strong inward impression I had that understanding these graces was critical to the body of Christ, I decided to continue my study and write a book about each; composing a Grace Trilogy.

My purpose for writing *Grace for Effectual Ministry* is to set forth for believers and ministers comprehensive understanding of how, in the New Testament, God calls men and women to unique ministries, strategically places them into the body of Christ, and stewards unique grace-gifts to them, enabling them to serve effectively in their unique ministries. The revelation contained in this book will help believers to not be "ignorant of spirituals" and will greatly assist the body of Christ in "being fruitful in every good work."

It is my prayer that *Grace for Effectual Ministry* will enrich your spiritual understanding and help you locate and become effective in the unique and important ministry to which God has called you and for which He has graced you. Enjoy as you learn. And may the grace of God be with you.

Introduction

The Mystery of Grace

In his letter to the Colossians, Paul apprised them of his continual prayers for them. He wrote,

"For this reason we also, from the day we heard of it, have not ceased to pray and make [special] request for you, [asking] that you may be filled with the full (deep and clear) knowledge of His will in all spiritual wisdom [that is, in comprehensive insight into the ways and purposes of God] and in understanding and discernment of spiritual things — That you may walk (live and conduct yourselves) in a manner worthy of the Lord, fully pleasing to Him and desiring to please Him in all things, bearing fruit in every good work..."

Colossians 1:9-10 Amp

Paul began praying intently for the Colossian believers after he heard that they had embraced the gospel and come into the faith. His constant prayer was that they would be filled with the knowledge of God's will — filled with all wisdom and spiritual understanding. His deep desire was that they would have "comprehensive insight into the ways and purposes of God." The answer to Paul's prayers would mean that these believers could please God with their lives and bear much fruit in the good works He had called them to.

In his unceasing prayer for the Colossians, Paul vocalized God's desire for believers in every place and in every generation. God desires that believers be filled with the knowledge of His will and have comprehensive insight into His ways. Just as natural understanding

enables people to be successful in the natural life, so spiritual understanding enables believers to be effective in spiritual life. When believers are fully filled with spiritual understanding, they will be able to
fulfill the will of God.

Throughout this study, we will learn that one of the primary ways
God accomplishes His purposes on earth is by calling people into His
kingdom, setting them into the body of Christ, stewarding unique
ministry graces to them and sending them forth to accomplish their
unique ministries. Growing in knowledge and spiritual understanding concerning this significant truth will help believers, ministers, and
churches to be much more fruitful.

Knowledge is the Starting Place

A few years ago, I spent an evening praying with a pastor and his
staff. As we prayed together, the Holy Spirit spoke these words over
and over again in my heart, "Knowledge is the starting place for all the
will of God."

It is true, of course, that in order to serve God effectively, believers
must be willing and zealous. In his letter to the Romans, Paul encouraged believers to be "fervent in spirit; serving the Lord" [Rom. 12:11].
The qualities of willingness and zeal, although essential, do not guarantee effective service. Only when these qualities are yoked together
with knowledge and spiritual understanding can believers serve effectively and bear much fruit for the Lord.

Paul's words to the Romans concerning the religious Jews reveal
the fruitlessness of zeal without knowledge. He said,

> *"For I bear them record that they have a zeal of God, but not accord-*
> *ing to knowledge. For they being ignorant of God's righteousness,*
> *and going about to establish their own righteousness, have not sub-*
> *mitted themselves unto the righteousness of God."*
>
> *Romans 10:2-3*

The Amplified Bible renders Paul's words this way,

*"...they have a certain zeal and enthusiasm for God, but it is not
enlightened and according to correct and vital knowledge."*
                                                    Romans 10:2 Amp

Although the Jewish people had a zeal and enthusiasm for God,
they failed to enter into His purposes because they were "not enlightened...according to correct and vital knowledge." A forfeiture of God's
will is the certain outcome of any spiritual endeavor when zeal is not
accompanied by correct and vital knowledge.

Zeal could be likened to the water in a river and knowledge likened to the river's banks. Without banks the river's water will simply
spread out on the ground, soak into the earth, and disappear. With
solid banks, on the other hand, the river's water will be contained
and have force and direction. Zealous believers who lack knowledge
are like rivers without banks. Their efforts are not guided in a clear
way, they have no force or direction, and they produce little. Believers whose zeal is channeled by knowledge, on the other hand, are like
mighty rivers with solid banks. They flow steadily, move with direction, generate power, and accomplish much good work.

Zeal could also be likened to the fuel that powers a car's engine
and knowledge likened to the car's transmission. When the engine
burns fuel, the car makes noise, produces heat and smoke, and sounds
impressive. The car goes nowhere, however, if there is no transmission
to deliver the power of the engine to the wheels. So, too, believers who
are full of zeal, but have no knowledge to transmit their zeal into effective service might make noise, produce smoke, and sound impressive,
but will accomplish very little in terms of consistent, fruitful work for
the Lord.

Zeal could also be likened to a fire and knowledge to a fireplace.
Without a fireplace, a fire cannot be harnessed for power-production
and may even be destructive. It may burn hot for a season, but eventually it simply burns itself out. So too, zeal that is not burning in the
"fireplace" of knowledge produces little, can actually cause trouble,
but often simply burns itself out. Just as a fireplace harnesses the fire
so that it can accomplish something positive and perpetual, so knowl-

edge harnesses zeal so that something positive and ongoing can be accomplished for the kingdom of God.

Like the banks of a river, the transmission of a car, and a fireplace, knowledge channels, transmits, and harnesses zeal for effective service. Zealous, knowledgeable believers will minister much more effectively and bear much more fruit than zealous, ignorant believers.

Don't be Ignorant of Spirituals

In his first letter to the Corinthian church, Paul wrote,

"Now concerning spiritual gifts, brethren, I would not have you ignorant."

I Corinthians 12:1

This scripture quote is from the King James Bible. In the original text the word "gifts" is not present. Apparently, the men who prepared the King James Version of the Bible thought that adding the word "gifts" would bring clarity. Unfortunately, however, adding the word "gifts" leaves the impression that Paul was exhorting believers to not be ignorant about the gifts of the Spirit. Paul was referring to much more than the gifts of the Spirit, however, when he urged the Corinthians to not be ignorant of "spiritual gifts."

The single Greek word translated "spiritual gifts" in I Corinthians 12:1 is the word *pneumatikon.* This word literally means, "spirituals." A more accurate translation of Paul's words would be: "Now concerning spirituals, brethren, I don't want you to be ignorant."

The Corinthian believers were zealous of spirituals. In fact, Paul commended them for their zeal [I Cor. 14:12]. He did not want them to remain ignorant of spirituals, however, because then effective ministry would not occur and the plans of God would not be accomplished. To enlighten the Corinthian believers, Paul commenced three full chapters of teaching about spirituals.

Like the Corinthian believers of Paul's day, many present day believers are ignorant of spirituals. Their ignorance makes it difficult for them to cooperate with God and keeps them from being as effective as they could be. Only when believers are properly instructed in spirituals can they harness their zeal, serve skillfully, and bear much fruit for the kingdom of God.

Three New Testament Graces

When, at any time in history or at any place in the world, important spiritual truths are ignored or improperly taught, the church at that time and in that place will lack the knowledge it needs to be victorious in life and effective in service. Paul told the church at Thessalonica that he earnestly desired to see them that he might "perfect that which is lacking in your faith" [I Thess. 3:10]. Like many churches, this church was deficient in some areas of truth. When truths are missing over an extended period of time the church becomes unhealthy and not fully functional.

One important truth that has been absent and often incompletely taught or wrongly taught is the truth of grace. Although the word "grace" is familiar to almost every believer, an awareness and proper understanding of New Testament grace has been, at best, limited.

One reason the church is not familiar with the doctrine of grace is because the very simplistic definition "God's unmerited favor" has, for a long time, been attached to it. Although this definition can bring some light to the nature and purpose of grace, it certainly does not do justice to the incredible, manifold grace of God. In some ways, this definition has obscured a proper understanding of grace.

Another reason the church is not familiar with the doctrine of grace is that most believers and ministers are unaware that there are three primary and distinct New Testament graces. Before we begin to study Grace for Effectual Ministry, let's briefly consider the three primary graces of the New Testament.

Saving Grace

Most believers are familiar with Saving Grace. One of the most well known scriptures about this grace comes from Paul's epistle to the Ephesians. He wrote,

"For by grace are ye saved through faith; and that not of yourselves: it is the gift of God."

Ephesians 2:8

In the most doctrinal epistle of the New Testament, Paul wrote this about saving grace,

"But not as the offense, so also is the free gift. For if through the offense of one many be dead, much more the grace of God, and the gift by grace, which is by one man, Jesus Christ, hath abounded unto many."

Romans 5:15

Another clear scripture about saving grace is found in Paul's letter to Titus. He wrote,

"For the grace of God that bringeth salvation hath appeared to all men."

Titus 2:11

Saving grace is the life transforming power of God which, because of His mercy and "the great love wherewith He loved us," He made available to all sinners through faith in Jesus Christ.

Although saving grace is available because of the mercy of God, saving grace is not synonymous with mercy and is far more than unmerited favor. If God only felt gracious toward sinners, nothing life-changing would happen to them. If God only bestowed unmerited favor, sinners would only experience temporary, natural blessings. But because of the great love wherewith God loved the human race, He made a plan and sent a Man so that sinners could be "saved by grace through faith."

When sinners hear the gospel of Jesus Christ and respond in faith, calling upon the name of the Lord, the quickening power of God is released in them and they are saved by grace through faith. The result of the life impacting grace of God is that one's spiritual condition is instantly and radically affected. The moment they believe, they are delivered from Satan, from sin, and from death. They are circumcised in heart and made new creatures in Christ. They become children of God and inheritors of an eternal inheritance.

In that moment of faith when the grace of God is released, sinners are cleansed from sin. They are justified from all their unrighteousness and exonerated from the "handwriting of ordinances" that was against them. Their heart of stone is extricated and replaced with a heart of flesh. They are washed, cleansed, delivered, sanctified, justified, raised, born-again, adopted, and translated from darkness into God's marvelous light because of the grace of God.

All the wonderful realities of salvation, including the forgiveness of sins, the crucifixion of the old man, the imparting of righteousness, the new birth, the giving of the Spirit, the promise of eternal life, and many other wonderful things are summed up in the familiar words, "For by grace are ye saved through faith" [Eph. 2:8]. Saving grace, made available to all sinners because of the great love of God and the completed work of Christ, is completely efficacious to transform sinners into saints, lost into found, enemies into family, and dead men into living sons.

Strengthening Grace

A New Testament grace the church is somewhat familiar with is Strengthening Grace. This grace is the power of God and of the Lord Jesus available to all believers by which they can be fortified in their inner man, helped in times of need, and basically, inwardly enabled to "do all things." Strengthening grace is one aspect of the "exceeding greatness of his power to usward who believe" [Eph. 1:20].

The apostle Paul received a life changing revelation of this strengthening grace. In the midst of great hardship, Jesus revealed to him this mighty available power that was sufficient for every temptation, circumstance, demonic buffeting, and heavenly assignment. "My grace is sufficient," Jesus told Paul, "for my strength is made perfect in weakness." Jesus referred to His grace as sufficient strength in times of weakness. Paul referred to this grace as "the power of Christ resting upon [him]" [II Cor. 12:9].

Paul's revelation of strengthening grace produced such a revolution in his life that he began to rejoice in tests and trials. He said, "Therefore I take pleasure in infirmities, in reproaches, in necessities, in persecutions, in distresses for Christ's sake: for when I am weak, then am I strong" [II Cor. 12:10]. Writing to the Philippians, he declared, "I can do all things through Christ which strengtheneth me" [Phil. 4:13]. In another place, he testified that in the midst of great trouble, crushing pressure, and beyond-strength difficulties, he lived by grace [II Cor. 1:8-12]. Paul informed Timothy that at his first trial, the Lord stood with him and strengthened him [II Tim. 4:17].

Strengthening grace is not God's power that changes circumstances. It is not God's power that heals bodies. It is not God's power that fixes relationships. It is not God's power that calms the storm. It is not God's power that protects from external danger. Yes, all these things are manifestations of God's power, but they are not described by the word grace.

Strengthening grace is the power of God which He delivers to believers' inner man which makes them, "Ready for anything and equal to anything that comes through Him who infuses me with inner strength" [Phil. 4:13 Amp]. It is the in-fusion of God's might which makes believers mighty and, therefore, able to do mighty things. A divine saline solution from a divine source, once infused, strengthening grace becomes the internal strength of believers. This heavenly adrenaline enables them to overcome, to resist, to continue, to self-govern, to run, to walk, to work, and to never fall. An awareness of this available help of God may have inspired Jude to write, "Now unto Him who is able to keep us from falling" [Jude 24].

By strengthening grace, believers are internally reinforced with God's might so that they can prevail in tests, trials, and temptations [Js. 4:4-7]. They are enabled to be longsuffering with difficult people [Col. 1:11] and empowered to deal with demonic afflictions [I Pet. 5:6-

10]. They are fortified internally; made strong in the Lord and in the power of His might [Eph. 6:10; II Tim. 2:1]. They are strengthened with might by God's Spirit in their inner man [Eph. 3:16; II Cor. 4:16]. Grace is supernatural internal help in a time of need [Heb. 4:16]. Hearts can be established by this grace [Heb. 13:9]. And by this grace, believers stand [Rom. 5:2].

Paul prayed that the Ephesian believers would know "the exceeding greatness of his power to usward who believe [Eph. 1:19]. He prayed that they would "be strengthened with might by his Spirit in the inner man" [Eph. 3:16]. He prayed for the Colossians to be "filled with the knowledge of His will" so they would be "strengthened with all might, according to His glorious power" [Col. 1:11]. Paul exhorted Timothy to "be strong in the grace that is in Christ Jesus" [II Tim. 2:1]. He exhorted the Ephesian believers to "be strong in the Lord and in the power of His might" [Eph. 6:10]. Clearly, it is not God's will for believers to be weak, but to be strong.

One of the most significant ways God assists believers in being strong is by the available provision of strengthening grace. Both Peter and James, writing to believers, revealed that "God gives grace to the humble" [I Pet. 5:5; Js. 4:6]. Jesus said to Paul, "My grace is...for you." Strengthening grace is not automatic; it is available. It is like a stored commodity; stored in God and in Christ, but available to believers.

In order to receive strengthening grace, believers need to "submit yourselves, therefore, unto God. " They must wait upon the Lord, come boldly to the throne of grace, humble themselves under God's mighty hand, submit themselves to God, and partake at the altar of grace [Is. 40:29-31; Heb. 4:16; I Pet. 5:6; Js. 4:6-7; Heb. 13:9-10].

Ministry Grace

The New Testament grace the church is least familiar with is Ministry Grace. This grace is "manifold" — extremely diverse. Ministry graces are the unique endowments of ministry ability God stewards to individual believers which enable them to serve effectively in the unique ministries they are called to and placed in the body of Christ to do. When believers discover, cultivate, and use the unique ministry graces stewarded to them, they render effectual ministry as unique members of the body of Christ.

Paul often testified about his special endowment of ministry grace. He said, "According to the grace of God given unto me, I am a wise master-builder" [I Cor. 3:10]. He spoke of "the dispensation of the grace of God given to me" [Eph. 3:1]. He testified, "I laboured more abundantly than they all: yet not I, but the grace of God which was with me" [I Cor. 15:10]. Paul was very conscious of the grace entrusted to him which enabled him to be a unique minister and to do unique ministry work.

Ministry grace is mentioned all throughout the New Testament. Paul taught the believers in Rome that they had "gifts that differ according to the grace given" to them [Rom. 12:6]. He informed the believers in Ephesus that every man had received a grace for service [Eph. 4:7-8]. The apostle Peter exhorted believers to minister to each other with the gifts they had received as "good stewards of the manifold grace of God" [I Pet. 4:10].

The unique endowments of ministry grace God stewards to believers is based upon His calling and His placing of each believer in the body of Christ. Just as believers do not choose their callings or their places in the body, they also do not choose the varieties or measures of the ministry graces stewarded to them. Believers are responsible, however, to discover their callings, find their places in the body, locate their grace endowments, and become effective in their ministries.

Outline

Before we begin our study of ministry grace, I want to explain how I organized the teaching for this book. In general, the early chapters deal with the doctrine of Grace for Effectual Ministry and the later chapters deal with the practical applications of this doctrine. The teaching moves from principle to practical application; from doctrine to doing. The later chapters will be more meaningful if you grasp the doctrine taught in the earlier chapters.

In Section One, you will learn that the apostle Paul was very conscious of and dependent upon the unique ministry grace stewarded to him. Very often in his writings, he attributed his ministry calling and his effectiveness to his unique endowment of grace. When you note the frequency with which Paul cited the role of grace in his ministry and the frequency with which grace and ministry are associated in contemporary Christian teaching, you cannot help but wonder if we have missed something very important.

In Section Two, you will learn what Grace for Effectual Ministry is. You will learn that when Jesus ascended on high, He distributed grace-gifts to each of His servants. You will learn that ministry graces are special endowments for special tasks. You will learn that ministry graces are distinct varieties and different measures of God's ability entrusted to different members of the body of Christ. You will learn that ministry graces are unique spiritual talents which motivate and enable believers to fulfill a variety of ministries. You will learn that there is a significant relationship between where believers are placed in the body of Christ and how they are graced.

In Section Three, you will learn that the ministry graces stewarded to believers are extremely diverse. You will learn that there are manifold graces for manifold ministries. You will learn that the different varieties and diverse measures of ministry grace enable believers to be effectual in many different ministries. You will learn that the unique blending of graces make believers perfectly suited to their special callings.

In Sections Four and Five, you will learn about the many different ministries believers can be called to and graced for. You will learn about the five spiritual leadership ministries — apostle, prophet, evangelist, pastor, and teacher. You will learn about many other valid New Testament ministries like helps, exhortation, gifts of healings, showing mercy, ruling, working of miracles, teaching, and giving. Learning about these many different New Testament ministries will help you determine which specific ministry you are called to and graced for.

In Section Six, you will learn that personal preparation is absolutely essential for effectual ministry no matter which specific ministry you are called to and graced for. You will learn how to do the critical work of preparation so that you can serve the Lord effectively and consistently during your tenure on earth.

In Section Seven, you will learn how to discover your grace, how to cultivate your grace, and how to administer your grace. Finally, you will be challenged to take your place in the body of Christ, employ your grace, and fulfill your ministry.

Section One

Grace
In
Paul's Ministry

I was made a Minister
According to the gift of the grace of God given unto me
By the effectual working of His power

1

Have You Heard of My Grace?

The apostle Paul was the most outstanding and exemplary minister of the New Testament. Excepting the Lord Jesus, he had more spiritual insight, operated in a greater intensity of ministry, taught more profoundly, ministered more powerfully, and made a deeper impact for the kingdom of God than any other minister.

This man with profound spiritual understanding, substantial spiritual gifting, and extensive ministry experience referred often in his writings to his own ministry. Sometimes he did so in order to certify himself as a man with divine credibility. Sometimes he did so to respond to false accusations. Sometimes he did so simply because ministry was such a significant aspect of his life.

Paul boldly declared who he was in ministry. He claimed that he was specially chosen. He testified that he was a chief apostle. He declared that he was a preacher and a teacher of the Gentiles. He considered himself an able minister and wise master-builder. He stated that his labors in ministry surpassed the labors of other apostles.

Paul not only boldly declared who he was in ministry, however. He also revealed what made him who he was in ministry. From his written revelations about what made him a minister, what made him an apostle, and what made him effectual, there emerge valuable insights about New Testament ministry. Certainly, it was the design of God that Paul's inspired writings be recorded for the benefit of future generations of believers and ministers.

Paul's Consciousness of His Grace

It is striking how often Paul referred to the special grace given to him. He said it was a gift of grace that made him an effectual minister. He cited grace as the operative inworking ability which motivated him toward and equipped him for his unique work. By grace he was an apostle to the Gentiles. By grace he was a wise master-builder and laid spiritual foundations. By grace he labored abundantly. According to Paul, who he was in ministry and what he accomplished in ministry was the result of the gift of grace given to him.

The gift of grace that made Paul an apostle and an effectual minister was not saving grace or strengthening grace. Certainly, Paul was saved by grace, but saving grace did not make him an effectual minister. Certainly, Paul had access to the throne of grace, but strengthening grace did not make him an effectual minister. The grace that made Paul an apostle and an effectual minister was the unique endowment of ministry grace stewarded to him by God.

The Grace Given to Me

In the third chapter of Ephesians, Paul identified himself as a prisoner of Jesus Christ and referred to his grace with these words,

"For this cause I Paul, the prisoner of Jesus Christ for you Gentiles, If ye have heard of the dispensation of the grace of God which is given me to youward..."

Ephesians 3:1-2

Paul wondered if the Ephesians had heard about the grace of God given to him for their benefit. The Amplified Bible renders his words just that way. It says,

"Assuming that you have heard of the stewardship of God's grace... that was entrusted to me to dispense to you for your benefit..."

Ephesians 3:2 Amp

If, by the words, "the grace of God which is given me," Paul had been referring to saving grace, he would not have described it as something entrusted to his care to dispense to others for their benefit, but as something given to him for his own benefit. If, by the words, "the grace of God which is given me," Paul had been referring to strengthening grace, he would not have described it as something entrusted to him for the benefit of others, but as something available to him for his own times of need.

The grace Paul was referring to in Ephesians 3:1-2 was not saving grace or strengthening grace, but was that unique ministry grace stewarded to him by God which made him an apostle and enabled him to minister effectively. It was that special indwelling endowment of ministry ability which enabled him to fulfill his unique ministry calling. The grace Paul was referring to was ministry grace.

Just a few verses later, Paul again cited the essential role of grace in his own ministry. He wrote,

"Whereof I was made a minister, according to the gift of the grace of God given unto me by the effectual working of His power."
Ephesians 3:7

Paul said that he was made a minister "according to the gift of the grace of God given to [him]." Again, he was not referring to saving grace or strengthening grace. The grace he was referring to that made him a minister was, rather, the unique endowment of ministry grace God had entrusted to him.

Paul followed immediately with these words in Ephesians 3:8,

"Unto me...is this grace given, that I should preach among the Gentiles the unsearchable riches of Christ...."
Ephesians 3:8

Paul wrote in a very possessive way about his grace. He did not write, "unto me is grace given." He did not write, "unto me is a grace given." He did not write, "unto me is some grace given." He wrote, "unto me...is this grace given." The unique "this grace" given to Paul made him a minister. It enabled him to preach Christ powerfully, teach truth profoundly, and lead the church effectively as an apostle to the Gentiles.

In his first letter to the church at Corinth, Paul wrote,

"According to the grace of God which is given unto me, as a wise master builder, I have laid the foundation..."

I Corinthians 3:10

Notice that Paul did not write, "According to the grace of God...I have laid the foundation." He wrote, "According to the grace of God which is given unto me...I have laid the foundation." Again, Paul was referring to the very specific ministry grace stewarded to him.

Near the end of that same letter, Paul wrote,

"...his grace bestowed upon me was not in vain; but I laboured more abundantly than they all: yet not I, but the grace of God which was with me."

I Corinthians 15:10

Paul did not attribute his extra-ordinary labors in ministry to his physical stamina, his emotional makeup, his excellent education, his deep commitment to the Lord, or even to saving grace or strengthening grace. Rather, he attributed his extra-ordinary labors to the "grace bestowed upon" him and "the grace of God which was with" him. According to Paul, his abundant labors in ministry were a direct consequence of the special ministry grace given to him.

Because of the Grace Given to Me

Twice in his epistle to the Romans, Paul referred to the special grace given to him. Notice how he took ownership of his grace by saying, "the grace given unto me." In chapter twelve, he wrote,

"For I say, through the grace given unto me, to every man that is among you..."

Romans 12:3

Paul claimed a right and a responsibility to speak to the church in Rome because of the special grace that had been given to him by God to be an apostle to the Gentiles. But why did he feel obliged to validate his right to speak to the Roman believers? Perhaps he suspected that they would ask, "What gives this man the right speak to us with such boldness? He didn't start this church. He didn't establish us. In fact, we have never seen this man!" Although those things were true, Paul did, in fact, have a basis for his bold instructions to this church. His legitimate spiritual basis and his boldness to speak were "because of" the ministry grace given to him.

Paul wanted the Roman believers to understand that his words were more than casual advice, personal opinion, or basic Christian encouragement. His words were divine directives that sprang out of his grace endowment. He claimed a right to speak, an ability to speak, and a responsibility to speak because of the special grace stewarded to him. His boldness was "through the grace given unto me." Near the end of his epistle, Paul wrote,

> *"Nevertheless, brethren, I have written the more boldly unto you in some sort, as putting you in mind, because of the grace that is given to me of God, That I should be the minister of Jesus Christ to the Gentiles..."*
>
> Romans 15:15-16

Again, Paul justified his strong exhortations to the Romans by referencing the special grace given to him. He could write boldly to them, he said, "because of the grace that is given to me of God, That I should be the minister of Jesus Christ to the Gentiles."

They Perceived the Grace Given to Me

In his epistle to the Galatians, Paul wrote,

> *"And when James, Cephas, and John, who seemed to be pillars, perceived the grace that was given unto me..."*
>
> Galatians 2:9

When Paul visited James, Peter, and John in Jerusalem, it was to confer with them about his apostolic work and seek their confirmation. Those men, being apostles themselves, realized that Paul had been assigned a specific commission and recognized that he had been stewarded a supernatural ability to fulfill that commission. According to Paul, they "perceived the grace" that was given to him.

What these spiritual leaders perceived at work in Paul was not saving grace or strengthening grace. Certainly, they knew Paul had been saved by grace. And they may have observed that he was strong in spirit because of strengthening grace. The presence of saving grace and strengthening grace could not, however, confirm Paul's calling and work as an apostle to the Gentiles. What these spiritual leaders recognized in Paul that emboldened them to confidently confirm his apostolic ministry was the unique ministry grace given to him by God. They "perceived the grace" that was given to him.

2

Made a Minister by Grace

Paul expressed the significant relationship between his unique grace and his unique ministry when he wrote,

"...I was made a minister, according to the gift of the grace of God given unto me by the effectual working of His power."

Ephesians 3:7

Paul said that he was "made a minister." The word "made" comes from the Greek *ginomai* and means, "to come into existence, to appear in history, or to come on the stage." When Paul was "made a minister" a unique ministry gift came into existence and appeared on the stage of history. Before he was saved by grace and graced for service, Paul was a Jewish sinner named Saul. When he was saved by saving grace, he became a Christian. When he was endowed with a unique gift of ministry grace, he became a minister.

When Jesus appeared to Paul on the road to Damascus, He not only offered him forgiveness of sins and the gift of eternal life; He also appointed him to be a minister. He told Paul,

"...I have appeared unto thee for this purpose...to make thee a minister..."

Acts 26:16

The Lord Jesus and the Father God had a specific purpose for apprehending Paul. They apprehended him because they needed an apostle for the Gentiles and a minister for the church. Apprehending Paul and assigning him a commission was not enough, however. Before Jesus and the Father could send Paul as an effectual minister to the Gentiles, they had to make him a minister.

God did a supernatural work in Paul on the day He apprehended him. Not only did He make him a new creation by saving grace; He also made him a minister by a gift of ministry grace. By the bestowing of a unique ministry grace, God brought into existence and onto the stage of history a ministry gift that had not been in existence before. From the moment of divine grace-giving, Paul began to be the minister God had called and ordained him to be.

Made a Deacon

The word "minister" Paul used in Ephesians 3:7 in the phrase, "I was made a minister," comes from the Greek *diakonos*. Often translated "deacon," *diakonos* likely came from the Greek *diako* which meant, "to run errands." During the time of temple service, stewards of the financial treasury were called deacons. These men were responsible to receive money, manage it, and distribute it both for temple service and for the needs of the poor.

Paul was made a deacon, not of a financial treasure, but of a unique spiritual treasure. He was chosen by God to "run errands" to the Gentile people and was entrusted with something divine to deliver. As a deacon of grace, he distributed the treasure of God's Word and the power of His Spirit both to the unsaved and to the church.

According to The Gift of Grace

Paul testified that he was made a minister "according to the gift of the grace of God." He did not claim to be a minister according to a special school that taught him. He did not claim to be a minister according to the endorsement of a synagogue that supported him. He did not claim to be a minister because of his keen intellect, his persuasive personality, or his practical skills. He did not claim to be a minister because his father was a minister or because his mother wanted a son in the ministry. He did not claim to be a minister because another minister laid hands on him and gave him a word of prophecy. Paul claimed that he was made a minister "according to the gift of the grace of God given to [him]."

The word "gift" Paul used in the phrase, "the gift of grace of God," comes from the Greek *dorea*. This word often denoted spiritual or supernatural gifts, but was also used concerning the monies cast into the temple treasury. The gift [*dorea*] that Paul received from God was the supernatural ministry grace-ability deposited into the mobile treasury of himself.

The word "given" Paul used when he wrote of "the gift of the grace of God given unto me" comes from the Greek *didomi*. This word means, "to supply or furnish; to give over into someone's care; to entrust something to be administered; or to give forth from one's self." Paul became a minister because God furnished him with, entrusted to him, and gave over into his care a gift of ministry grace. As a mobile spiritual repository, Paul carried his wonderful gift of grace throughout the known world, ministering to the unsaved, to believers, to local churches, and to other ministers.

By the Effectual Working of His Power

Paul said that the giving of grace to him was "by the effectual working of [God's] power" [Eph. 3:7]. The words "effectual working" come from the Greek *energeia*. *Energeia* refers to supernatural power which, when released in someone, produces a significant result.

Most often *energeia* describes God's power which accomplishes His purposes. *Energeia* was the power of God which raised Christ from the dead [Eph. 1:19; Col. 2:12]. *Energeia* is that power by which Christ will transform mortal bodies into immortal bodies when He comes again [Phil. 3:21]. Interestingly, *energeia* also describes the power of Satan which will energize the man of sin to accomplish his terrible last days deeds [II Thess. 2:9]. In Ephesians 3:7, *energeia* denotes the dynamic power God released into Paul which made him a minister and supernaturally enabled him to accomplish his works.

The word "power" in Ephesians 3:7 is the Greek *dunamis*. This word means, "inherent power — the power residing within a person or thing." *Dunamis* is, "the power which can accomplish anything intended." Our English word "dynamite" derives from *dunamis.*

Paul was made a minister when ministry grace was stewarded to him by the *energeia* of God's *dunamis.* There was a divine release when God stewarded ministry grace to Paul. Something powerful transpired. An impartation was effected. Ministry ability was stewarded. A supernatural giving of God occurred as He transmitted to Paul a gift of apostolic grace and made him an apostle. Paul was made a minister, as the Amplified Bible says, by, "the gift of God's...grace... bestowed on me by the exercise — the working in all its effectiveness — of His power."

Paul wrote these similar words to the Colossian believers about the divine ability stewarded to him which made him a minister,

> *"...I am made a minister, according to the dispensation [stewardship] of God which is given to me for you, to fulfill the word of God..."*
>
> Colossians 1:25

The word "made" Paul used here is the same Greek word *ginomai* he used in his letter to the Ephesians when he said he was "made" a minister by grace. Although Paul did not use the specific word "grace" in these words to the Colossians, there is little doubt that he was referring to that same divine ability stewarded to him which he termed "grace" in his epistle to the Ephesians.

Paul also referred to being endowed with supernatural ability for ministry in his first letter to Timothy when he wrote,

> *"And I thank Christ Jesus our lord, who hath enabled me, for that he counted me faithful, putting me into the ministry..."*
>
> I Timothy 1:12

Paul said that Jesus had put him into the ministry. The word "putting" comes from the Greek *tithemi* and means, "to place, to make for one's use, to establish." The word "enabled" is the Greek *endunamoo* which literally means, "inward *dunamoo*." To be enabled, then, means, "to be inwardly endued with the power to accomplish whatever is willed." The Father God and the Lord Jesus not only put Paul into the ministry; they also put a supernatural ministry grace into Paul!

A Minister Because of Grace

Paul's words from Ephesians 3:7, Colossians 1:25, and I Timothy 1:12 could be summarized this way:

"By a supernatural and energetic working of God's dunamis — His dynamic power which can accomplish whatever He intends — a special gift of ministry grace was stewarded to me. By that indwelling gift of ministry grace which I now possess, I am supernaturally endowed and enabled to be an effectual minister."

It was by a divine decision that Paul was chosen. It was by a divine calling that he was apprehended. But it was by a divine grace-giving that Paul was made a minister and equipped for his calling. Paul was appointed to the office of apostle and commissioned to go to the Gentiles by the purposing of God, but he was eminently fit for and supernaturally enabled to perform that ministry by the unique ministry grace stewarded to him!

3

Apostle to the Gentiles by Grace

The unique ministry grace stewarded to Paul was a significant determining factor in fitting him to be an apostle to the Gentiles. In Ephesians 3:1-2, he referred to his grace-calling with these words,

"...Paul, the prisoner of Jesus Christ for you Gentiles, If ye have heard of the dispensation of the grace of God which is given me to youward..."

Ephesians 3:1-2

Paul recognized that he was a prisoner of Jesus Christ, but he was also aware that he was a prisoner for the Gentiles. The Gentiles were the people God had in mind when he called and graced Paul.

In his encounter with Jesus on the road to Damascus, Paul was commissioned to go to the Gentiles. Testifying years later before King Agrippa, Paul recounted these words that Jesus spoke to him,

"...I have appeared unto thee for this purpose, to make thee a minister and a witness...Delivering thee from the people, and from the Gentiles, unto whom now I send thee..."

Acts 26:16-18

God's purpose for apprehending Paul on the road to Damascus went far beyond introducing him to Jesus Christ as Savior. In that divine encounter, Paul was called to ministry, made a minister, and sent to the Gentiles. Jesus' words, indelibly branded upon his heart, left Paul no doubt about what his calling and his commission were.

Paul's confidence concerning his calling was not only rooted in the words Jesus spoke to him on the road to Damascus, however. He was also confident of his calling because he was conscious of the ministry grace that was stewarded to him. In Ephesians three, he wrote,

> *"Unto me, who am less than the least of all saints, is this grace given, that I should preach among the Gentiles the unsearchable riches of Christ..."*
>
> *Ephesians 3:8*

Paul said, "Unto me...is this grace given." And then he said, "that I should preach among the Gentiles." Paul was very aware that he had been entrusted with the grace to preach the gospel to the Gentiles.

Toward the Gentiles

From Paul's epistle to the Galatians, we learn that after he had been laboring in his ministry for a number of years, he went to Jerusalem and communicated with the other apostles about his work among the Gentiles. After he shared about his ministry with those apostles, they acknowledged his calling and endorsed his ministry. Recounting that event, Paul wrote,

> *"...they saw that the gospel of the uncircumcision was committed unto me, as the gospel of the circumcision was unto Peter; (For he that wrought effectually in Peter to the apostleship of the circumcision, the same was mighty in me toward the Gentiles:)..."*
>
> *Galatians 2:7-8*

The word "saw" Paul used comes from the Greek *eido* and means, "to know, to perceive, to discern." The apostles in Jerusalem discerned that Paul had been entrusted with the mission of bringing the gospel to the Gentiles. They perceived that the same God who worked effectually in Peter for his ministry to the circumcision was mighty in Paul for his ministry to the Gentiles.

Paul said that the same God who worked in Peter "to" the circumcision was mighty in him "toward" the Gentiles. Both "to" and "toward" come from the Greek preposition *eis* which can be translated "unto, toward, for, or among." Peter was God-called, God-sent, and God-endowed to go to and labor among the Jews. Paul was God-called, God-sent, and God-endowed to go to and labor among the Gentiles. Because God was actively at work in Peter and Paul, they were putting forth ministry power and producing fruit. The unique in-workings of God in those two men produced the unique, effectual out-workings of their ministries.

After reporting that the apostles in Jerusalem recognized his commission, Paul wrote,

> *"And when James, Cephas, and John...perceived the grace that was given unto me..."*
>
> *Galatians 2:9*

Peter, James, and John not only "saw" that the responsibility of preaching the gospel to the Gentiles had been committed to Paul; they also "perceived" the unique endowment of ministry grace that had been stewarded to him. The word "perceived" comes from the Greek *ginosko* and means, "to know by experience and observation." The apostles in Jerusalem knew from their own experience of God's ministry grace and from their interaction with Paul that God had indeed specially grace-endowed him for an apostolic mission to the Gentiles.

What the apostles perceived in Paul was that apparent, undeniable, supernatural in-working God-ability which both motivated him toward and enabled him to labor abundantly among the Gentiles. Paul called the supernatural, inworking ability that the apostles perceived in him "grace."

Paul also referred to his special endowment of grace for the Gentiles in his letter to the Romans when he wrote,

> *"Nevertheless, brethren, I have written the more boldly unto you... because of the grace that is given to me of God, That I should be the minister of Jesus Christ to the Gentiles..."*
>
> *Romans 15:15-16*

The Amplified Bible expresses Paul's words this way,

"...I have written to you the more boldly...because of the grace... bestowed on me by God in making me a minister of Christ Jesus to the Gentiles..."

Romans 15:15-16 Amp

He had written similar words to the Romans earlier when he said,

"For I speak to you Gentiles, inasmuch as I am the apostle of the Gentiles, I magnify mine office."

Romans 11:13

Paul's grace endowment was a significant determining factor in his ministry. He was an apostle to the Gentiles because of the grace given to him. If you had asked Paul, "How do you know you are an apostle to the Gentiles?" he may have answered, "I know because I am graced for the Gentiles."

4

Abundant Labors by Grace

Although Paul was supernaturally called for his ministry, that supernatural calling did not enable him to do the work of his ministry. And although the love of Christ constrained him to reach out to people, the love of Christ could not equip him to meet those peoples' needs. What was it, then, that enabled Paul to labor effectively and fulfill his ministry? According to Paul, it was the grace bestowed upon him. In I Corinthians, he wrote,

> "...and his grace which was bestowed upon me was not in vain; but I laboured more abundantly than they all: yet not I, but the grace of God which was with me."
>
> I Corinthians 15:10

Paul said that the grace bestowed on him was "not in vain." The word "vain" comes from the Greek *kenos* which means, "empty; especially with a reference to quality." The grace given to Paul was not in vain; it was not lacking in quality or empty of results.

The NIV Bible renders Paul's words to the Corinthians this way,

> "...His grace to me was not without effect."
>
> I Corinthians 15:10 NIV

The grace that God bestowed upon Paul was not without effect. Rather, it was very effective and made him very effective. Because of the richness of the grace stewarded to him, Paul was able to labor in a very abundant manner and produce much good fruit.

More Abundant Labor

Paul testified that he "laboured more abundantly" than all the other apostles. The words "more abundantly" come from the Greek word *perissoteron* which means, "over and above, exceeding abundantly, superior, or more excellent." Paul took no personal credit for his exceeding abundant, superior, and excellent work, however — work that surpassed the work of other apostles — but credited his grace endowment. The Amplified Bible renders his words this way,

> "...His grace toward me was not [found to be] for nothing — fruitless and without effect. In fact, I worked harder than all of them [the apostles], though it was not really I, but the grace...of God which was with me."
>
> I Corinthians 15:10 Amp

Paul labored more than other apostles in preaching and teaching, in prayer, in healings, in miracles, in travel, in counsel, in friendship, in writing, in leadership, and in training. He traveled over a great part of the known world of his day. Although he endured incredible hardships, suffered extreme difficulties, and was sorely persecuted for his work, he was a premier instrument of God in converting souls, establishing believers, building churches, and overseeing the affairs of God.

According to Paul, his abundant labors were an out-working of the abundant grace bestowed upon him. In other words, his significant ministry labors proceeded from his significant grace endowment. If Paul had been unaware of the grace bestowed upon him, he would not have cooperated with it. If he had been slothful and neglected his grace, it would have laid dormant within him. If, for any reason, Paul had failed to discover, cultivate, and labor by the grace entrusted to him, his grace would have been bestowed "in vain."

I Strive According to His Mighty Inworking

Paul referred to his unique ministry endowment in his epistle to the Colossians with these words,

"...I am made a minister, according to the dispensation [steward-ship] of God which is given to me for you...we preach, warning every man, and teaching every man in all wisdom; that we may present every man perfect in Christ Jesus..."

Colossians 1:25-28

A divine ability was stewarded to Paul for the benefit of the church. By means of that ability, he preached Christ, "warning every man, and teaching every man in all wisdom" [Col. 1:28]. By means of that ability, he brought sinners to Christ and believers to maturity. Paul confirmed that it was really God's divine inworking that made his labors so prolific when he wrote,

"Whereunto I also labour striving according to his working, which worketh in me mightily."

Colossians 1:29

The word "labour" in this verse comes from the Greek *kopiao*. This verb is closely related to the noun *kopos* which means, "a striking or a beating which results in weariness." Paul labored diligently, even to weariness, in his ministry of saving the lost and bringing the saved to maturity. The word "striving" he used is the Greek *agonizoma* which means, "to contend as in battle, to agonize toward the accomplishing of a task."

The word "working" in the phrase, "according to his working which worketh in me mightily," is the Greek *energeia*. *Energeia* is that energy which, when released within a person, produces something. Because God was working supernaturally in Paul [*energeia*], Paul was supernaturally empowered to work [*kopiao*].

The phrase, "which worketh in me mightily," comes from the Greek words *en dunamei* which mean, "an inward working of divine power which enables one to accomplish anything they intend to accomplish." Paul used the phrase *en dunamei* to specify that it was God's ability at work in him that enabled him to do his work.

The NIV Bible renders Paul's words to the Colossians this way,

"To this end I labour, struggling with all his energy, which so pow-erfully works in me."

Colossians 1:29 NIV

The BBE version of the Bible says,

"And for this purpose I am working, using all my strength by the help of his power which is working in me strongly."

Colossians 1:29 BBE

I prefer to render Paul's words to the Colossians this way:

"I labor continually, even to weariness, in my ministry of preaching and teaching. My agonizing and striving in ministry is not, how-ever, a manifestation of my own mental efforts, emotional strength, or physical capacity, but a manifestation of the powerful working of God in me. Because God is mightily and energetically at work in me, I can work mightily and accomplish what He wills."

Paul labored super-abundantly from the inside in order to accomplish his ministry on the outside. He strived in his visible ministry according to God's invisible working in him. He worked out of the divine in-working of God.

5

A Wise Masterbuilder by Grace

In the Old Testament, God chose men and endowed them with supernatural wisdom to build the tabernacle under Moses' leadership and to build the temple under Solomon's leadership [Ex. 31:2,6; II Chron. 2:13-14]. He "put wisdom" in these men's hearts so they "knew how to work all manner of work" [Ex. 35:35]. By the means of special endowments these men knew "how to work all manner of work" and made everything the Lord commanded [Ex. 36:1-39:31].

In a similar way, God chose Paul and endowed him with a supernatural grace-ability to build believers' lives and to build the New Testament temple; the church. Paul spoke of his skill to build with these words,

> *"According to the grace of God which is given unto me, as a wise masterbuilder, I have laid the foundation..."*
>
> *I Corinthians 3:10*

The word "masterbuilder" Paul used to describe himself is the Greek *architekton*. This word comes from *arche*, "rule, beginning," and *tekton*, "an artificer," and means, "a principal artificer." The Amplified Bible uses both "skilful architect" and "master builder" to translate *architekton*. In Bible times the *architekton* both designed works and participated in their construction. This word accurately describes Paul's work in laying the foundation of the church in Corinth and of other churches in other places. The inception of many early churches and their ongoing spiritual construction devolved upon him.

What made Paul a wise masterbuilder? Was he a wise master-builder because of years of Scripture study? Was he a wise master-builder because he had been mentored by an older wise masterbuilder? Was he a wise masterbuilder because he had been born with unusually high intelligence? Although all these things could enhance his minis-try, Paul claimed to be a wise masterbuilder because of the grace given to him.

If we take the words "as a wise masterbuilder" out of I Corinthi-ans 3:10, Paul's words read this way,

> *"According to the grace of God which is given unto me...I have laid the foundation."*
>
> *I Corinthians 3:10*

By using the words "according to" Paul connected his grace en-dowment to his skillful ministry. Basically, he assigned the credit for his work to the grace stewarded to him. According to Paul, the reason he was skillful in laying foundations and building churches was be-cause God had entrusted him with foundation laying grace.

The Amplified Bible renders Paul's words this way,

> *"According to the grace — the special endowment for my task — of God bestowed on me, like a skillful architect and master builder I laid [the] foundation..."*
>
> *I Corinthians 3:10 Amp*

The men who prepared the Amplified Bible very accurately de-picted the grace given to Paul as the "special endowment for [his] task." Paul's task was to build the church. Therefore, God stewarded to him foundation laying and church building apostolic grace.

6

I Am What I Am by Grace

In I Corinthians 15:8-11, Paul informed the church at Corinth of his unique calling to apostolic ministry, of his abundant labors in that ministry, and of the special grace which enabled him to fulfill that ministry. He reported his profound experience of being called into ministry with these words,

"And last of all he was seen of me also, as of one born out of due time."

I Corinthians 15:8

When Jesus appeared to Paul on the road to Damascus, He commissioned him to be an apostle to the Gentiles. Paul revealed his feelings of being unworthy for this apostleship when he said,

"For I am the least of the apostles, that am not meet to be called an apostle, because I persecuted the church of God."

I Corinthians 15:9

Paul had been a destroyer of the church. He had withstood the kingdom of God. He had persecuted, imprisoned, and killed Christians. Because of his terrible past, he identified himself as "the least of the apostles" and said he was not fit to be called an apostle. After declaring himself unfit to be called an apostle, however, he penned these familiar words,

"But by the grace of God I am what I am..."

I Corinthians 15:10

Many Christians suppose that when Paul wrote, "But by the grace of God I am what I am," he was referring to how he had become a Christian by God's saving grace. They think he was testifying that although he did not deserve to be saved, he was, in fact, saved by grace. Some actually use Paul's words as part of their own testimony, saying, "I was so sinful and terrible in the past, but by the grace of God I am what I am; I am saved and a child of God."

Paul was not, however, referring to becoming a Christian by saving grace when he wrote, "But by the grace of God I am what I am." Notice the word "But" in his message. It is a word of contrast which connects what he wrote about the effect of grace to what he had just written about being an apostle. He wrote, "I am not fit to be an apostle," and then wrote, "But by the grace of God I am what I am."

Paul was informing the Corinthians that he had been made an apostle by the ministry grace God stewarded to him. He was testifying about who he was in ministry and why he was who he was in ministry. Who was Paul? He was an apostle. And why he was an apostle? He was an apostle because of the ministry grace God had stewarded to him.

After Paul declared, "But by the grace of God I am what I am," he wrote,

> "...and his grace which was bestowed upon me was not in vain; but I laboured more abundantly than they all: yet not I, but the grace of God which was with me."
>
> I Corinthians 15:10

These words, in which Paul acknowledged the profound effect of the ministry grace bestowed upon him, further confirm that when he wrote, "But by the grace of God I am what I am," he was not referring to being saved by saving grace, but to being made an apostle by ministry grace.

Paul also penned words to the church at Ephesus contrasting his destructive past and his present fruitful work as a minister because of the ministry grace given to him. He wrote,

"Unto me, who am less than the least of all saints, is this grace given, that I should preach among the Gentiles the unsearchable riches of Christ..."

Ephesians 3:8

Paul wrote that he was "less than the least of all saints." This was his self-evaluation based on his past merits. In the very same sentence, however, he described himself as one called to preach to the Gentiles "the unsearchable riches of Christ." This was his self-evaluation based on the ministry grace given to him. On the basis of his past, Paul estimated himself to be less than the least of all saints. On the basis of the ministry grace bestowed upon him, however, he estimated himself to be a minister to the Gentiles.

Paul was humble enough to admit his personal unworthiness for an apostolic ministry, but he was also bold enough to confess that he was, in fact and by grace, an apostle. He was realistic about his past and realistic about his grace-gifting. Although he debased himself, he boasted of his grace and magnified the office for which it qualified him. Because of the special grace entrusted to him, Paul was eminently qualified and supremely equipped to minister as an apostle to the Gentiles.

Section Two

What is Grace for Effectual Ministry?

Having then gifts differing
According to the grace
That is given to us

7

God's New Testament Way

God can work in many different ways in the church age to accomplish His purposes. He can send angels to do His bidding. He can speak to men through visions and dreams. He can impress things upon men's hearts by His Word and by His Spirit. He can do things by His manifested presence.

Most often, however, the way God accomplishes His purposes in the church age is by saving human vessels, calling them into service, stewarding ministry graces to them, and then sending those called and grace-endowed vessels to do works and to speak words; making divine deliveries to those who are in need.

How God Worked in the Old Testament

Throughout the Old Testament, God called, anointed, and sent men and women to accomplish His purposes. The calling of God and the anointing of His Spirit was primarily for kings, prophets, judges, and priests. Others, however, were also called and endowed. The men who labored in the construction of the tabernacle of Moses, for example, were specially called by God and endowed by His Spirit for their task.

When the anointing of Gods' Spirit came upon called individuals, they were supernaturally empowered — changed sometimes, as it were, into different men — and enabled to accomplish works for God [I Sam. 10:6]. When the Spirit of God lifted from these individuals, they would return to "normal."

In the Old Testament, the anointing of God's Spirit was always upon men, not within them. The coming upon of the anointing was sometimes referred to by the phrase "the hand of the Lord." In Elijah and Elisha's case, the anointing was represented by a physical mantel. In some cases the anointing was represented by oil.

When the Hebrew children cried out for deliverance from Egypt, God called Moses, put His Spirit upon him, and sent him to Egypt to deliver His people [Ex. 3:7-10]. Moses was supernaturally endowed to deliver Israel from bondage and to lead them in the will of God. Later, God chose Joshua to lead Israel into the promised land of Canaan. When Moses laid his hands on Joshua the anointing of God's Spirit came upon him, enabling him to fulfill his calling as the new leader of Israel [Deut. 34:9].

Many years later, when Israel had been without a prophetic voice for a long time, God closed the womb of a woman named Hannah until she became so desperate for a child that she made a promise to God. If He would give her a son, she would lend that son back to Him all the days of his life. God gave Samuel to Hannah and Hannah gave Samuel back to God. At a young age, God anointed Samuel to stand in the office of the prophet [I Sam. 3:1-21]. By the anointing of God's Spirit, Samuel delivered God's word and accomplished God's purposes.

A double portion of the anointing that was upon the prophet Elijah came upon Elisha when he picked up Elijah's mantle [I Kings 2:13-14]. One time, when asked to prophesy, Elisha requested that a skilled musician come and play. When the musician played, the "hand of the Lord" came upon him and he prophesied the plan of the Lord [II Kings 3:15].

There is a vivid example of the effect of the anointing from the life of Saul. After Saul met Samuel while searching for his father's donkeys, Samuel informed him that on his journey home he would meet prophets coming down from a high place. The Spirit of God would come upon him, Samuel said, and he would prophesy and be turned into a different man. What Samuel foretold came to pass. When Saul came into the proximity of the prophets, the anointing came upon him. He prophesied so profoundly that people wondered if he was called to the prophet's office [I Sam. 10:1-13].

Later, a more abiding anointing came upon Saul that enabled him to stand in the office of the king. That anointing remained upon him until his persistent disobedience caused God to remove him from office and take the anointing of the Spirit from him [Acts 13:22]. After God removed Saul, He chose David, a young shepherd boy and a man after His own heart, to be king over Israel [Ps. 78:70]. David was anointed with the Spirit and fulfilled all God's will [Acts 13:22].

In the Old Testament the anointing also came upon men and women called by God to serve as judges. These judges governed the people of God and delivered Israel from their enemies. Samson was one of these judges. The anointing of God's Spirit that would come upon him enabled him to perform mighty physical acts. When the anointing lifted from him, however, he was like any other man.

Other Old Testament men like Jeremiah and Isaiah were specially called by God and stewards of His anointing. They fulfilled God's will in their own generations, working by His power and speaking by His Spirit. By the anointing, these Old Testament men and women ministered the power of God, spoke His divine directives, and fulfilled His purposes.

The Way God Worked Through Jesus

During the three and a half years that Jesus ministered on the earth, He preached, taught, and did mighty works. He declared that the Spirit of the Lord was upon Him, empowering Him for service [Lk. 4:18-19]. John the Baptist stated that Jesus was given the Spirit without measure [Jn. 3:34]. Peter confirmed that Jesus' effectual ministry was the result of the anointing of the Holy Spirit when he said,

> *"How God anointed Jesus of Nazareth with the Holy Ghost and with power: who went about doing good, and healing all that were oppressed of the devil; for God was with him."*
>
> *Acts 10:38*

God the Father fully manifested Himself through Jesus in words and works. Everything He wanted to reveal about Himself — His wisdom, His love, His forgiveness, His miracle power, His healing virtue — was revealed through Jesus. When someone saw Jesus work, they were seeing God work. When someone heard Jesus speak, they were hearing God speak. Jesus did His mighty deeds, spoke His life-changing words, and executed His earthly ministry by the anointing of the Holy Spirit [Is. 61:1-3; Lk. 4:16-21].

Greater Works Because I Go to My Father

Jesus' ministry lasted about three years. When the time for His suffering and death drew near, He finished His ministry and began to prepare for His death [Jn. 17:4]. At that time, He spoke these profound words to His disciples,

> *"Verily, verily I say unto you, He that believeth on me, the works that I do shall he do also; and greater works than these shall he do; because I go to my father."*
>
> John 14:12

Jesus told His disciples that they would do the same works He had done and even greater works. He prefaced His radical declaration with the words "Verily, verily" because He wanted His disciples to embrace His profound words as a statement of fact that announced the future work of the church.

According to Jesus, the reason His disciples would be able to do the same works He did and greater works was "because I go to my father." What was it about Jesus returning to His Father that would enable His disciples to do greater works?

First, before ascending to heaven, Jesus would authorize believers to use His name in preaching, healing, delivering, and prayer [Mt. 28:18-20; Mk. 16:17-18]. Second, after ascending to heaven, He would send forth the Holy Spirit to empower the church [Lk. 24:49; Acts 1:8]. Third, when He ascended to heaven, He would apportion diverse kinds and different measures of ministry grace to equip different members of His body to serve in unique ministries [Eph. 4:7-11].

When Jesus ascended to heaven, He not only entrusted His ministry commission to the church; He also stewarded to the church the full measure of His ministry gifting. By that stewarded gifting the church is supernaturally enabled to do His works and even greater works. Like Jesus, the church has been enabled to accomplish the works of God by the stewarded ability of God.

The Way God Works Through the Church

In the New Testament, God accomplishes His purposes and meets the needs of people by working through the church. Just as Jesus of Nazareth accomplished God's will by God's stewarded anointing so the church accomplishes God's will by God's stewarded graces. God's primary *modus operendi* in the New Testament is to minister by the grace-endowed church.

The apostle Paul offered a striking insight into this way of God when he declared that his purpose for preaching the gospel and teaching believers was,

> *"To the intent that now unto the principalities and powers in heavenly places might be known by the church the manifold wisdom of God, According to his eternal purpose which he purposed in Christ Jesus our Lord..."*
>
> *Ephesians 3:10-11*

Notice Paul's words "by the church." It is "by the church" that God's wisdom is manifested in the sight of principalities and powers. And this is part of God's "eternal purpose." The Amplified Bible renders Paul's words this way,

> *"[The purpose is] that through the church the complicated, many-sided wisdom of God in all its infinite variety and innumerable aspects might now be made known to the angelic rulers and authorities (principalities and powers) in the heavenly sphere. This is in accordance with the terms of the eternal and timeless purpose which*

He has realized and carried into effect, in [the person of] Christ Jesus our Lord..."

Ephesians 3:10-11 Amp

According to Paul, one of God's eternal purposes is to demonstrate His many-sided wisdom "through the church." By so doing, He not only reaches the lost, meets the needs of His people, and accomplishes His plans and purposes in earth; He also gives a stinging demonstration of His tender mercies, His excellent truth, His divine power, and His irresistible purposes to the principalities and powers in heavenly places!

The primary way God manifests His manifold wisdom through the church is by means of the manifold graces He stewards to the church [I Pet. 4:10]. When God-called, God-placed, God-graced members of the church locate, cultivate, and minister effectively by their unique grace-giftings, the wisdom and power of God is displayed and the will of God is wrought.

When Jesus was on the earth, He said, "If you have seen me, you have seen the Father." When believers minister effectively by their grace-gifts, the church will be able to say, "If you have seen us, you have seen the Father." It is God's plan that the church minister by His manifold grace and accomplish His manifold purpose.

It is very important to understand that when God calls sinners by His gospel it is not only to save them from sin, adopt them as children, and give them an eternal inheritance. He also calls sinners to eventually employ them as co-workers in His heavenly business. God's calling, then, is not only an invitation to heaven; it is also a summons to service while on earth. This reality is very clear in Ephesians 2:10 where Paul wrote,

"For we are his workmanship, created in Christ Jesus unto good works, which God hath before ordained that we should walk in them."

Ephesians 2:10

When sinners hear and believe the gospel call, they are not only born again in Christ Jesus unto heaven; they are also created in Christ Jesus "unto good works." Paul was referring to this very reality when he exhorted Timothy with these words,

> *"[God] hath saved us, and called us with an holy calling, not according to our works, but according to his own purpose and grace..."*
> II Timothy 1:9

Manifold Grace for Manifold Works

To accomplish His purposes in the New Testament, God entrusts different varieties and various measures of His ministry grace to different believers. His mighty grace-givings enable some believers to be pastors, some to be apostles, some to be healers, some to be evangelists, some to be teachers, some to be prophets, some to be exhorters, some to be helpers, some to be showers of mercy, some to be workers of miracles, some to do practical service, some to prophesy, some to administrate, some to rule, and some to give. The New Testament grace-givings of God are so substantial that once unregenerate men and women, and sometimes the meanest, weakest, and least skilled of all, become effective servants of Christ!

The manifold grace of God is divided to the church just as a great river divides itself into many distributaries. There is One Source of all ministry, but there are many different streams destined for many different places. It is the plan of God that the many dry places on earth be satisfied by the many heavenly graces carried by the many members of the body of Christ!

Concerning the way God works in the New Testament, then, we find this progression: First, God purposes to accomplish particular works. Then, He chooses individuals to accomplish those works. Then, He calls those individuals by the gospel and saves them by saving grace. Then, He sets those members in the body as it pleases Him and stewards specific ministry graces to them. Then, He sends those saved, placed, and grace-gifted members to specific places and specific people to labor in specific ministries and to meet specific needs. God purposes. God chooses. God calls. God saves. God places. God graces. God sends. This IS God's New Testament Way!

8

The Parable of the Talents

In Matthew 25, Jesus taught a parable about how the kingdom of heaven works. This parable, commonly called the Parable of the Talents, wonderfully illustrates God's stewarding of ministry graces for New Testament ministry. Jesus began this parable by saying,

> *"For the kingdom of heaven is as a man travelling into a far country, who called his own servants, and delivered unto them his goods. And unto one he gave five talents, to another two, and to another one; to every man according to his several ability; and straightway took his journey."*
>
> *Matthew 25:14-15*

In this parable a householder planned to travel to a far country. Because he wanted his business to prosper in his absence, he called his servants and "delivered unto them his goods." The word "delivered" comes from the Greek *paradidomi* and means, "to give over into another's hands or into another's power to keep, manage, and use."

To each servant the householder gave talents according to their individual abilities. The word "gave" comes from the Greek *didomi* which means, "to supply, to furnish, or to give a gift." The householder expected each servant to work faithfully with the talents entrusted to their care and to make increase for him while he was gone.

After entrusting his goods to his servants, the householder departed on his journey. Jesus continued the parable saying,

> *"Then he that had received the five talents went and traded with the same, and made them other five talents. And likewise he that had*

received two, he also gained other two. But he that had received one went and digged in the earth, and hid his lord's money."

Matthew 25:16-18

Two servants went into the marketplace and conducted business with the talents stewarded to them. The servant who had been given five talents gained another five. The servant who had been given two talents gained another two. By working faithfully and skillfully with the talents stewarded to them, these two servants made increase for the householder.

The servant who was stewarded one talent did not trade with his talent, but buried it in the earth. He "hid his lord's money." Jesus continued to teach saying,

"After a long time the lord of those servants cometh, and reckoneth with them. And so he that had received five talents came and brought other five talents, saying, Lord, thou deliveredst unto me five talents: behold, I have gained beside them five talents more. His lord said unto him, Well done, thou good and faithful servant: thou hast been faithful over a few things, I will make thee ruler over many things: enter thou into the joy of thy lord."

Matthew 25:20-21

After a lengthy absence the householder, now called "the lord of those servants," returned and reckoned with his servants. Each was required to give an account of their stewardship. What had they done with the talents stewarded to them? Had they been faithful? Had they worked diligently and skillfully? Had they made increase for the householder?

The first servant was able to give a good report because he made a proportional increase with the talents stewarded to him. Using his five, he gained five more and was able to return ten talents to his lord. Because he was faithful and skillful, the householder made him ruler over many things and invited him to enter into the joy of his lord.

The second servant was also able to give a good report. Using the two talents stewarded to him, he gained two more and was able to return four talents to his lord. This servant received the same commendation as the first servant. He was made a ruler over much and invited to enter into the joy of his lord.

Now let's read the report of the servant who was stewarded one talent,

> *"Then he which had received the one talent came and said, Lord, I knew thee that thou art an hard man, reaping where thou hast not sown, and gathering where thou hast not strawed: And I was afraid, and went and hid thy talent in the earth: lo, there thou hast that is thine. His lord answered and said unto him, Thou wicked and slothful servant, thou knewest that I reap where I sowed not, and gather where I have not strawed: Thou oughtest therefore to have put my money to the exchangers, and then at my coming I should have received mine own with usury. Take therefore the talent from him, and give it unto him which hath ten talents. For unto every one that hath shall be given, and he shall have abundance: but from him that hath not shall be taken away even that which he hath. And cast ye the unprofitable servant into outer darkness: there shall be weeping and gnashing of teeth."*
>
> *Matthew 25:24-30*

Notice the length of the third servant's report. He could not render a favorable report to his lord, but offered a lengthy excuse for why he had failed to make any gain. Because he was fearful and lazy, he did not use his lord's talent, but hid it in the earth. Consequently, he was only able to return to the householder what had originally been stewarded to him.

The householder was angry with the third servant calling him "wicked and slothful" and "unprofitable." This servant was dealt with in a very harsh manner. The householder took his talent away and gave it to the servant who had ten. Then he was cast into outer darkness.

The Revelation of Graces Stewarded

The parable of the talents illustrates how the Lord Jesus stewards grace-gifts to His servants and reveals His expectation that they will use those grace-gifts to make increase for His kingdom while He is gone. It makes clear the fact that there are rewards for those who faithfully employ what has been stewarded to them and consequences for those who fail to do so.

In this parable, Jesus is the man who travelled to a far country. After He finished His work on earth, He ascended on high and entrusted His goods — grace-talents — to his servants. The three servants in the parable represent believers. All believers are called to serve in God's kingdom and entrusted with special grace-gifts according to God's purpose and according to their individual abilities.

The talents, or goods, in this parable represent the diverse grace-gifts Jesus stewards to His servants. Every believer is stewarded a unique grace-gift or gifts and, therefore, is spiritually talented in some way. Every believer can say, "I have the goods!" Whatever spiritual talents each believer is given, they are responsible to locate, cultivate, and use those talents to make increase for the kingdom of God till Jesus comes again.

In telling this parable, Jesus said, "he that had received the five talents went and traded with the same." The word "traded" comes from the Greek *ergazomai* and means, "to work, to labor, or to minister." *Ergazomai* was used by Paul in I Corinthians 16:10 where he said of Timothy that he "worketh the work of the Lord." It was also used in I Corinthians 9:13 concerning Old Testament priests who "minister about holy things." Like the servants in the parable, believers are expected to "trade" with the grace-gifts stewarded to them.

Some believers, because they lack teaching, do not realize that grace-talents have been stewarded to them. Consequently, they do not locate and cultivate their gifts or employ them for the benefit of God's kingdom. Other believers do nothing with the grace-gifts stewarded to them because of fear or laziness or because they are not committed to the advancement of God's kingdom. Other believers, desiring to make gain for themselves, invest their talents "in the earth."

Wise and diligent believers, understanding that grace-gifts have been entrusted to them and realizing that they will give an account to their Lord, are faithful to locate, cultivate, and employ their gifts. They make increase for the kingdom of God according to what has been stewarded to them. Because they are faithful and skillful, they bring gain to God's kingdom and will be richly rewarded on the day of reckoning.

9

Unique Grace-Gifts

Like the man who traveled to a far country in the Parable of the Talents, when Jesus ascended to heaven, He commissioned the church to continue His work and stewarded to His servants the necessary spiritual gifts. Paul wrote of this stewarding of spiritual gifts in the fourth chapter of his letter to the Ephesians. There, he revealed that when Jesus ascended to heaven, He endowed believers with unique grace-gifts and, by so doing, enabled the church to continue His ministry.

Salvation and Vocation

At the beginning of the fourth chapter of Ephesians, Paul encouraged believers to live worthy of their calling, saying,

> *"I therefore, the prisoner of the Lord, beseech you that ye walk worthy of the vocation wherewith ye are called..."*
>
> *Ephesians 4:1*

The word "vocation" means, "a calling that is heavenly in its origin, heavenly in its nature, and heavenly in its destination." When men and women hear the gospel message and accept it, they are not only answering God's invitation to a common eternal inheritance in heaven; they are also answering His summons to fulfill a unique service while on earth.

Paul highlighted believers' common salvation with these words,

> *"There is one body, and one Spirit, even as ye are called in one hope*

of your calling; One Lord, one faith, one baptism, One God and
Father of all, who is above all, and through all, and in you all."

Ephesians 4:4-6

Notice how often Paul used the word "one" in the above verses. Believers have one Father and share one faith. They are members of one body and indwelt by one Spirit. They have one hope of heaven and serve one Lord. Concerning salvation, all believers have the same and are the same in Christ.

After emphasizing believers' common salvation, Paul changed his focus and emphasized believers' unique vocations and grace-giftings. He wrote,

"But unto every one of us is given grace according to the measure
of the gift of Christ."

Ephesians 4:7

Notice that Paul used the word "But" to preface his statement that grace is given to every believer. "But" is a word of contrast. In Ephesians 4:7, it notifies the reader that Paul's statement about grace being given to every believer is in contrast to what he had written in the previous verses about believers having things in common.

When Paul stated, "But unto every one of us is given grace," he was not referring to the truth that all believers are saved by one saving grace. If he had been, he would have written, "And we have all been saved by one grace." Paul was also not referring to the truth that all believers can be strengthened by strengthening grace. If he had been, he would have written, "And we can all be strengthened by one grace."

Paul prefaced his statement in Ephesians 4:7 with the word "But." That puts his statement about grace being given to believers in contrast with his previous statements about all believers having the same things. Paul was revealing that although believers have many things in common in Christ, God has stewarded unique ministry graces to each believer. Believers do not share the same callings, the same placings in the body, or the same grace-giftings for service.

The Measure of the Gift of Christ

Paul taught that the ministry graces given to believers are "according to the measure of the gift of Christ" [Eph. 4:7]. The word "measure" comes from the Greek *metron* and means, "a determined extent or a portion measured off." In Ephesians 4:7, the phrase, "the measure of the gift of Christ," signifies those pre-determined varieties and portions of Jesus' full ministry gift that are measured out to different members of the body of Christ as grace-giftings.

In John 3:34, John the Baptist used the word *metron* when he said concerning Jesus that "God giveth not the Spirit by measure" to Him. Jesus did not have a measure of the Spirit. He had the full measure of the Spirit; the full measure of the ministry gift of God. No member of the body of Christ has the full measure of the gift of Christ. Rather, each member of the body has a *metron*; a measure or a portion.

The NIV Bible renders Paul's words in Ephesians 4:7 this way,

> *"But to each one of us grace has been given as Christ apportioned it."*
>
> *Ephesians 4:7 NIV*

To apportion means, "to divide and distribute according to a plan." When Jesus left the earth, He divided the full measure of His ministry gift to the church, distributing different ministry graces to different members according to His pre-determined plan.

A Confirming Word from the Old Testament

Paul supported his statement in Ephesians 4:7 about the measuring out of ministry graces by quoting the Holy Spirit's words from Psalm 68:18. This confirms that what Paul was teaching was not an invention of his own, but a New Testament reality foretold in the Old Testament. He wrote,

> *"Wherefore he saith, When he ascended on high, he led captivity captive, and gave gifts unto men."*
>
> *Ephesians 4:8*

Psalms 68:18 literally says, "thou hast received gifts for men." The word "received" comes from the Hebrew *laqach* which means, "to procure, to select, to choose, or to lay hold of." In Psalm 68:18, the Holy Spirit foretold Jesus' work of choosing and giving unique ministry gifts to New Testament believers.

The word "Wherefore" Paul used in Ephesians 4:8 establishes a connection between what he wrote in Ephesians 4:7 about ministry graces being measured to believers and what the Holy Spirit said in Psalm 68:18 about gifts being given unto men. The words "Wherefore he saith" could be replaced with, "That is what God meant when He said." Let's make that replacement and render Ephesians 4:7-8 this way:

> *"But unto every one of us is given grace according to the measure of the gift of Christ. That is what God meant when He said, When Jesus ascended on high, he gave gifts unto men."*

In Psalm 68:18, the Holy Spirit foretold through David that when Jesus ascended to heaven, He would select and distribute gifts to His servants. In Ephesians 4:7, the Holy Spirit testified through Paul that grace is given to every believer according to the measure of the gift of Christ. The single truth communicated is that when Jesus left the earth, He endowed His body with the full measure of His ministry gifting by distributing different grace-gifts to different members.

Following the Theme of Grace

In Ephesians 4:11, Paul continued teaching about ministry grace by stating that some believers are graced to be apostles, prophets, evangelists, pastors, and teachers. Since verses nine and ten are not in the main vein of Paul's teaching, but are a typical Pauline side-journey, we can connect verses seven and eight to verse eleven and read Paul's words this way,

> *"But unto every one of us is given grace according to the measure*

of the gift of Christ. Wherefore he saith, When he ascended on high, he...gave gifts unto men...And he gave some, apostles; and some, prophets; and some, evangelists; and some, pastors and teachers..."

Ephesians 4:7-8, 11

The word "given" Paul used in Ephesians 4:7 when he said, "unto every one of us is given grace," is the Greek *didomi. Didomi* means, "to give forth from one's self, to give over to another's care, to supply something necessary, or to entrust something to be administered." The word "gave" Paul used in Ephesians 4:8 when he said that Jesus "gave gifts unto men" is also *didomi.* The word "gave" he used in verse 11 in the phrase, "and he gave some, apostles," is, again, *didomi.* Paul's use of the word *didomi* in these three verses confirms that they are intimately related.

All Members Are Graced to Minister

In Ephesians 4:12-15, Paul briefly stated the responsibilities of those called and graced to be apostles, prophets, evangelists, pastors, and teachers. Returning to the ministry of all believers in verse sixteen, he wrote,

"From whom the whole body fitly joined together and compacted by that which every joint supplieth, according to the effectual working in the measure of every part, maketh increase of the body unto the edifying of itself in love."

Ephesians 4:16

In Ephesians 4:16, Paul concluded the short teaching on grace and ministry that he introduced in Ephesians 4:7. It is interesting to note that the words "every man" in Ephesians 4:7 and the words "every part" in verse sixteen are both the Greek *hekastos.* Clearly, Paul's teaching in verse sixteen about the effectual working of every body part is connected to his statement in verse seven that every believer is graced for service. The word "measure" [*metron*] in verse seven is also used in verse sixteen. Again, it is clear that all these verses are related.

The words "effectual working" that Paul used in Ephesians 4:16 to describe the way each part of the body should work comes from the Greek *energeia*. This word is only used in the New Testament of superhuman power. Every member of the body of Christ can minister effectually and supernaturally and supply something vital because of the grace given to them.

Each Part Has Divine Ability

Notice how the Amplified Bible renders Paul's words in Ephesians 4:16,

"For because of Him the whole body (the church, in all its various parts closely) joined and firmly knit together by the joints and ligaments with which it is supplied, when each part [with power adapted to its need] is working properly (in all its functions), grows to full maturity, building itself up in love."

Ephesians 4:16 Amp

This verse teaches that when each body part, with power adapted to its need, is working properly in all its functions, the body of Christ grows to full maturity. What is the "need" of each "part" in this scripture and what is the "power adapted" to each part's need?

The "need" of each part is not personal in the sense that a part is lacking something it needs for itself. The "need" of each part, rather, is to possess a specific supernatural endowment so that it can accomplish its specific ministry task. For example, if a believer is called and commissioned to teach, he needs a teaching endowment. If a believer is called to pastor, he needs a pastoral endowment. If a believer is called to be an apostle, he needs an apostolic endowment. If a believer is called to show mercy, he needs a mercy endowment. If a believer is called to exhort, he needs an endowment to exhort. Members of the body of Christ can only function effectively in their ministries if God gives them the ability/endowment they "need."

The "power adapted" to each part's need are the unique ministry graces the Lord stewards to believers which enable them to be effectual in their ministries. Ministry graces, then, are the supernatural endowments, the divine abilities, God stewards to every member of the body so they can "work properly" and be effective.

This, then, is how New Testament ministry works: To "every one of us is given grace according to the measure of the gift of Christ" and then "according to the effectual working in the measure of every part" the body is edified. In other words, Christ divides and distributes different ministry graces to the different members of His body and then, as each graced member labors effectively in their place by the enabling of ministry grace, the body of Christ is edified and the will of God is accomplished.

As effectual ministry is rendered by called, placed, and graced members, the body of Christ grows, the church is edified, the needs of people are met, and the plans of God are accomplished. The church, graced with the full measure of the gift of Christ and ministering by His grace, is truly "the fullness of him that filleth all in all" [Eph. 1:23].

10

Charis – Charisma

The word "grace" comes from the Greek *charis*. The word "gift" comes from the Greek *charisma*. That there is a close relationship between *charis* and *charisma* is obvious even from the spelling of the two words. Their relationship goes far beyond a similarity in spelling, however.

The word *charisma* means, "a manifested *charis*." In his Greek dictionary of New Testament Words, W.E. Vine defines *charisma* as, "a gift of grace," or, "a gift involving grace on the part of God as the Donor." Another Greek dictionary defines *charisma* as, "gifts denoting extraordinary powers, distinguishing certain Christians and enabling them to serve the church of Christ, the reception of which is due to the power of divine grace operating on their souls by the Holy Spirit." These definitions are accurate and enlightening concerning ministry grace.

Two Kinds of Charisma

The word *charisma* is used in the New Testament to describe two different kinds of ministry. A *charisma* can be the outward expression, in words or works, of a particular temporary manifesting of the Holy Spirit. This kind of ministry is rightly described by Paul as the "manifestation of the Spirit" because it is, in fact, the Holy Spirit who manifests [I Cor. 12:7]. When the Holy Spirit moves upon a believer and they cooperate with Him, there will be a *charisma* [gift] of the Spirit [I Cor. 12:4]. The nine *charisma* of the Spirit as recorded in I Corinthians twelve are divided to believers as the Spirit wills, are the result of the cooperation of believers and the Holy Spirit, and are occasional in their manifestation [I Cor. 12:11]. They are for unique circumstances, to meet specific needs, and to speak into particular situations.

A *charisma* can also be the consistent outward expression, in words or works, of a permanent inward endowment of ministry grace. This *charisma*, unlike the *charisma* of the Spirit, is not intermittent and unpredictable, but consistent and predictable. Because stewarded ministry graces [*charis*] reside permanently in believers, they can always be employed to express a gift [*charisma*].

Charisma Is According to the Charis Given

New Testament ministry gifts [*charisma*] are often described as "according to" a grace [*charis*] given. The words "according to" mean, "in agreement with," or, "on the basis of." They are employed to make apparent the relationship between two or more things, sometimes revealing the unseen source of what can be seen. They connect cause and effect and reveal the means by which things are accomplished.

In the context of grace for effectual ministry the words "according to" draw attention to the significant relationship between unique graces stewarded and unique ministries rendered. They reveal the harmony between what is at work within — stewarded graces — and what shines out — ministry gifts. They connect invisible inward graces [*charis*] with visible outward ministries [*charisma*].

Paul's Ministry

Paul often employed the words "according to" when expressing the vital relationship between the ministry grace stewarded to him and his unique ministry. In Ephesians 3:7, he wrote,

> *"I was made a minister, according to the gift of the grace of God given unto me."*
>
> Ephesians 3:7

In I Corinthians 3:10, he stated the same fact with these words,

"According to the grace of God which is given unto me, as a wise masterbuilder, I have laid the foundation..."

I Corinthians 3:10

Paul was a minister, a wise masterbuilder and a foundation layer "according to" — by means of and in harmony with — the special grace given to him. To the Colossian believers, he wrote,

"Whereof I am made a minister, according to the dispensation [stewardship] of God which is given to me for you..."

Colossians 1:25

Paul told the Colossians that he was made a minister "according to" what God had stewarded to him. Although he did not use the word grace in this verse, it is clear that he was referring to that endowment of ministry ability which, in other places, he termed grace.

Believers' Ministries

The words "according to" are used other places in the epistles to demonstrate the significant relationship between graces given and ministries rendered. In Romans 12:6, Paul wrote,

"Having then gifts differing according to the grace that is given to us..."

Romans 12:6

Believers' ministry gifts [*charisma*] differ "according to" the grace [*charis*] given to them. In other words, the ministry gift each believer possesses and the ministry they render is directly dependent upon the grace stewarded to them. Paul's words from Romans 12:6 could be rendered this way,

"Our spiritual gifts and unique abilities for ministry are not the same. They differ depending upon the variety of ministry grace God has given to each of us."

In his first epistle, Peter expressed the significant relationship between ministry graces and ministry gifts this way,

> *"As every man hath received the gift, even so minister the same one to another, as good stewards of the manifold grace of God."*
>
> I Peter 4:10

Peter exhorted believers to minister to one another using the gift [*charisma*] they had received from the Lord. When they did so, he said, they would be good stewards of the manifold grace [*charis*] of God. Basically, Peter told believers,

> *"When you minister with your unique gift, you are being a good steward of the unique grace God entrusted to you."*

Stewarded graces are the source of spiritual giftings and the origin of effectual service. They are the well-spring of ministry; the invisible, inward endowments of divine ability which enable believers to produce visible, outward results. The particular spiritual gift each believer possesses and expresses [*charisma*] is a direct result of the particular ministry grace [*charis*] stewarded to and cultivated by them.

11

Stewarded Ministry Ability

Ministry graces are the particular abilities God stewards to believers which enable them to be effective in particular ministries. When believers recognize, cultivate, and use their grace-gifts, they meet the needs of the lost, meet the needs of the body of Christ, and bring God's purposes to pass. The stewarding of unique ministry graces precedes and produces unique ministries.

Stewards of Ministry Grace

The Greek word for steward — *oikonomos* — comes from two words which together mean, "to arrange a house." In Bible times, stewards were men hired by householders to manage their houses or estates. Stewards were given the responsibility, the authority, and the means to administrate what belonged to the householder. They managed his affairs, collected receipts, and paid expenditures. They were often responsible to deal out proper portions of goods to the householder's children. Some stewards were administrators of a king's finances or a city's finances.

The word "steward" is used metaphorically of believers because believers are entrusted with grace-gifts, granted authority, and given responsibility to minister on God's behalf. They are, in a sense, "hired" to serve in His household by administrating His heavenly gifts.

Paul notified the church at Ephesus of his grace stewardship when he wrote,

"Assuming that you have heard of the stewardship of God's grace...
that was entrusted to me to dispense to you for your benefit."

                                        Ephesians 3:2 Amp

Paul not only described himself as a preacher, a teacher, and an apostle, but also as a steward of grace. He was not the owner of his grace, but the manager and administrator of it. The grace entrusted to him was not a personal gift given to him for his own benefit, but a ministry ability stewarded to him for the benefit of others. Grace was given by God the owner to Paul the steward for the benefit of others.

The apostle Peter described all believers as stewards of grace when he wrote,

"As every man hath received the gift, even so minister the same one
to another, as good stewards of the manifold grace of God."

                                        I Peter 4:10

Peter declared that "every man hath received the gift." The word "received" comes from the Greek *lambano* which means, "to receive what is offered, to take possession of, or to lay hold of a thing in order to use it." God expects every believer to take possession of the ministry grace He offers and, as a good steward, use that grace to minister to others.

Following his exhortation that believers be good stewards of grace, Peter wrote,

"If any man speak, let him speak as the oracles of God; if any man
minister, let him do it as of the ability which God giveth..."

                                        I Peter 4:11

Believers are to minister with "the ability which God giveth." The word "ability" comes from the Greek *ischus*. This word refers to an inward ability or inherent personal power that manifests itself in an outward manner. In Luke 10:27 *ischus* is used to describe the way believers are to love God outwardly with all the strength and love they have within. In II Thessalonians 1:9 *ischus* signifies the inherent power of the Lord Jesus Christ that is visibly expressed as glory. In II Peter 2:11 *ischus* is used to describe angels which are mighty. In the scripture above, Peter used *ischus* to denote the supernatural abilities God gives to believers by which they are enabled to speak and work effectively.

Believers are to minister by the *ischus* which God "giveth." The word "giveth" comes from the Greek *choregeo* and means, "to procure and supply all things necessary to fit out a chorus; to supply or furnish abundantly." God abundantly supplies to the members of His body the abilities they need in order to perform effectively in their assigned parts. When the chorus called the body of Christ recognizes, embraces, and makes use of the abilities God has supplied, its performance will command a standing ovation!

Stewarded Spiritual Talents

The Amplified Bible renders Peter's words to believers about being stewards of grace this way:

> *"As each of you has received a gift (a particular spiritual talent, a gracious divine endowment), employ it for one another as [befits] good trustees of God's many-sided grace — faithful stewards of the extremely diverse [powers and gifts granted to Christians by] unmerited favor."*
>
> *I Peter 4:10 Amp*

Paul's words to the Romans concerning grace are very similar. He wrote,

> *"Having gifts (faculties, talents, qualities) that differ according to the grace given us, let us use them..."*
>
> *Romans 12:6 Amp*

According to Peter, every believer has been stewarded a "particular spiritual talent." According to Paul, every believer has a different spiritual faculty, spiritual talent, or spiritual quality.

In the natural realm, particular talents are resident in certain people. A person's talent is a native ability which they have discovered and developed and are now noted for. Often parents will say concerning their grown children who enjoy success in a particular endeavor, "They had a talent in that area since they were young children." The mother of a veterinarian may say, "My son always had a way with animals." The parents of a skilled musician may remark, "Our daughter took to music right away. It was so natural for her."

People often determine their careers by their natural talents. If a person is gifted in mathematics, they may pursue a career in engineering, physics, or another related field. If a person has a talent and love for music, they may pursue a vocation in music. If a person is specially physically endowed, they may pursue a career in sports. If a person has a deep natural compassion for people, they may pursue a career in nursing.

Spiritually, we can recognize a similar thing. After believers are born again and have grown spiritually, it becomes apparent that they possess certain spiritual talents. These spiritual talents are not the result of unique personalities, specific genetic backgrounds, or different social upbringings, but are the result of God-stewarded ministry graces. Often these grace-talents seem native; almost natural. And they are native, in a sense, because God puts them in believers. Over time, these graces become woven into the fabric of their lives. When believers find their places in the body of Christ and serve according to the graces stewarded to them, it is hard to imagine them doing anything else.

Stewarded Equipment

In the business world companies hire a variety of employees to assist them in accomplishing their overall vision. A road construction company, for example, hires truck drivers, mechanics, accountants, foremen, paving operators, grader operators, and other kinds of employees to enable them to build roads.

In order for each employee of a road construction company to perform the task they are hired to do, they must be supplied with the proper equipment. If an employee is hired to load trucks with gravel, he is supplied with a loader. If an employee is hired as an accountant, he is supplied with office equipment. If an employee is hired to sweep the road surface, he is supplied with a power broom. The equipment provided to company employees does not benefit them personally, but enables them to do their job effectively and benefit the company.

Like owners of companies, God has a vision. To facilitate His vision, He "hires" believers and stewards supernatural equipment to them. If a believer is "hired by God" to teach, teaching grace will be stewarded to him and he will have a supernatural ability to teach. If a believer is "hired by God" to pastor, pastoral grace will be stewarded to him and he will have a divine ability to pastor. If a believer is "hired by God" to give, then the grace of God to make money will be stewarded to him so that he can prosper abundantly and give liberally. If a believer is "hired by God" to administrate, the grace to administrate will be stewarded to him and he will possess a special wisdom to administrate. If a believer is "hired by God" to work miracles, a grace to work miracles will be stewarded to him and he will be enabled to work miracles. The stewarding of particular ministry graces enable believers to labor effectively in their unique tasks and contribute to the overall success of God's business.

Graces Stewarded to Vessels

In the natural realm, vessels are created for the purpose of retaining and safely delivering the contents consigned to them. Water entrusted to a vessel can be carried from its source to a place of thirst and dispensed to meet a need. A water-vessel makes it possible for a person who cannot make direct contact with the well to drink from the well.

On a ministry trip to the country of Estonia in early 1990, I noticed that the grocery stores were filled with food products from other countries. There was juice from France, milk from Finland, and cereal from Germany. Each unique product was in a unique container. By the means of containers, each product was preserved and delivered to the people of Estonia. In the process of getting a product from source to need the container is critical!

In the New Testament, God thoughtfully consigns different graces to different human vessels and then sends those vessels to dispense what has been entrusted to them. While speaking to Ananias about Saul, Jesus said,

> *"...he is a chosen vessel unto me, to bear my name before the Gentiles, and kings, and the children of Israel...."*
>
> *Acts 9:15*

Paul was a "chosen vessel" entrusted with a special grace and assigned the task of carrying Jesus' name to the Gentiles, to kings, and to the children of Israel.

Believers are vessels in God's house [II Tim. 2:20]. They are containers of valuable graces. When they minister by the graces stewarded to them, they discharge gifts from God into the world and into the body of Christ. In this way, people receive supernatural, heavenly blessings from the Lord. Like the woman in the Old Testament whose oil did not fail, believers will never exhaust the supply of ministry grace that flows out of their vessels!

Grace Couriers

One way to ensure that things are delivered in a timely manner to the right people is to send them by a reliable courier. If, for example, I wanted to send a book to a missionary in China, I could send it with someone I trusted who was going to China to visit that missionary. The trusted courier would deliver the book in a timely fashion to the person for whom it was intended.

At different times in my own travels, I have carried personal mail, special gifts, office supplies, and even sums of money on behalf of others. Every time I delivered one of these items, I was thanked by the sender of the gift and by the recipient of the gift.

There are people all over the world with significant needs. But Jesus and the Father are in heaven. How do they deliver their goods to the people they want to bless? They do so by entrusting their goods to believers. God-sent grace couriers travel to the designated people and lovingly administer the grace-gifts entrusted to them. The grace-couriers will be thanked by the Sender and by the recipients of the heavenly goods.

Ministry graces are the special abilities God stewards to believers which remain in their care to be used as He directs. They are varieties of supernatural abilities deposited into the treasury of human vessels which enable those vessels to accomplish their tasks in the kingdom of God. These special graces are not lent to believers for a brief moment and then reclaimed. They do not come upon, lift, come upon, and lift again. These unique ministry graces, rather, remain in the care of believers and enable them to accomplish their unique and significant ministries.

12

Special Endowments for Special Tasks

The specific task God assigns each believer determines the specific variety of ministry grace He endows them with. This truth is beautifully expressed by the Amplified Bible's rendering of Paul's words,

"According to the grace (the special endowment for my task) of God bestowed upon me, like a skillful architect and master builder I laid [the] foundation..."

I Corinthians 3:10 Amp

I don't know if the men who drafted the Amplified Bible were aware of the significant revelation about ministry grace they brought out in their rendering of I Corinthians 3:10. In any case, their amplification of the word "grace" is very accurate. They referred to grace as a "special endowment for [a] task."

God had assigned Paul a specific task. To enable him to fulfill that task, God specially endowed him. Paul's task was to lay spiritual foundations as a wise masterbuilder. The special endowment which enabled him to fulfill that task was the ministry grace God bestowed upon him.

Financial Endowments

Financial endowments are sometimes made by wealthy individuals. The general purpose of any endowment is to enable others to pursue and accomplish the special interest of the one who made the endowment. Endowments are not random gifts or spur of the moment investments, but are well thought out financial plans. By making financial endowments, endowers seek to ensure that interests they hold dear will be pursued by others, sometimes even after their death.

The person who makes an endowment chooses someone to manage his endowment. The chosen manager will oversee the endowment and administer it at the time and in the manner specified by the endower. No matter what other needs are present or how tempted the manager may be to use the endowment in another way, it can only be used as specified by the endower.

If a wealthy man had a strong interest in Spanish students becoming marine biologists, he could make a financial endowment to a particular university specifying that every year a full scholarship be granted to the most qualified Spanish student studying in that field. The university, as manager of the endowment, would be responsible to administer the appropriate amount of money each year to a student who met the criteria.

Another individual might make an endowment to a charitable organization that cares for the poor, specifying that $5,000 be given each year to a single mother who was raising a physically handicapped child. The charitable organization, as manager of the endowment, would be responsible to administer that money each year to a single mother who met the pre-determined criteria.

Old Testament Endowments

In the Old Testament, God enabled men to accomplish the special tasks He assigned by endowing them with special abilities. For example, when He wanted a tabernacle built, He called Bezaleel and Aholiab and filled them with "the spirit of God, in wisdom, and in understanding, and in knowledge, and in all manner of workmanship" [Ex. 31:2, 6]. He "put wisdom" in these men's hearts so they "knew how to work all manner of work" [Ex. 35:35]. By the means of special endowments these men knew "how to work all manner of work" and made everything the Lord commanded [Ex. 36:1-39:31].

Specially endowed men also participated in the building of Solomon's temple. When Solomon requested skilled and cunning men from Huram, he sent him those men and said,

"And now I have sent a cunning man, endued [endowed] with understanding...skilful to work in gold...silver...brass...iron...stone... timber...fine linen...graving..."

II Chronicles 2:13-14

Near the beginning of his reign, Solomon requested for himself and received from God a substantial endowment of wisdom to rule Israel. Realizing that he was not qualified to perform the leadership task God had assigned him, he had asked for wisdom, saying,

"And now, O LORD my God, thou hast made thy servant king instead of David my father: and I am but a little child: I know not how to go out or come in...Give therefore thy servant an understanding heart to judge thy people, that I may discern between good and bad: for who is able to judge this thy so great a people."

I Kings 4:7-9

Although Solomon had been chosen by God to lead the nation of Israel, he felt like a child who didn't know how to go out or come in. Because he felt inadequate, he asked God to grant him wisdom; the ability he needed for the work God called him to. God answered Solomon with these words,

"Because thou hast asked this thing...for thyself understanding to discern judgement; Behold, I have done according to thy words: lo, I have given thee a wise and an understanding heart..."

I Kings 3:11-12

God gave Solomon a "wise and understanding heart." By that special endowment of wisdom, he was able to serve as king and fulfilled the work God had called him to.

New Testament Grace Endowments

Immediately prior to His final ascent into heaven, Jesus commissioned the church to continue His ministry. He told His disciples,

> *"All power is given unto me...Go ye therefore, and teach all nations...Go ye into all the world, and preach the gospel to every creature...as my Father hath sent me, even so send I you..."*
>
> *Matthew 28:18-19; Mark 16:15; John 20:21*

Jesus not only commissioned the church to continue His ministry. He also endowed the church with the full measure of His ministry ability so that she could fulfill the great task given to her. Notice these words about that divine endowing,

> *"But unto every one of us is given grace according to the measure of the gift of Christ. Wherefore he saith, When he ascended on high, he...gave gifts unto men..."*
>
> *Ephesians 4:7-8*

Because of His deep love for the human race, Jesus supernaturally endowed the church, ensuring that the work He began would continue and succeed after He was gone. Some in the church were endowed with apostolic grace-gifts. Some were endowed with pastoral grace-gifts. Some were endowed with teaching grace-gifts. Others were endowed with healing grace-gifts, exhortation grace-gifts, giving grace-gifts, teaching grace-gifts, practical service grace-gifts, and administrative grace-gifts.

Peter's words as rendered by the Amplified Bible offer us wonderful insight into New Testament grace endowments. He wrote,

> *"As each of you has received a gift (a particular spiritual talent, a gracious divine endowment), employ it for one another as [befits] good trustees of God's many-sided grace..."*
>
> *I Peter 4:10 Amp*

Every believer has received a "gracious divine endowment." These divine endowments enable believers to accomplish things they could not accomplish by their own means. Without grace endowments, no believer — not even the strongest, wisest, richest, smartest, and most personally developed — would have the means to accomplish the ministry they are called to. Grace endowments make effective ministry possible!

In the context of teaching the Corinthian church about ministry, Paul wrote,

> *"Now there are distinctive varieties and distributions of endowments [extraordinary powers distinguishing certain Christians, due to the power of Divine grace operating in their souls by the Holy Spirit]."*
>
> *I Corinthians 12:4 Amp*

The Amplified Bible's rendering of I Corinthians 12:4 expresses the doctrine of grace for effectual ministry in a profound way. It reveals that Christians are different from one another because of the "distinctive varieties and distributions of endowments" given to them. It reveals that every Christian possesses a unique "extra-ordinary power" for service "due to the power of Divine grace" operating in them.

Paul's and Peter's Grace Endowments

Paul wrote to the churches of Galatia about his and Peter's unique commissions and unique grace endowments. His words highlight the significant relationship between the task God assigns each believer and the grace endowment which enables them to accomplish that task. He wrote,

> *"...the gospel of the uncircumcision was committed unto me, as the gospel of the circumcision was unto Peter; (For he that wrought effectually in Peter to the apostleship of the circumcision, the same was mighty in me toward the Gentiles:) And when James, Cephas, and John...perceived the grace that was given unto me..."*
>
> *Galatians 2:7-9*

The apostle Peter was commissioned by God to go to the circumcision. Therefore, God "wrought effectually in Peter to the apostleship of the circumcision." God assigned Peter the task of ministering to the Jews and, therefore, endowed him with the ability to minister to the Jews. Peter's commission and his endowment were harmonious.

The apostle Paul was commissioned by God to go to the Gentiles. Therefore, God "was mighty in [him] toward the Gentiles." God assigned Paul the task of ministering to the Gentiles and, therefore, endowed him with the ability to minister to the Gentiles. Paul's commission and his endowment were harmonious.

Supernatural Sufficiency for Service

Paul referred to his supernatural endowment for service in his second letter to the Corinthians when he wrote,

> *"Not that we are sufficient of ourselves to think anything as of ourselves; but our sufficiency is of God; Who also hath made us able ministers..."*
>
> II Corinthians 3:5-6

Paul and his partners did not consider themselves to be sufficient of themselves for their ministries. The word "sufficient" comes from the Greek *hikanos* and means, "enough, or sufficient in ability." The word "of" comes from the Greek *ek* and denotes the point of origin of something. According to Paul, there was nothing that originated within himself or within any of his ministry associates that made them sufficient for their ministry assignments.

Paul did not say, however, that he and his partners were insufficient for their tasks. He said, rather, "but our sufficiency is of God." Here the word "sufficiency" comes from the Greek *hikanotes* and means, "the ability or competency to accomplish a thing." Paul's sufficiency was "of God." In other words, God the Source endowed Paul and his partners with a divine competency to accomplish their ministry assignments.

The Amplified Bible renders Paul's words this way,

"...but our power and ability and sufficiency are from God."
II Corinthians 3:5

In verse six, Paul said that God made he and his ministry partners "able ministers." The word "able" comes from the Greek *hikanoo* which means, "to equip one with adequate powers to perform duties." Paul and his ministry associates were endowed by God with adequate powers and the necessary sufficiency to perform their ministry duties!

Paul confirmed that he was endowed with supernatural ability in his first letter to Timothy when he wrote,

"And I thank Christ Jesus our lord, who hath enabled me, for that he counted me faithful, putting me into the ministry..."
I Timothy 1:12

Paul said that the Lord had "enabled" him. The word "enabled" comes from the Greek *endunamoo* which literally means, "inward *dunamis.*" To be enabled means, "to be inwardly endued with the power to accomplish whatever is willed." The Lord Jesus not only put Paul into the ministry; He also put *dunamis* into Paul so that he could accomplish his ministry.

A few years ago, I was speaking with the pastor of a church where I was ministering. During our conversation, he asked for my advice concerning a problem in his church. I got quiet and listened to my heart to see if the Holy Spirit had anything special to say. Before I could think, I heard myself ask this pastor, "Are you sure you are called by God to be a pastor?" He thought for a moment and answered in the affirmative. Then I asked him, "Are you sure you are called by God to pastor this church?" Again, he answered in the affirmative. Then I told him, "It is not possible that you are truly called to pastor this church and don't know what to do." He looked at me in a kind of surprised way and said, "You know, you are right. I actually do know what to do. I was just a little unsure of myself."

When God calls any believer to any assignment, He endows them with the supernatural sufficiency and the adequate power to accomplish that assignment. God will never give a believer an assignment that supersedes the divine sufficiency He has granted. No believer, then, should ever suppose that he is under-endowed for his task!

Timothy's Grace Endowment

Paul exhorted Timothy to pay attention to his special inward ministry endowment with these words,

> *"Neglect not the gift that is in thee, which was given thee by prophecy, with the laying on of the hands of the presbytery."*
> *I Timothy 4:14*

Timothy's gift [*charisma*] was not a special anointing that came upon him unexpectedly or an occasional manifestation of the Spirit. His gift was a resident inward endowment of God-ability that had been imparted to him during a sacred time of prayer, prophecy, and laying on of hands. This gift was "given" to Timothy. "Given" comes from the Greek *didomi* which means, "to give over or to commit to someone's care something to be administered." According to Paul, Timothy could either neglect his resident inward endowment or he could cultivate and use it.

Weymouth translates I Timothy 4:14 this way,

> *"Do not be careless about the gifts with which you are endowed."*
> *I Timothy 4:14*

The Amplified Bible renders Paul's words to Timothy this way,

> *"Do not neglect the gift which is in you, that special inward endowment, which was directly imparted to you by the Holy Spirit..."*
> *I Timothy 4:14 Amp*

According to the Amplified Bible, Timothy's grace-gift was a "special inward endowment" directly imparted to him by the Holy Spirit.

In his second letter to Timothy, Paul exhorted him with these words,

"Wherefore I put thee in remembrance that thou stir up the gift of God, which is in thee by the putting on of my hands."

II Timothy 1:6

Again, Paul reminded Timothy of his indwelling *charisma*, or grace-gift, and exhorted him to pay attention to it. Evidently, Timothy's resident gift did not stir him up. Rather, Timothy was to stir up his resident gift.

In some cases, as with Paul and Timothy, God can impart or enhance a grace-gift through the laying on of hands. I remember a meeting I attended in 1981 before I started to travel in my teaching ministry. Kenneth E. Hagin was teaching in that meeting, but he also took time to lay hands on those who were going into full time ministry. I went forward in that service and he laid his hands on me. While driving home after that meeting I said to myself, almost without conscious thought, "I am ready to teach now." I believe that a grace to teach was either imparted to me at that time or that a teaching grace I already possessed was actuated or enhanced.

In a meeting I conducted several years ago something similar happened. A young musician in the church where I was ministering approached me after my teaching and asked me to lay hands on him to enhance his music ministry. Initially I hesitated, but then felt prompted by the Holy Spirit to do so. When I laid hands on him, I felt something go into him and watched as he fell to the floor. I knew that something special had transpired. A year later this young man reported to me that his ministry had changed significantly, that his song writing had been greatly enhanced, and that he and his wife had won an award as amateur Christian musicians.

More recently, I felt impressed by the Holy Spirit to lay hands on a teaching elder in a local church. I sensed that God wanted to add something to that person in terms of teaching ability. I followed the leading of the Holy Spirit, laid hands on that person, and ministered a brief word of knowledge to them. Several months later the pastor of the church remarked to me that the person I had ministered to was noticeably more effective in their teaching.

Grace endowments continue to be measured out by the Lord Jesus right up to this present day. For every need in the world and for every purpose of God a vessel is called, saved, placed in the body of Christ, and endowed with a unique ministry grace. By the means of supernatural grace endowments, chosen vessels accomplish the unique tasks God assigns them in His kingdom.

13

The Measure of Faith

In his epistle to the Romans, Paul penned these enlightening words concerning diverse graces and the diversity of ministries they produce,

"For I say, through the grace given unto me, to every man that is among you, not to think of himself more highly than he ought to think; but to think soberly, according as God hath dealt to every man the measure of faith. For as we have many members in one body, and all members have not the same office: So we, being many, are one body in Christ, and every one members one of another. Having then gifts differing according to the grace that is given to us, whether prophecy, let us prophesy according to the proportion of faith; Or ministry, let us wait on our ministering: or he that teacheth, on teaching; Or he that exhorteth, on exhortation: he that giveth, let him do it with simplicity; he that ruleth, with diligence; he that sheweth mercy, with cheerfulness."

Romans 12:3-6

Paul exhorted the Roman believers not to think too highly of themselves but to think soberly according to what God had dealt to them of "the measure of faith." He followed his exhortation with an explanation of why they should do so. They should do so "For" — because — there are many members in the one body and the many members don't have the same function. They should do so because each believer has been given a unique place in the body of Christ and a unique grace-gift for ministry.

To understand what Paul was teaching in these verses, we must realize that Romans 12:3-8 is a whole section of thought. Verse three is an exhortation and the following verses are the truth which validates the exhortation. Verse three must, therefore, be interpreted with verses four through eight in mind. Only by examining Romans 12:3-8 as a complete section of thought can we understand what "the measure of faith" is and grasp the important truth Paul intended to communicate.

Think Soberly

In Romans 12:3, Paul wrote,

"For I say, through the grace given unto me, to every man that is among you, not to think of himself more highly than he ought to think; but to think soberly, according as God hath dealt to every man the measure of faith."

Romans 12:3

The word "think" Paul used in his exhortation that believers should not "think of [themselves] more highly" than they ought is the Greek *phroneo* which means, "to have an opinion of one's self, to be modest, to not exceed the bounds of modestly." The word "soberly" which described how these believers should think of themselves comes from the Greek *sophroneo* and means, "of sound mind, of moderate estimate." The Romans should not overestimate themselves, but should think soberly about themselves, according to "the measure of faith" dealt to them by God.

What was Paul referring to when he wrote about "the measure of faith" that the Romans were to think of themselves according to? He was referring to the unique abilities God measures to believers to equip them for different ministries and the faith to function which arises when they properly assess what has been dealt to them. Let's consider several reasons why this understanding of "the measure of faith" is accurate.

The Context

That "the measure of faith" in Romans 12:3 refers to the diverse ministry abilities dealt to believers and the confidence to minister by those abilities is clear when one examines the context in which these words are found. After exhorting believers to think of themselves according to "the measure of faith" dealt to them, Paul explained why they must do so. He began his explanation with the preposition "For" and, by so doing, vitally connected verse three with verses four, five, and six. He wrote,

"For as we have many members in one body, and all members have not the same office: So we, being many, are one body in Christ, and every one members one of another. Having then gifts differing according to the grace that is given to us..."

Romans 12:4-6

Paul presented a three-fold reason why believers must soberly estimate themselves according to "the measure of faith" dealt to them. First, they must do so because the many members of the one body "have not the same office"[vs. 4]. The word "office" comes from the Greek *praxis* and means, "a doing, to practice, or to function." Because the members of the body of Christ do not have the same function, each believer must soberly rate "the measure of faith" dealt to them so they can determine their function in the body.

Second, believers must soberly estimate themselves according to "the measure of faith" dealt to them because the members of the body of Christ are many [vs. 5]. In verse five, Paul was developing the line of reasoning he introduced in verse three and expanded in verse four. That is why he used the words, "So we." His words in verse five were a continuation of what he wrote in verses three and four.

When Paul said, "So we, being many," he was not referring to the quantity of believers in the one body, but to the diversity in gifting and function of the members of the one body. Because the members of the body of Christ are "many" — very diverse in gifting and function

— each must determine what unique part they are and what they are uniquely gifted to do.

Third, believers must soberly estimate themselves according to "the measure of faith" dealt to them because the members of the body have "gifts differing according to the grace that is given" [vs. 6]. Because each believer is uniquely grace-gifted, each believer must soberly estimate themselves.

The words "Having then" connect verse six to Paul's previous words in verses three, four, and five and indicate that he was preparing to summarize his short exhortation. His words could be rendered this way:

"Since, as I have already said, believers have gifts that are different depending upon the grace given to them..."

Paul's statement in verse six that believers have different gifts because of the different graces given to them was another way of stating that believers have been dealt different measures of faith [vs. 3], that believers do not have the same function in the body [vs. 4], and that believers are diverse in terms of ministry [vs. 5].

The examples of grace ministry Paul offered in verses six through eight strengthen his exhortation in verse three and support his teaching in verses four through six. This further confirms that Romans 12:3-8 concerns believers' proper estimation of and faithful use of the diverse measures of ministry abilities God deals to the different members of the body of Christ.

The context in which Paul exhorted believers to judge themselves according to "the measure of faith" dealt to them strongly suggests that the phrase "the measure of faith" is simply another way to describe those pre-determined portions of ministry ability which God distributes to different members of the body of Christ and the faith to function in those ministries.

Dealt and Measure

That "the measure of faith" in Romans 12:3 refers to the diverse ministry abilities God stewards to believers and the confidence to minister by those abilities is further confirmed by Paul's use of the words "dealt" and "measure." The word "dealt" comes from the Greek *merizo* and means, "a part, a portion, or to divide into parts." The word "measure" comes from the Greek *metron* and means, "a determined extent or a portion measured off."

According to Paul, God has dealt — apportioned or divided — different measures — parts or portions — of something to the different members of the body of Christ. By exhorting believers to think of themselves according to the "measure" God had "dealt" to them and then following up in the next few verses with teaching about ministry, Paul made it clear that he was referring to God's action of measuring out unique abilities to different members of the body of Christ to enable them to minister in unique ways.

Why Faith?

Why did Paul use the word "faith" in the phrase "the measure of faith" if he was teaching about ministry giftings? He used the word "faith" because of the vital connection between believers properly assessing what God has dealt to them in terms of ministry grace and the confidence they will have to minister when they properly assess that grace. The sober assessment of ministry graces stewarded and the accompanying faith to minister by those graces are so interrelated that in this context Paul simply referred to the ministry abilities dealt to believers and the confidence to minister by them as "the measure of faith."

The word faith can mean, "a conviction of the truth of anything." Just as faith to receive becomes alive when believers comprehend what promises have been given to them in Christ, so faith to function becomes alive when believers discover what special ministry graces have been dealt to them. The revelation of a promise genders faith to receive. The sober estimation of a ministry grace-gift stewarded genders faith to function.

We could say, then, that a faith to function is part of each ministry grace dealt. In other words, when believers properly estimate themselves according the ministry abilities dealt to them, they will be confident to function in their unique ministries. No doubt, this is why Paul also exhorted believers in this context to minister in their giftings according to their "proportion of faith" [Rom. 12:6].

So What is the Measure of Faith?

The Amplified Bible helps us understand what the measure of faith is by its rendering of Romans 12:3. It says,

"I warn everyone among you not to estimate and think of himself more highly than he ought...but to rate his ability with sober judgement..."

Romans 12:3 Amp

Notice the words "rate his ability." Rating one's ability with sober judgement is the same as thinking soberly about one's measure of faith.

Paul was alerting believers to the fact that unique and diverse ministry abilities had been dealt to them and exhorting them to soberly rate those abilities. Once they had soberly rated what had been dealt to them, they should function in their unique grace-giftings according to their proportion of faith.

We could render Paul's words in Romans 12:3-6 as follows:

"Because I have been graced as an apostle to the Gentiles, I am qualified to speak to you. I exhort each one of you not to think more highly of himself than he should. Rather, estimate yourself soberly, according to the variety and measure of ministry ability God has dealt to you. When you do this, you will see yourself properly as a member of the body of Christ who has been entrusted with a unique ability and a specific function. When you soberly evaluate the ability for ministry that has been measured to you, you will be bold and confident to function in your ministry."

"Yes, it is true that you are all members of one body and are one

in Christ. It is also true, however, that you differ from one another in calling and function. You have many different assignments and many different abilities, but are one body in Christ, being members of one another. Now that I have established the truth that each of you possesses different gifts for ministry depending upon the unique graces given to you, I exhort you to make use of your special grace-gifts and function in your unique ministries according to your proportion of faith."

14

A Benefit for Others

Grace for effectual ministry is fundamentally different than the other two primary New Testament graces in that it does not benefit the person to whom it is given, but benefits those to whom the graced person is sent. This fact is evident in these words Paul wrote to the Ephesians,

> *"If ye have heard of the dispensation of the grace of God which is given me to you-ward..."*
>
> *Ephesians 3:2*

Paul described the grace that God had given to him as "to you-ward." This grace was not "Paul-ward" as was the grace by which he was saved. And it was not "Paul-ward" as was the grace by which he could be inwardly strengthened. The ministry grace given to Paul was "Ephesian-ward." In other words, Paul's unique gift of grace was ultimately for the benefit of others.

The Amplified Bible renders Paul's words this way,

> *"Assuming that you have heard of the stewardship of God's grace... that was entrusted to me to dispense to you for your benefit."*
>
> *Ephesians 3:2 Amp*

Paul said that the grace entrusted to him was "to dispense to you for your benefit." His grace was to be dispensed to the Gentiles for their blessing, their help, and their enrichment. The Gentiles would be benefitted because something supernatural was going to come to them from God through Paul.

Paul penned similar words to the Colossians when he wrote,

"In it [the church] I became a minister in accordance with the divine stewardship which was entrusted to me for you — as its object and for your benefit..."

Colossians 1:25 Amp

The Colossians were the "object" — the target, the final destination — of the divine stewardship entrusted to Paul. He was made a minister for their "benefit." We could say, then, that when God called and graced Paul, He had the Colossians in mind.

Peter confirmed that ministry graces are given for the benefit of others when he wrote,

"As every man hath received the gift, even so minister the same one to another, as good stewards of the manifold grace of God."

I Peter 4:10

The "gift" Peter referred to which "every man hath received" was not a personal gift to be enjoyed, but a ministry grace to be employed for the benefit of others. Grace-gifts received are to be ministered "one to another." They are not supposed to terminate at the persons to whom they have been stewarded. Grace-gifted believers, then, are intermediaries. They are like UPS delivery persons who are entrusted with packages to deliver to certain addresses. Those who use their grace-gifts as they should are described as "good stewards of the manifold grace of God." The true beneficiaries of ministry graces, however, are those ministered to by grace-endowed believers.

Children's Giving of Gifts

Most Christians enjoy the Christmas season. During this season, they think about the fact that God so loved the world that He sent the gift of His Son. To imitate God's giving, Christians also give gifts. Everyone likes to be involved with this giving of gifts; even the young children. The young children have a problem, however. Their problem is that they do not have the means to supply the gifts they want to give.

Most parents solve this problem by purchasing gifts on behalf of their children, wrapping those gifts, and placing those gifts under the tree. At present opening time, the parents place these gifts in their children's hands and whisper to them who the gift is for. As they remain seated, the children proudly take the gift, walk to the person it is for, hand it to them, and exclaim, "This gift is from me!" The person who receives the gift opens it, shows excitement, and tells the child, "Thank you so much for your special gift!"

Because of their thankful hearts, believers desire to serve God by ministering to others. They have a problem, however. They do not have the means within themselves to provide what others need. God has solved this problem by entrusting unique grace-gifts to believers and then directing them to the right people. If those people will receive what is being offered to them by God through a grace endowed believer, they will be enriched. They will say, "Thank you for blessing me with your precious gift!" And ultimately, they will give thanks to God.

15

A Divine Inward Motivation

Ministry grace is not only a divine inward ability which enables believers to labor skillfully; it is also that divine internal impetus, that inward spiritual force, which influences believers toward certain ministries and certain people. Ministry graces not only equip believers for unique ministries; they also produce persistent inward urgings which propel believers toward the intended beneficiaries of their grace-gifts.

Believers sometimes refer to the persistent inward urgings of grace as their calling. And these urgings can, in fact, be their calling. God's callings do not always come by a vision, a burning bush, a prophetic word, or some other spectacular, external experience. For many believers the persistent inward urgings of the ministry grace that God has stewarded to them is their calling.

God's Old Testament Way

In the Old Testament, God often called men in ways that could be seen, heard, or felt. When He appeared to Moses, He manifested Himself in the burning bush. Later, He made Moses' hand leprous and then clean again to confirm to him that he was called to a special work [Ex. 4:6-7].

Joseph received a dream from the Lord when he was young. That dream influenced the course of his life, kept him from dangerous snares, and helped him fulfill his calling [Gen. 37:5-11]. When God chose Saul to be king of Israel, He notified him by the words of Samuel the prophet and by anointing oil [I Sam. 10:1]. Later, God sent Samuel to the house of Jesse to designate David as king by anointing him with oil [I Sam. 16:13]. Elisha knew he was called to the prophetic office because Elijah cast his mantle upon him [I Kings 19:19].

Sometimes God called His Old Testament servants by speaking to them in an audible word of the Lord. Other times, as with Gideon, He sent angels with special messages. In some cases, He revealed His plans by giving special dreams or visions. Often, He spoke through prophets. In the Old Testament the callings of God most often came in physical, audible, and external ways.

God's New Testament Way

In the New Testament, God has access to the hearts of His people in a way He did not have in the Old Testament. When calling believers to service, then, He does not often manifest Himself to the natural senses by giving a vision, speaking in an audible voice, or directing through the ministry of a prophet.

Occasionally, those who are called to profound ministries may be visited by the Lord in a vision or called in some other special way. Some may receive a word of prophecy concerning what they are to do for the Lord. For most, however, there will be no burning bush, no mantle thrown, no special vision, no anointing oil, and no prophetic word. How, then, are believers to know what they are called to do? This is where an understanding of the motivating nature of grace for effectual ministry is very helpful.

Unique grace endowments are a primary reason believers are motivated toward different ministries and different people groups. They are a primary reason that one believer is motivated to teach Sunday school at his church in Boston and another is motivated to evangelize in Nepal. They are a primary reason that one believer is motivated to raise up a business in South Africa to support missionaries and another is motivated to quit his job and serve as a missionary in Ireland. They are a primary reason that one believer is motivated to save the lost in Europe and another is motivated to raise a spiritual standard in the South Pacific. Different grace endowments motivate different believers toward different ministries, different people, and different places.

Sometimes those who are not called and graced in the same way as another believer cannot relate to that believer's drive toward a particular ministry. When they observe what that believer is motivated to do, they may think to themselves, "Why would anyone want that ministry?"

Who, for example, would want to do missions work in the jungle? Who would want to labor where there is persecution and hardship? Who would want to work with people who don't bathe, who are illiterate, or who are abusive? Who would want to clean the church? Who would want to pastor a church? Who would want to give themselves to prayer? Who would want to stay home alone and raise the children? Who would want a miracle ministry? Who would want to oversee an orphanage? Who would want to care for the broken-hearted? Who would want to be an apostle to a remote region of the world? Who would want to work in the nursery?

Thinking naturally, we could answer every question with an emphatic, "No one!" But the special graces given to believers motivate them beyond the realm of human preference and urge them, irresistibly at times, to reach out and minister to those for whose benefit they are called and graced.

You might say to me, "Brother Guy, I don't feel anything like that motivating me." If you will take time to listen to your heart in seasons of prayer, worship, study, and waiting upon God, the inner working of grace will be there stirring you toward some ministry. That inward motivation may be strong or it may be gentle, but it will be there. If you have absolutely no motivation to serve the Lord, perhaps you have not been saved by grace.

When my youngest brother was a college student, he took a little break from pursuing the things of God. Spiritually, he was at a standstill. I decided to visit him one weekend when he was at my parents' home. As I stood with him in the kitchen, I told him, "There is something in you from God. There is a calling on your life. From time to time it surfaces from your heart into your thinking, but you push it down, not wanting to make a decision about it. There will come a time, however, when you cannot push it down any more. You will have to make a decision about what is working in you and say yes or no." Eventually my brother yielded to that inner stirring and entered the ministry to which he was called and for which he was graced.

Recently, I met a man who is an evangelist. He knows he is an evangelist and everyone else knows he is an evangelist. In our few brief conversations, it was interesting to note what came out of his mouth. He was always talking about how much God loved people and how wonderful it was to be saved. He told many testimonies about people who had turned to the Lord when he witnessed to them.

What motivates this evangelist is different from what motivates me. I think about bringing believers to maturity. I think about full stature Christians. I think about establishing strong local churches and raising up effective spiritual leaders. I think about sound doctrine and healthy believers. I am concerned about teaching, writing, and helping believers with maturity, character, commitment, and preparation for service.

What is the difference between myself and the evangelist? Is it a difference in salvation, revelation, or doctrine? Is it a difference in commitment? Is it a difference in personality? No. Our difference is in calling and gracing. The evangelist is motivated toward and passionate about saving the lost. I am motivated toward and passionate about developing believers and building strong local churches.

Paul's Divine Inward Motivation

Paul's record of his second visit to Jerusalem offers valuable insight into the motivating nature of ministry grace. He wrote,

> "But contrariwise, when they saw that the gospel of the uncircumcision was committed unto me...the same was mighty in me toward

the Gentiles: And when James, Cephas, and John, who seemed to be
pillars, perceived the grace that was given unto me..."

Galatians 2:7-9

The spiritual leaders in Jerusalem perceived that God was mightily at work in Paul "toward the Gentiles." Paul said they "perceived the grace" that was given unto him. The Amplified Bible renders his words this way,

"For He Who motivated and fitted Peter and worked effectively
through him for the mission to the circumcised, motivated and fitted
me and worked through me also for [the mission to] the Gentiles."

Galatians 2:8 Amp

The Amplified Bible provides a wonderful insight into the motivating nature of ministry grace. It reveals that Peter was not only "fitted" to go to the circumcised; he was also "motivated" to go to the circumcised. It reveals that Paul was not only "fitted" to go to the Gentiles; he was also "motivated" toward the Gentiles. The same God worked in Peter and Paul, but He was "pushing" them toward two different people groups.

Referring to his ministry grace in his letter to the Ephesians, Paul wrote,

"If ye have heard of the dispensation of the grace of God which is
given me to you-ward..."

Ephesians 3:2

Paul described the grace stewarded to him as "to you-ward." His grace motivated him toward the intended recipients of his grace; namely, the Gentiles. The grace stewarded to Paul was a principal factor in determining which people he would minister to.

Thrust Out Into Service

On one occasion during His ministry, Jesus looked out upon the multitudes that were scattered like sheep without a shepherd. Commenting on their serious need, He told His disciples,

> *"...The harvest truly is plenteous, but the labourers are few; Pray ye therefore the Lord of the harvest, that he will send forth labourers into his harvest."*
>
> Matthew 9:37-38

The words "send forth" Jesus used come from the Greek *ekballo*. *Ekballo* is made up of *ek*, which means, "out of or away from," and *ballo*, which means, "to thrust, to cast, to pour, or to insert." In the New Testament *ekballo* is most often translated "cast out." It can mean, "to drive out or to send forth," and implies the notion of violence. It can also mean, "to strongly thrust some thing or some person out of one realm into another."

I was not aware of the meaning of *ekballo* when I prayed for my younger brother in 1994. A Spirit-filled medical doctor who trains other doctors and does disaster relief, he had been asked to travel to Rwanda, Africa to minister to the medical needs of war refugees. As I prayed for him, I continued to hear the word "insertion" in my spirit. I could see that he was being inserted into a specific place, for a specific time, to meet a specific need. He was already equipped, well trained, and motivated. Now was his season to minister out of his special grace to a needy people. It would have been very difficult for him to ignore the thrusting out of the Lord into that waiting field of ministry.

I'm sure you are familiar with the story of Jonah. He was the man God called to preach repentance to the people of Nineveh. Not wanting to go to Nineveh, however, Jonah ran from God's calling. How did God respond to his disobedience? Did He look for a second Jonah? Did He give up on Nineveh? No. Jonah was the man God had ordained for Nineveh and he was going there or he was going to die. By manipulating outward circumstances in an extreme way, God "motivated" Jonah to do His will.

The way the Lord of the harvest thrusts forth New Testament believers is seldom as physical or dramatic as the way He thrusted forth Jonah. The primary way God thrusts believers into their ministries is by endowing them with ministry graces and directing them by His Spirit. Ministry graces serve as a divine stimulus, motivating believers toward their particular fields of ministry.

Motivational Gifts

Several years ago a teaching developed in the church called "Motivational Gifts." In this teaching, believers were encouraged to determine their ministry giftings by evaluating their personalities. People who liked to tell others what to do were considered "prophetically motivated." People who like to study and teach were considered "teaching motivated." People who were shy, quiet, and kind were considered "mercy motivated." People who liked to talk a lot were considered "evangelistically motivated."

One problem that resulted from this teaching was that believers were granted liberty to manifest their personalities and call it a ministry gifting. Who believers are in terms of personality and who they are in terms of grace-gifting may not, however, be the same. In fact, some believers may be graced to minister in ways that do not fit their personalities. It is possible, for example, that a believer with a quiet and shy personality be called and graced as an evangelist. This believer could never lean on an outgoing personality, but would have to depend upon his indwelling grace-gift. His ministry would obviously be according to the ability which God gave him [I Pet. 4:11].

Another believer might be very dynamic in personality and a leader in the business world, but be graced to help in the church. If this person misjudged his calling by rating his personality and intelligence instead of rating his grace, he would cause problems in the church. If he tried to take the lead in spiritual things, others would probably allow him to do so because he was a "natural" leader. The spiritual results of his actions, however, would be minimal and could even be disastrous.

I am a testimony to the fact that there can be a difference between one's personality and one's grace for ministry. In my own personality, I am not outgoing. I prefer to study, write, read, or to compose music. I do not naturally prefer the atmosphere of a crowd or enjoy the responsibility of teaching a congregation. In fact, when I hear other ministers say how much they enjoy preaching and teaching, I cannot relate. I am, however, called and graced to teach. Although I do not naturally prefer this ministry, I cannot ignore the motivating, directing, and enabling power of the teaching grace that has been entrusted to me.

It is possible, of course, that believers' personalities and their grace-giftings be complementary. Some outgoing individuals may be called and graced to be evangelists. Some naturally merciful individuals will be graced to show mercy. Some analytical believers may be called and graced to teach. When we observe some individuals functioning in their ministries, we will say, "They are certainly a natural for that ministry." It is wrong, however, to make any absolute rule in this area. The only thing we can say for sure is that each believer must locate their calling and grace, cultivate their gift, and fulfill their ministry.

Grace Motivation is Proper Motivation

Some believers are motivated to minister because they come from a background of hard work. Some are motivated to minister because they have a deep need to feel useful or significant. Some are motivated to minister because they want to gain acceptance or praise among other Christians. Some are motivated to minister because they are success oriented or because they see potential for financial gain. Paul revealed that some even preached Christ because of a party spirit when he wrote,

> "Some indeed preach Christ even of envy and strife; and some also for good will: The one preach Christ of contention, not sincerely..."
> Philippians 1:15-16

Carnal motivations can produce ministries, but they will not be ministries born out of the purposes, callings, and gracings of God. Although believers who minister from carnal motivations may seem, for a time, to produce good fruit, all ministry that is not motivated by God's calling and enabled by His gracing will be far less profitable, if not unprofitable, for His kingdom. The proper motivation for ministry proceeds from a heavenly commission, from a love for God and for people, and from the unique ministry graces God stewards.

The ministry graces God stewards to believers are like divine catalysts which ignite ministry activity. They are divine provocateurs which compel certain works of service. They are the sparks which, if yielded to and cooperated with, become great spreading fires. They continue to urge, to impel, and to insist on being followed. Stewarded graces initiate a desire to minister which can only be satisfied by doing the ministry the grace is urging.

By the inworking pressure of ministry grace, God pours believers into thirsty places, thrusts them out into ready fields, and strategically inserts them into others' lives. If believers are serious about the Lord and take time to listen to their hearts, they will recognize a consistent inner urging to do specific works of service for Him.

16

Ministry Graces Make Believers Who They Are

On the basis of the grace given to him, Paul declared, "I was made an apostle...I am an apostle...I am what I am." Paul never said, "God uses me in an apostolic way," or, "I am endeavoring to accomplish apostolic work." Because apostolic grace was stewarded to him, Paul was an apostle. Because he was an apostle, apostolic work and apostolic fruit followed.

The unique graces stewarded to believers reside permanently within them. Over time and with use these graces become grafted into their lives till they are no longer believers who have a ministry gift, but believers who are a ministry gift.

People Are, People Do

In the natural realm, people have unique personality traits and native abilities because of their genetic makeup. Scientific studies of identical twins have confirmed this fact. In one study, male twins separated at birth married women with the same name, owned the same breed of dog, worked the same kind of job, and enjoyed the same kinds of food. They liked what they liked and did what they did because of who they were.

My parents had four sons. In many ways, my brothers and I are similar. Our voices are similar. We have similar noses. We have similar personalities. We have similar interests. The primary reason we are similar is because we have the same genetic makeup.

Have you ever wondered why the Dutch act Dutch? They act Dutch because they are Dutch. Have you ever wondered why the Chinese act Chinese? They act Chinese because they are Chinese. Have you ever wondered why men act like men? It is because they are men. Have you ever wondered why women act like women? It is because they are women. Have you ever wondered why intelligent people act intelligent? It is because they are intelligent. Have you ever wondered why people gifted in music write and perform music? It is because they are musicians. It is very natural for people to be and to do who they are.

When a person enters into an occupation based on their native abilities, what they do is a natural outgrowth of who they are. And what they do over time becomes a primary way they are defined by others. We might hear people say things like, "Bob is an electrician," or, "Mary is a musician."

Believers Are, Believers Do

Just as it is natural for people to be and then to do according to their natural endowments, so it is natural for believers to be and then to do according to their spiritual endowments. After ministry graces are bestowed by God, they become infused into believers' spiritual makeup, worked into the core of their being. As these graces are nurtured and employed, they become more and more something believers are and not just something they do.

If a believer is stewarded an apostolic grace and recognizes and develops that grace, he will be an apostle, do the works of an apostle, and bear the fruit of an apostle. If a believer is stewarded pastoral grace and recognizes and develops that grace, he will be a pastor, perform the duties of a pastor, and bear the fruit of a pastor. If a believer is stewarded exhorting grace and recognizes and develops that grace, he will be an exhorter, do the work of exhorting, and bear the fruit of an exhorter.

It is true, then, that the most spiritually-natural thing for an evangelist to do is evangelistic work. The most spiritually-natural thing for an exhorter to do is exhort. The most spiritually-natural thing for a helper to do is to help. The most spiritually-natural thing for a miracle worker to do is to work miracles.

I can say concerning myself that it is spiritually-natural for me teach. It is also spiritually-natural for me to minister in music. I do not feel inadequate when I minister in these ways. I do not feel out of place or beyond my ability. Why is this? It is because I am a teacher. It is because I am a musician. Why am I a teacher? Why am I a musician? I am these ministries because I was called and stewarded a grace to teach and a grace to minister in music and have cultivated those grace-gifts.

Because of God's stewarding of ministry graces, believers will find themselves motivated toward and doing the works of the ministries they are graced for; unless, of course, they are neglecting the graces stewarded to them. When believers take their place in the body and serve with their unique grace-gifts, they will have a sense of peace and contentedness because of the harmony between who they are in grace-gifting and what they are doing in ministry.

17

What About the Anointing?

Concerning the subject of ministry, the term "anointing" is quite familiar; especially in charismatic circles. It is most commonly used to describe that ability of God which makes believers effective in ministry. Often the word "anointing" is used of those who are in spiritual leadership ministries. For example, when a pastor or other spiritual leader is effective, someone may say, "They are really anointed." When a minister senses God ministering through him, he might say, "I am really sensing the anointing."

In light of its current popularity, especially in more charismatic circles, it is interesting to note that the word "anointing" is not used in the epistles in reference to ministry. Even the apostle Paul, from whom we learn so much about New Testament ministry, only used the word "anointing" one time. Speaking of himself in II Corinthians 1:21, he said that God had established and anointed him. We cannot determine if Paul used the word "anointed" in that scripture to denote the special ability God had stewarded to him for ministry or to denote the gift of the Holy Spirit he had received as part of his salvation.

Paul did, of course, acknowledge and teach about the nine manifestations of the Spirit [I Cor. 12:6-11]. And he certainly depended upon the power of the Holy Spirit in his own ministry [I Cor. 2:2; Acts 13:9-12; Rom. 15:19]. He also requested prayer for himself that utterance be given unto him [Col. 4:3]. He did not, however, employ the word "anointing" when speaking about his own ministry or ministry in general.

Paul did not use the word "anointing" in his comprehensive and important instructions to Timothy and Titus concerning ministry. He did, however, exhort Timothy several times to pay attention to his indwelling ministry endowment. In his first letter, he exhorted Timothy to not neglect the grace-gift [*charisma*] that was in him [I Tim. 4:14]. In his second letter, he exhorted Timothy to stir up his indwelling gift [*charisma*]. In both of these exhortations, Paul referred to Timothy's ministry ability as an indwelling grace-gift.

It is also interesting that none of the other men who wrote epistles employed the word "anointing" in the context of ministry. In his first epistle, the apostle John spoke about the anointing that abides within believers and teaches them all things [I Jn. 2:27]. In this context, the word "anointing" clearly refers to the indwelling Holy Spirit and His role in teaching, guiding, and warning believers.

In response to these thoughts, you might say, "Does it really matter what word we use to describe God's endowments of ministry ability? Is it wrong to say we are anointed?"

When teaching New Testament doctrine and bringing spiritual understanding to the church, it is important to strike a balance between accuracy and over-caution. We should not be so cautious about the words we choose that we become afraid to speak. We also should not argue over words when the choice of a word is not a major issue. Sometimes what seem to be differences in doctrine are simply differences in word choice.

On the other hand, accuracy is important. The words we choose and use shape our thinking, our doctrine, and, finally, the way we function. The more accurate we are in our choice and application of New Testament words — words which the Holy Ghost has chosen [I Cor. 2:13] — the more accurate our doctrine will be and the clearer our understanding will be. The more we understand spiritual things — especially how things work in ministry — the more effective we will be [Col. 1:9-10; I Cor. 12:1].

In the context of teaching about the ministry abilities God stewards to believers, it would not be wrong to use the word anointing, spiritual talent, heavenly endowment, gifting, grace-gift, or ministry gift. In one sense, any one of those words would be legitimate. On the other hand, as I said, accuracy is important.

The words "grace" [*charis*] and "grace-gift" [*charisma*] are the primary words used in the epistles to refer to the ministry abilities stewarded to and resident within believers which enable them to minister in their unique ministries. Who believers are in the body of Christ and the ministries they regularly engage in are not the result of special manifestations of the Spirit or a special anointing, but are the result of stewarded and permanent indwelling grace-gifts.

In light of this, I believe that concerning New Testament ministry, the word "anointing" is best used to describe the occasional, sometimes unpredictable, manifestations of the Spirit of God which enable believers to function in unusually effective ways. The manifestation of the Spirit, as Paul taught in I Corinthians 12:7-11, takes believers beyond knowledge, beyond preparation, and beyond human strength and power of persuasion. It also takes believers beyond the capacity of the ministry abilities they possess because of their resident grace-gifts. By the "anointing" — or the manifestation of the Spirit — believers are empowered to speak in extra-ordinary ways and perform extra-ordinary works as God determines.

Because it is so important to understand the different ways God has designed for the church to work in ministry, I deal briefly with ministering in the "manifestation of the Spirit" near the end of this study and show how that aspect of ministry can work beautifully in conjunction with believers' more permanent and consistent ministries as uniquely graced body members. It is important for believers to understand that God can use them in different ways, and in complementary ways, to meet the needs of people and accomplish His will.

It is true that the Holy Spirit has a central and significant place in New Testament ministry. We must not underestimate His essential role. He is the Paraclete and helps believers in every way [Jn. 14:16-17]. He empowers for service [Acts 1:8]. He gives utterance [Rom. 15:18-19; I Cor. 2:4]. He manifests through believers in the nine manifestations of the Spirit [I Cor. 12:7-11]. He guides and directs believers in their individual ministries [Acts 8:29; 10:19-20; 16:6-7].

Concerning believers' unique places in the body and their more permanent callings and giftings for ministry, however, the epistles point to a primary and significant divine agent which makes believers who they are and enables them to do what they do in ministry. That God-stewarded and resident divine ability is ministry grace.

Section Three

Varieties of Ministry Grace

There are diversities of gifts
But the same Spirit
Differences of administrations
But the same Lord
Diversities of operations
But the same God which worketh all in all

18

Diversity of Grace Gifts

Grace endowments are very diverse. That statement is simple, but concerning New Testament ministry it is significant. Believers are not called to the same ministries and are not grace-gifted in the same ways. Rather, there are a great variety of grace ministries and a great variety of grace endowments which enable those ministries.

Grace endowments are very diverse. This is a revelation you must embrace. Without this revelation, you may attempt to emulate someone else's ministry. Without this revelation, you may think your part in the body of Christ is not necessary. Without this revelation, you may try to be all things to all people or feel pressure to meet every need. That is not the way New Testament ministry works. That is not spiritual understanding.

In this section, you will learn that there are many varieties of ministry grace. You will learn that within each variety there are further varieties and different measures. You will learn that some ministries are the result of one primary grace while other ministries result from a combination of graces. You will learn that different believers can be graced with different measures of the same grace. Ministry graces and the ministries they gender are extremely diverse.

The Reality of Diversity

From Paul's writings, we know that the Corinthian believers strongly desired to be used in ministry; they were "zealous of spirituals" [I Cor. 14:12]. We also know, however, that they lacked spiritual understanding. Paul, a knowledgeable and experienced minister, sought to help them. After exhorting the Corinthians not to be ignorant of spirituals in I Corinthians 12:1, he began to teach them about spirituals. The first truth he stressed was that ministry is very diverse. He wrote,

> *"Now there are diversities of gifts, but the same Spirit. And there are differences of administrations, but the same Lord. And there are diversities of operations, but it is the same God which worketh all in all."*
>
> I Corinthians 12:4-6

In this passage, Paul referenced three different aspects of New Testament ministry: gifts by the Spirit, administrations by the Lord, and operations by God. The Greek word he chose to emphasize the diversity in each of these three different areas of ministry was *diaireses*. This word — twice rendered "diversities" and once "differences"— comes from *dia* which means, "apart," and *haireo* which means, "to take." *Diaireses* literally means, "to strongly take apart." After emphasizing that there was diversity in these three general areas of ministry, Paul went on to teach about these areas of ministry more specifically.

In I Corinthians 12:7-11, Paul taught about the nine diverse manifestations of the Spirit. In working through believers the Holy Spirit takes Himself apart, manifesting differently through different believers to meet different needs. Some believers manifest gifts of healings by the Spirit. Some manifest prophecy by the Spirit. Some interpret tongues by the Spirit. Some manifest the word of knowledge by the Spirit. The full ministry of the Holy Spirit is manifested through the church, but He manifests differently through different believers.

In I Corinthians 12:12-27, Paul taught about the diverse ways the many members in the one body serve. One member sees. Another hears. Another speaks. Another smells. One is a hand. One is a foot. One is an ear. One is an eye. The whole ministry of Jesus is manifested through the one body of Christ, but different members manifest different aspects of His ministry.

In I Corinthians 12:28-30, Paul taught about the diverse operations some believers are enabled by God to function in. Some believers operate in the office of the apostle. Some operate in the office of the teacher. Some operate in the office of the prophet. Some operate in working of miracles. Some operate as interpreters of tongues. Some operate as administrators. Some operate as healers. Some operate as helpers. God operates fully through the church, but He operates differently through different believers.

There is one God, one Lord, and one Spirit. But God the Father, God the Son, and God the Spirit work differently through different believers. By so doing, They gender the diverse ministries which meet the diverse needs of people and accomplish His diverse purposes.

It is critical to the effectiveness of the church that believers embrace the reality of diversity. Certainly, there is a "believer's ministry." In one sense, all believers can preach the gospel. In one sense, all believers can teach. In one sense, all believers can lay hands on the sick and cast out devils. In one sense, all believers are apostles; they are sent ones. In one sense, all believers can help. There is an aspect of truth in the statement that every believer can do the works of Jesus.

Far more prevalent in the New Testament, however, is the reality that believers are uniquely called, uniquely placed, and uniquely graced to fulfill unique ministries. In reality, no believer can accomplish the whole ministry of Jesus by himself. No member is used in all the manifestations of the Spirit. No member can hold all the offices in the church. It is true, of course, that working as one body the church should manifest the fullness of the Spirit, do the full ministry of Jesus, and fully perform the divine operations of God. Individually, however, each member can only function effectually in the unique ministry they are called to and graced for.

Variety of Inworkings, Variety of Outworkings

In I Corinthians 12:6, Paul wrote,

"And there are diversities of operations, but it is the same God which worketh all in all."

I Corinthians 12:6

The word "operations" Paul used in this verse is the Greek *energema*. This word means, "what is wrought or produced." The word "worketh" Paul used when he said that the same God "worketh all in all" is the Greek *energeo*. This word is made up of *en* which means, "in," and *ergon* which means, "to work." *Energeo* means, "to work in, to be active in, or to be operative in."

When God works within believers [*energeo*] there is an outworking called "diversities of operations" [*energema*]. The "diversities of operations" are the many different ways believers operate in ministry because of the unique way God is working in them. By first working within, supernaturally grace-energizing believers, God accomplishes His will without.

According to Paul, God who divinely inworks, works "in all." He doesn't only work in believers who are called to be pastors, apostles, or teachers. He works in all believers, divinely enabling them to render unique ministries. The Amplified Bible confirms this reality with these words,

> *"And there are distinctive varieties of operations — of working to accomplish things — but it is the same God Who inspires and energizes them all in all."*
>
> I Corinthians 12:6 Amp

Divine Cause, Divine Effects

Notice how the NASB Bible renders I Corinthians 12:6,

> *"And there are a variety of effects..."*
>
> I Corinthians 12:6 NASB

The principle of cause and effect states that every effect has a cause. That means if something happens, something caused it to happen. If there is no causal agent, there is no effect.

Different effects are usually the result of different causes. The rainbow is caused by sunlight passing through rain. Sunlight is caused by the burning of gases on the sun. Sound is caused when the vibration of an object sets air in motion.

It can also be true that a single agent produces a variety of effects. Electricity is one cause, but it can produce a variety of effects depending upon what appliance it flows into. Electricity flowing into a light bulb makes light. Electricity flowing into a heater makes heat. Electricity flowing into a fan produces wind.

Electrical appliances are called "appliances" because they apply electricity to produce specific effects. A stove applies electricity to produce heat for cooking. A refrigerator applies electricity to produce cold for preserving foods and liquids. A phone charger applies electricity to recharge a battery. Electricity can be employed by many different appliances to produce many different effects.

Believers are like appliances and ministry grace is like electricity. In the same way that electricity flows into different appliances and produces different effects, so God's ministry grace stewarded to different believers produces many different divine operations.

The Williams translation renders I Corinthians 12:6 this way,

> *"...but it is the same God who does all things by putting energy in us all..."*
>
> *I Corinthians 12:6 Williams*

What are the "all things" the "same God" does? The "all things" He does are the many different ministry operations He accomplishes throughout the world. And how does God do these "all things?" He does them by "putting energy in us all." When God energizes believers by stewarding special grace-gifts to them, they are enabled to operate effectively in many different ministries.

If someone needs encouragement, a believer grace-energized by God to exhort can meet that need. If a person is sick, a believer who is grace-energized by God with gifts of healings can meet that need. If a person is unsaved, a believer who is grace-energized by God as an evangelist can meet that need. If a person needs to become established in the faith, a believer who is grace-energized by God to teach can meet that need. God, of course, is the one who meets every need. He does so, however, by uniquely gracing each believer. Paul illustrated this very reality when he said, "I have planted, Apollos watered; but God gave the increase" [I Cor. 3:6].

Extremely Diverse Varieties of Grace

Peter wrote these words about ministry graces,

> *"As each of you has received a gift (a particular spiritual talent, a gracious divine endowment), employ it for one another as [befits] good trustees of God's many-sided grace — faithful stewards of the extremely diverse [powers and gifts granted to Christians by] unmerited favor."*
>
> I Peter 4:10 Amp

The Amplified Bible refers to ministry grace-gifts as "particular spiritual talent[s]" and "extremely diverse powers and gifts granted to Christians." Notice that ministry graces are "particular" and "extremely diverse" rather than general and similar. Because the needs of people all over the world are extremely diverse the ministry graces granted to believers are extremely diverse.

One believer may evangelize on the city streets of America. Another may preach in the jungles of Asia. One may study and translate the Word of God into foreign languages. Another may show mercy to those bound in a life of prostitution. One may administrate in a large church. One may work miracles, but have no ability to teach. Another may teach skillfully, but have no special ability to work miracles or heal the sick.

One believer may hold large seminars in major cities teaching one specific subject. Another may travel from local church to local church delivering unique messages to each church. One believer may prophesy of future events. Another may prophesy unto edification, exhortation, and comfort. Another may function in the office of the prophet. One may pastor a small village church in a remote region of the Amazon forest. Another may pastor a large church in a metropolitan city. One may come along side a pastor as a helper.

One believer may work with children. Another may support ministries with financial gifts. One may minister to the handicapped. One may feed the hungry by raising money and buying food. Another may teach people how to develop good work habits so that they can feed themselves and others. One may minister in music by leading others in worship. Another may use music as a tool in evangelistic outreach.

Diverse varieties of grace are bestowed upon believers to equip them for the diverse ministries which meet the diverse needs of people, both in the body of Christ and in the world. By the means of diverse grace-giftings the many different aspects of God's power and ability are manifested in the earth. When believers discover, cultivate, and employ their diverse grace-gifts the manifold needs of people are met and the manifold purpose of God is accomplished.

19

Uniquely Placed
Uniquely Graced

Throughout the New Testament the church is called the body of Christ and compared to the human body. In I Corinthians twelve, Paul wrote,

> "...the body is one, and hath many members...For the body is not one member, but many...And if they were all one member, where were the body? But now are they many members, yet but one body... Now ye are the body of Christ, and members in particular."
>
> I Corinthians 12:12, 14, 19, 20, 27

Paul also referred to the church as a body in his letter to the Romans when he wrote,

> "For as we have many members in one body, and all members have not the same office [function]: So we, being many, are one body in Christ, and every one members one of another."
>
> Romans 12:4-5

In I Corinthians 12:27, Paul described the members of the body of Christ as "members in particular." The word "member" comes from the Greek *melos* and means, "of diversity, but all essential to effectivity." The words "in particular" mean, "one of the constituent parts of a whole." The many members of the body of Christ are diverse, but every one is essential to the effectiveness of the whole body.

One Salvation, Many Vocations

In the human body, every cell possesses the same genetic information. The eye cells, ear cells, hand cells, heart cells, and all other cells have the same DNA. Every cell could rightly say, "I have the same identity as every other cell."

In the same way, every member of the body of Christ has the same identity in Christ. Jude confirmed this when he wrote,

> *"Beloved, when I gave all diligence to write unto you of the common salvation..."*
>
> Jude 3

Believers share a common salvation. They are identical in terms of covenant blessings, promises, inheritance, relationship with the Father, eternal destination, and many other things [Eph. 4:4-6]. In this sense, believers do not differ from one another. Every believer can rightly say, "I am the same as every other member in the body of Christ."

Although the cells in the human body are identical in genetic makeup, they differ in constitution, in placing, and in function. In the early weeks of a fetus' development cells begin to diversify and migrate to different places in the body to become different body members. Some cells become bones. Some become kidneys. Some become blood. Some become skin. Some become eyes. Some become the heart. By the unseen hand of divine direction, cells migrate to different places, develop special characteristics, and become capable of performing unique and necessary tasks. Because of this fact, every cell in the human body could say, "I am different than the other cells in the body and am competent to perform a unique task."

Diversity in placing, in constitution, and in function is also a reality concerning members of the body of Christ. Different members are graced with different spiritual abilities and guided by the unseen hand of divine direction to different places in the body. Each member, by virtue of his unique placing and grace-gifting, is able to perform a unique function. Each member of the body of Christ can say, "I am different than other members of the body. By virtue of my unique place and my special grace, I am qualified to perform a unique ministry."

Although believers are the same in salvation, they are not the same in vocation. Although they serve one Master, their tasks and their tools are not the same. And although they will finally arrive at a common destination, they do not currently work in the same places. There are many different ministries that the many different members of the body of Christ are placed and graced to do.

God Places, God Graces

In I Corinthians twelve, Paul revealed that when people are saved, they are not only baptized into Christ, but are also baptized into the body of Christ [I Cor. 12:13]. Paul declared God's role in placing believers into the body of Christ when he wrote,

> *"But now hath God set the members every one of them in the body, as it hath pleased him. And if they were all one member, where were the body? But now are they many members, yet but one body."*
>
> *I Corinthians 12:18-20*

God has set the members in the body as it pleased Him. The word "pleased" comes from the Greek *thelo* which means, "as determined, as purposed, as resolved." The word "set" comes from the Greek *tithemi* which means "to place, to set down, to establish or ordain." If God did not purposely and wisely set the members into the body there would be no functional body of Christ and no fulfilling of the works of Jesus.

In Romans twelve, Paul revealed that the diverse ministries of the members of the body of Christ are the result of diverse graces given. He wrote,

> *"For as we have many members in one body, and all members have not the same office [function]: So we, being many, are one body in Christ, and every one members one of another. Having then gifts differing according to the grace that is given to us..."*
>
> *Romans 12:4-6*

God summons believers to service, thoughtfully sets them into the body of Christ, and endows them with special ministry graces. God uniquely places and God uniquely graces.

When the graced members of the body of Christ function under the direction of the one Head, their diverse abilities contribute to the effectiveness of the whole body. Many and marvelous works can be accomplished by the body of Christ because of the unique and marvelous ways God places and graces the members!

Every Member is Important

To help believers grasp the significance of their ministries as members of the body of Christ, Paul wrote these words:

"If the foot shall say, Because I am not the hand, I am not of the body; is it therefore not of the body? And if the ear shall say, Because I am not the eye, I am not of the body; is it therefore not of the body? If the whole body were an eye, where were the hearing? If the whole were hearing, where were the smelling?"

I Corinthians 12:15-17

Some members of the body of Christ think they are unimportant because they are not called and graced to do what other members are doing. This thinking is wrong, however, and must be corrected. If believers do not have right thinking concerning their unique placing and gracing, they will abdicate their places, fail to minister by their graces, and become a reason that some needs go unmet and some plans of God remain unfulfilled.

Just think about this: If the whole body was a preacher, who would do the work of practical service? If the whole body was a teacher, who would be evangelizing? If the whole body was laboring on the evangelistic field, who would be home paying the bills? If the whole body was a helper, who would be exhorting? If the whole body was a pastor, who would go lay foundations for new churches?

Who believers are in terms of "body part" is because of who God was pleased to make them. So, if God was pleased to make you a little toe, be pleased. If He was pleased to make you a heart, be pleased. If he was pleased to make you a helper, be pleased. If He was pleased to make you a prophet, be pleased. If He was pleased to make you an exhorter, be pleased. If He was pleased to make you a miracle worker, be pleased. Become firmly established in your place, become skilled in your grace, and do your part!

20

The Manifold Grace of God

In his first epistle, the apostle Peter penned these significant words concerning graces and gifts,

"As every man hath received the gift, even so minister the same one to another, as good stewards of the manifold grace of God."
                                                                    I Peter 4:10-11

Peter described the grace of God as "manifold." The word "manifold" comes from the Greek *poikilos* and means, "variety, different kinds, different aspects, or multiple." Saving grace and strengthening grace, although abundant, are not "manifold." Ministry grace, however, is manifold. There are many varieties of ministry grace. These many varieties enable the many members of the body of Christ to accomplish many different ministries.

The Body of Christ, A Variegated Flower

The word "manifold" can mean "parti-colored" or "variegated." "Parti-colored" means, "to show different colors or tints." "Variegated" means, "to have marks of a different color." It can also mean, "to diversify in external appearance especially with different colors," or, "to make interesting by variety."

A variegated flower is composed of different colors which are separate and distinct. One variegated flower might be composed of a distinct red color, a distinct green color, and a distinct blue color. Another variegated flower might be composed of a distinct purple color and a distinct yellow color.

The body of Christ is like a variegated flower. It is one flower, but it is not one color. The grace-gifted members of the body of Christ are unique; each beautiful in their own right. Jesus is sometimes called the Lily of the Valley. The body of Christ could be called the Divinely Variegated Lily of the Valley.

It might be the beautiful color blue of one member that attracts a sinner to the Lord. It could be a vibrant yellow that turns a backslider from his destructive ways. It may be a soft hue of green that comforts someone in distress. It may be a beautiful purple that brings healing to someone dying of cancer. It may be a bright red that establishes believers in the faith. Displayed in unity of purpose the manifold graces of the many members make the body of Christ complete, beautiful, and effectual.

The Rainbow of Grace

The manifold grace of God can be illustrated by the diffraction of light into its many colors. Science calls a beam of light a "wave train" because light is actually made up of different color waves that travel together. Undiffracted, the wave train of light is perceived simply as light. When the wave train of light is diffracted, however, its many different colors are expressed.

The word "diffract" comes from a Latin word which means, "to break apart." A common incidence of the diffraction of light is when sunlight passes through rain. When this happens light is broken apart into its manifold colors and manifests on the other side of the rain as a rainbow. A rainbow, then, is a manifestation of light that has passed through the diffracting agent water.

The diffraction of light into its various colors is a wonderful illustration of how the manifold grace of God is expressed through the church. God has taken the whole ministry of Christ, diffracted it, and given different aspects of His ministry to different parts of the body of Christ. When Jesus was in the world, He was the Light of the world [Jn. 9:5]. Now, however, the church is the light of the world.

When the church expresses the light of Jesus in all its manifold colors, the world will experience the manifold goodness of God. They will come to know Him as Savior. They will experience His compassion. They will learn the Truth. They will be delivered in times of trouble. They will be healed in their bodies. They will be encouraged. They will be helped. They will be directed. They will be supported. When all the members of the body of Christ minister by their grace-gifts, the full spectrum of the ability of God and the ministry of Jesus will be manifested in the earth.

Manifold is Many-sided

The way the Amplified Bible renders I Peter 4:10 gives us further insight into the manifold grace of God. It reads,

> *"As each of you has received a gift (a particular spiritual talent, a gracious divine endowment), employ it for one another as [befits] good trustees of God's many-sided grace..."*
>
> I Peter 4:10 Amp

The Amplified Bible uses the word "many-sided" to describe ministry grace. Unlike Jesus, believers cannot say of their works, "If you have seen me, you have seen the Father." Believers can only say, "If you have seen me, you have seen one aspect, or one part, of God."

People have many aspects to their personalities. A man in his work setting may appear as conservative, intense, and unfriendly. The same man at home with his family, may appear as liberal, unconcerned, and loving. That same man playing a sport with his friends may appear as competitive and passionate. This one man expresses many aspects of his personality because he has many roles to fill, many works to accomplish, and many needs to meet.

When believers labor according to their unique graces, the body of Christ manifests the manifold grace of God. When a teacher teaches, the teaching element of God's grace is manifested. When an exhorter exhorts, the exhorting element of God's grace is manifested. When a shower of mercy shows mercy, the mercy element of God's grace is manifested. When a man gives a cup of cold water, the serving aspect of God's grace is manifested. When a man works miracles, the miracle aspect of God's grace is manifested. In whatever way God graces each believer to minister, that element of His manifold grace will be manifested through them.

21

Varieties and Proportions

Within each general variety of ministry grace there can be further varieties and different proportions. These further varieties and different proportions cause variations and different levels of effectualness within the same general areas of grace ministry.

A good illustration of variety within the same general area of grace ministry are the human hands. The right and left hand are, for all purposes, identical in constitution. Typically, however, one hand is dominant. Isn't it interesting that if you are right handed, your left hand almost never feeds you or writes a letter? Although both hands are capable of functioning in the same way, they have been assigned slightly different responsibilities by the head.

Another illustration of variety within the same general area of grace ministry are the four fingers on each hand. Although all the fingers are similar, each has a distinct capacity and function. The ring finger, for example, is different in function than the index finger. Have you ever pointed at something with your ring finger? Probably not. The ring finger, although certainly a finger, is not equipped to point. The pinky finger is not as strong as the middle finger. It has unique capabilities, however. If you play the piano or guitar, you know that the pinky finger is essential to a skilled performance.

We could also consider the illustration of a football team. Every person on a football team is a football player. Some players, however, are on the offensive team, while others are on the defensive team. Yet others are on the specialty teams. One football player on the offensive team may be the quarter-back while another is the center. One football player on the defensive team may cover a receiver while another may rush the quarterback. Some players never get on the field during a regulation game, but are a vital part of preparing the first team in practice sessions. Although each football player is a football player there are many varieties of football players.

Examples of Varieties within Variety

The ministries of Paul and Peter demonstrate variety within the same general area of grace ministry. Both men were apostles. Paul, however, was called and graced to be chief apostle to the Gentiles while Peter was called and graced to be chief apostle to the Jews [Gal. 2:8-9].

We can also note varieties of apostolic ministry among the twelve apostles of the Lamb. For example, not all the apostles were noted for their miracle ministries. When a woman from Joppa named Tabitha died, the disciples sent for Peter to come and raise her from the dead [Acts 9:36-42]. Why did they send for Peter and not for John, Matthew, or Nathaniel? They sent for Peter because he was noted among the apostles as having a healing and miracle ministry. In fact, he had such a reputation for healing that people tried to get in his shadow [Acts 5:15]. We never read this kind of report concerning John or James or any other apostle of the Lamb, including Peter's brother Andrew.

Several apostles of the Lamb were graced to write. Peter is noted for his two epistles. John wrote one gospel and three epistles. We have no gospels or epistles, however, from Nathaniel, Thomas, or Andrew. Certainly, these men were apostles of the Lamb. Their apostolic gracings, however, were of a slightly different variety.

From Paul's writings, we know about a man named Epaphroditus. This man was an apostle to the church at Philippi, but he also ministered in practical service to Paul [Phil. 2:25-30]. His ministry of serving was so valuable that Paul said his work was the work of Christ.

Among modern day apostles there can also be many different varieties. One apostle may labor for a lifetime in a remote region of the world. Another may labor in many different countries and be well known. Some apostles may stay for a season in the churches they found, establishing new believers in doctrine. Others may function more like evangelists, bringing sinners into the kingdom and founding churches and then turning those churches over to a pastor.

There are also varieties of grace within the general grace of the teacher. One teacher may pastor a local church. His primary grace may be to teach, but he will have a significant proportion of pastoral grace mixed in. This is a common reality and may be what Paul intended to communicate in Ephesians four when he said that Jesus gave "some to be pastors and teachers" [Eph. 4:12]. In the Greek language the words "pastors and teachers" could designate one man.

One teacher may be graced to travel from church to church throughout the world in a ministry similar to that of Apollos. Another may teach in a particular Bible School. One teacher may have a mix of prophetic grace in his teaching and bring very tailored messages. Some teachers may have a complementary grace to write.

In my ministry, I most often teach messages that speak specifically to the people in the place where I am at the time. Often pastors inform me that what I taught in their church was exactly what they needed. Sometimes my message was a continuation of a series they had been teaching. Why does this happen? It happens because there is an element of prophetic grace mixed in with my teaching grace.

Variety within a general area of grace ministry is also typical for those called and graced to be pastors. No two pastors are exactly alike. Some are evangelistic. Some are strongly gifted to teach. Others are able to administrate. Some pastors will oversee churches in rural areas. Other pastors will oversee churches in large cities. Some pastors may be called and graced to oversee more than one local church.

Variety within general areas of grace ministry can also be noted in the ministry of gifts of healings. Even the name of this ministry suggests variety by using the plural gifts and healings. Some who are called and graced with gifts of healings will have profound results in dealing with tumors and cancers. Others will have significant results with deafness. Others might have a high success rate with women who want to become pregnant. Philip seemed to be specially gifted in ministering to the lame and those with palsies [Acts 8:7]. This diversity within the ministry of gifts of healings equips the church to deal with many different kinds of sickness and diseases.

Shades of Grace

In the color world there are primary colors. There is a true blue. There is a true red. There is a true yellow. These primary colors can be blended, however, to make other unique colors. Green is created by mixing blue and yellow. Orange is made by mixing yellow and red. There can also be shades of each color. In the blue family, for example, there is royal blue, sky blue, and aquamarine blue. These different blues are created by adding other colors to the primary color blue.

In the spiritual realm there are also primary graces. There is the grace of the pastor. There is the grace of the evangelist. There is a grace to show mercy. There is a grace to rule. There is a grace to give. There is a grace to exhort. Unique ministries can be created, however, when God combines two or more graces in a believer or when He adds portions of secondary graces to one's primary grace. By blending graces in believers, God creates ministries that are perfectly tailored to the needs of the people to whom the graced vessels will be sent.

22

Different Measures of Grace

Within each general area of grace ministry, there can be different proportions of the same grace. In other words, believers who have been stewarded the same variety of grace and are doing the same kind of ministry can exhibit different degrees of effectiveness depending upon the measure of that grace stewarded to them.

In the parable of the talents each servant received talents. A different amount, however, was entrusted to each. One servant received five talents, another two, and another one. The different amount each received was clearly a factor in the results they produced [Mt. 25:14-30].

In Romans 12:6-8, Paul said,

"Having then gifts differing according to the grace that is given to us, whether prophecy, let us prophesy according to the proportion of faith; Or ministry, let us wait on our ministering: or he that teacheth, on teaching; Or he that exhorteth, on exhortation..."

Romans 12:6-8

The word "proportion" Paul used in this scripture comes from the Greek *analogia* and is where we get our English word "analogy." Paul exhorted the one who was graced to prophesy to do so according to his "proportion of faith." He did not mean that if a believer exercised more faith, he would be able to prophesy in a more profound way. He meant, rather, that those who were graced to prophesy should not attempt to prophesy beyond the measure of prophetic grace they were confident had been stewarded to them. They should minister, rather, in a way that was proportionate to how they had been called and graced. That same principle of wisdom is true for every ministry.

In one local church there could be several believers graced to prophesy. One may prophesy at a level that brings exhortation, comfort, and edification. Their inspired utterances might encourage others to praise the Lord or to hold fast in difficult times. Another may prophesy about changes that need to be made in the church. This kind of prophecy would not only be exhortation, but also revelation in that it specified changes which must be made in order to avoid future trouble. Another may prophesy about future events. These would be examples of prophesying in different proportions.

Different proportions of teaching grace can also be stewarded. One teacher may teach primarily what others have taught him. Another teacher may dig out truths or recover truths that have been neglected. I have heard some teachers get off into doctrinal error because they stretched beyond their measure of teaching grace. They estimated themselves too highly, pushed beyond their proportion of teaching grace, and, trying to be something they were not graced to be, wandered into unsound teaching.

Paul's words concerning his own ministry reveal that there can be different measures of apostolic grace within the apostolic office. In I Corinthians fifteen, he wrote,

> "...his grace which was bestowed upon me was not in vain; but I laboured more abundantly than they all [other apostles]: yet not I, but the grace of God which was with me."
>
> *I Corinthians 15:10*

Paul reported that his ministry labors were greater than the labors of all other apostles. He was clear, however, that his greater labors were a result of the grace stewarded to him. Apparently, the measure of apostolic grace dealt to Paul was greater than the measure of apostolic grace dealt to other apostles.

All believers should minister in agreement with the portion of grace measured to them. If a believer is graced to evangelize, he should evangelize according to the measure of evangelistic grace stewarded to him. If he is graced to reach out to his community and draw sinners into his local church, he should not attempt to launch a world-wide evangelistic ministry. If, on the other hand, he is graced to harvest souls in a foreign nation, he should not stay home.

If a believer is graced to pastor, he should pastor in agreement with the pastoral grace stewarded to him. One pastor may be operating at his full spiritual capacity when overseeing 120 people. Another may be able to pastor a larger congregation or, perhaps, more than one congregation. Another pastor may function as a pastor to pastors because of the measure of pastoral grace stewarded to him.

If a believer is graced to show mercy, he should do so according to the grace given to him. One shower of mercy may minister in his own local church, touching fellow believers one by one. Another believer graced to show mercy may open an orphanage in a foreign nation to help children who have no home.

If a believer is graced to serve, he should do so in proportion to the measure of serving grace given to him. One server may lend a helping hand in the natural care of a local church. He might vacuum, straighten chairs, or clean an office. Another server may move to a foreign country to assist a missionary couple. Another server may hold a recognized position of service in a local church as did the seven deacons who cared for the Grecian widows in Jerusalem.

Whatever each believer does in terms of ministry, whether teaching, ruling, prophesying, showing mercy, administrating, giving, evangelizing, helping, pastoring, or any other ministry, it should be in proper relationship to the variety and the measure of ministry grace he has received from the Lord.

23

Diverse Grace Ministries

There are many wonderful ministries that believers can be called to and graced for in the New Testament. Sometimes, unfortunately, valid ministries are not recognized and embraced. Some churches, for example, acknowledge that pastors, teachers, administrators and exhorters are valid ministries, but do not acknowledge or embrace the more supernatural ministries like apostles, prophets, gifts of healings, diverse tongues, interpretation of tongues, and working of miracles. Other churches overemphasize supernatural ministries and, by so doing, leave the impression that ministries like administration, showing mercy, exhortation, helps, and ruling are not important. A limited or lopsided view of New Testament ministry can establish boundaries in thinking that keep believers from functioning in ministries they are called to. As a consequence, the church and the world will be robbed of God-ordained, need-meeting, grace-endowed ministries.

In Ephesians 4:7, Paul taught that "unto every one of us is given grace according to the measure of the gift of Christ." After stating that every believer is graced for service, he listed five ministries that some believers are graced for, saying,

> *"And he gave some, apostles; and some, prophets; and some, evangelists; and some, pastors and teachers..."*
>
> *Ephesians 4:11*

Some members of the body of Christ are called and graced for one of the five spiritual leadership ministries. Some are called and graced to be apostles. Some to be prophets. Some to be evangelists. Some to be pastors. And some to be teachers. Like all New Testament ministries, these five ministries are the result of God's unique calling, placing, and gracing.

In I Corinthians 12:28-30, Paul presented another list of valid New Testament ministries. He wrote,

> *"And God hath set some in the church, first apostles, secondarily prophets, thirdly teachers, after that miracles, then gifts of healings, helps, governments, diversities of tongues. Are all apostles? are all prophets? are all teachers? are all workers of miracles? Have all the gifts of healing? do all speak with tongues? do all interpret?"*
>
> *I Corinthians 12:28-30*

In this list, Paul included three spiritual leadership ministries and several "after that" ministries. In this list are what we might call supernatural ministries and natural ministries. The diversity of ministries presented in this one passage underscores the reality that there are, in fact, many different New Testament ministries.

After teaching the Roman believers that their different ministries were a result of the different measures of faith and varieties of grace entrusted to them, Paul offered this short sampling of grace ministries,

> *"[He whose gift is] prophecy, [let him prophesy]...[He whose gift is] practical service, let him give himself to serving; he who teaches, to his teaching...(He who exhorts, encourages), to his exhortation; he who contributes, let him do it in simplicity and liberality; he who gives aid and superintends, with zeal and singleness of mind; he who does acts of mercy, with genuine cheerfulness and joyful eagerness."*
>
> *Romans 12:6-8 Amp*

This list, like the list of ministries in Ephesians four and I Corinthians twelve, contains a diversity of ministries. There is a ministry of prophecy, of practical service, and of teaching. There is a ministry of exhortation, of giving, of ruling, and of showing mercy.

Grace Ministries from the Ministry of Jesus

In His earth ministry, Jesus was a pastor; the Shepherd of God's sheep. He was an evangelist; declaring the kingdom of God and calling men to repentance. He was an apostle; sent unto the world and unto His own. He was a prophet; pointing to the past, prophesying of the future, and revealing the thoughts of men's hearts. He was a teacher; opening the scriptures and revealing the will, the ways, and the wisdom of God. He taught the Jews in the synagogues, instructed the masses in the countryside, and trained His own disciples.

Jesus was a healer of all manner of physical disease and sickness. He restored the blind, the deaf, the lame, and lepers and healed the broken hearted. He cast out devils and raised the dead. He was a worker of miracles; multiplying fishes and loaves, calming storms, and turning water into wine. He was a servant doing practical service, such as washing His disciples' feet. He was a minister to children, blessing them through the laying on of hands.

Jesus was an exhorter; He knew how to speak a word in season to the weary. He was a mentor; making disciples of simple men and training some of them to be spiritual leaders. He prayed for the lost and made intercession for His own. He was a shower of mercy, granted forgiveness to sinners and backsliders, and reached out to the poor and needy.

The many different works Jesus did during His earth ministry foreshadow the many different ministries that members of the body of Christ might be called to, graced for, and engage in. Any ministry which emulates or reasonably imitates a ministry Jesus functioned in while He was on earth could qualify as a New Testament ministry.

What About My Ministry?

In the next two sections, we will examine many different New Testament ministries. Learning about these ministries will help you in several ways. First, your thinking concerning ministry will be expanded. Second, you will learn to appreciate, receive from, and cooperate with other believers' ministries. Third, you will be assisted in locating and further refining your own ministry.

It's important to be aware that the Bible offers no explicit description of any New Testament ministry. The Bible does not state, for example, what the apostle or pastor does. It does not specify the role and activity of the prophet and evangelist. Nowhere does it offer a job description for those called to the working of miracles, gifts of healing, interpreting of tongues, administration, helps, or showing mercy.

Our understanding of each particular New Testament ministry must be gained, then, in two ways. First, by definition — by understanding the meaning of the word that labels that ministry. Second, by implication — by finding places in the Bible where that ministry is in action. In the next two sections, I will offer a general description of many New Testament ministries. It is important, however, not to give too narrow a description of any of these ministries since the Scriptures do not do so.

After you finish the next two sections, you may ask, "Where is my ministry?" Just remember that there are varieties and measures in each grace ministry. Every unique ministry, including yours, can be located in one of the grace ministries we study in the next two sections. Let's proceed now to examine the various ministries we have introduced, first examining the five spiritual leadership ministries and then examining the many "after that" ministries.

Section Four

Spiritual Leadership Ministries

*And he gave some apostles
And some prophets and evangelists
And some pastors and teachers*

24

The Five Spiritual Leadership Ministries

Some believers are called and graced by God for one of the five spiritual leadership ministries – apostle, prophet, evangelist, pastor, or teacher. Believers called to these ministries are stewarded leadership ability, granted leadership authority and expected to fulfill leadership responsibility. They may not be superior to others in their personal Christian lives, but they are unique in their callings and giftings and have significant responsibilities in the church. A pastor, for example, has authority and responsibility for teaching, leading, and overseeing in the church that an exhorter does not have. Certainly, both the pastor and the exhorter are important. The exhorter cannot say, "I am not important in the body because I am not a pastor." The pastor cannot say, "I don't need the exhorter."

When those who are called and graced to be spiritual leaders embrace their callings, prepare themselves, locate and cultivate their grace-gifts, and function skillfully in their ministries the church will grow in knowledge, strength, and love, will minister skillfully, and will accomplish the plans of God. When, on the other hand, those who are called and graced to be spiritual leaders fail to understand their callings, fail to mature, fail to locate and cultivate their grace-gifts, and fail to fulfill their ministries, the church will remain ignorant, weak, and ineffective and the plans of God will be hindered, perverted, and maybe even thwarted.

I use the term Spiritual Leadership Ministries to describe the apostle, prophet, evangelist, pastor, and teacher because of the unique leadership calling and unique leadership responsibilities these five ministries share. Describing them as Spiritual Leadership Ministries is at the same time accurate and helpfully broad. There are other terms, however, that can help us understand these important ministries.

Other Descriptive Terms

The five spiritual leadership ministries could be characterized as Headship Ministries or Ministries of Governance. These terms express the important role of apostles, prophets, evangelists, pastors, and teachers in teaching, correcting, modeling, overseeing and directing the affairs of the church. These terms also help portray how the governance of God flows from the Head of the church to the church through these ministries.

The other ministries in the church could be termed Body Ministries or Ministries of Service. Although these other ministries supply very necessary things — healings, miracles, practical service, finances, encouragement, support — they are not responsible for the doctrinal soundness, the spiritual health, and the overall ministry effectiveness of the church.

Another way to describe the five spiritual leadership ministries is as Vital Organs. In the human body there are organs which must be present and functioning properly in order for the body to remain viable. No human body can remain alive without a good heart, clear lungs, a healthy brain, or a sound liver. These vital organs are essential for existence.

All other ministries could be described as Important Members. These ministries, although important to the body, are not necessary to keep the body viable. A person can live, for example, if he is missing an eye. He will, however, lack depth perception and peripheral vision. A person can live even if he is missing both legs. He will never win a running race, however, and will be hindered in many aspects of his life.

It is true, of course, that the church cannot function at full capacity unless every Important Member is healthy, in their place, and contributing. The church cannot even remain viable, however, unless the Vital Organs are healthy, in their place, and functioning.

Spiritual leaders serve under the direction of the Head of the church; stars in His right hand. They oversee the flock of God as undershepherds, feeding the sheep, providing pasture and defending against wolves. They teach doctrine and defend against unsound doctrine. They spend time in watchings, fastings, and prayers. They model the spiritual life for the benefit of the body. They diligently prepare others for service, bringing them to maturity and helping them enter into their own unique and important ministries.

Spiritual Leadership Offices

In the context of teaching the Ephesian believers about ministry grace and God's design for the church, Paul listed all five spiritual leadership ministries. He wrote,

> *"Wherefore he saith, When he ascended up on high, he...gave gifts unto men...And he gave some, apostles; and some, prophets; and some, evangelists; and some, pastors and teachers..."*
>
> *Ephesians 4:8, 11*

The words, "gave gifts unto men," from Ephesians 4:8 have been interpreted by some to mean that Jesus gave apostles, prophets, evangelists, pastors, and teachers as gifts to the church. Although these ministries are indeed gifts to the church, what Paul was specifically teaching was that Jesus has stewarded to some believers the grace-giftings to be and to do these five ministries. Paul's words could read this way,

> *"When Jesus ascended on high, He gave ministry gifts to believers. To some He gave the grace-gifting to be apostles; to some the grace-gifting to be prophets; to some the grace-gifting to be evangelists; to some the grace-gifting to be pastors; and to some the grace-gifting to be teachers."*

In I Corinthians 12:28-30, Paul presented three of the spiritual leadership ministries — the apostle, prophet, and teacher. He wrote,

"God hath set some in the church, first apostles, secondarily prophets, thirdly teachers, after that miracles, then gifts of healings, helps, governments, diversities of tongues. Are all workers of miracles? Have all the gifts of healing? do all speak with tongues? do all interpret?"

I Corinthians 12:28-30

Paul distinguished the three spiritual leadership ministries in this list of ministries by numbering them first, second, and third. Many opinions have been offered as to why he numbered them as he did. Some say Paul numbered these three ministries based on the order they appeared in the early church. Some say he numbered them as he did because the apostle is the most important and authoritative ministry in the church, the prophet is second in importance and authority, and the teacher is third. Some say Paul numbered these ministries based on God's design for establishing local churches. According to this theory, apostles should always lay the foundation of churches.

In the early days of the church it was, in fact, primarily apostles who pioneered churches. The church in Antioch, an exception to this pattern, was not founded by apostles, but by dispersed believers from Jerusalem [Acts 11:19-21]. It is true, however, that after the Antioch church was started, it was first ministered to by apostles [Barnabas and Paul], then by prophets from the church in Jerusalem [Judas and Silas], and finally, there were also teachers in that church [Acts 11:22-27; 13:1]. This example of how the church in Antioch was established may confirm the first, second, third pattern Paul presented in I Corinthians 12:28.

In fact, however, no one can be certain why Paul numbered the three spiritual leadership ministries as he did. It is my own opinion that he did so because the apostle is the New Testament ministry which carries the most spiritual authority and is most responsible for laying sound foundations and overseeing the affairs of God. The prophet and teacher follow closely behind in terms of responsibility for establishing doctrine, maturing believers, building and guiding the church, and overseeing the affairs of God.

Although we cannot be certain why Paul numbered the three spiritual leadership ministries as he did, it is evident that he wanted those three ministries to be distinguished from the other ministries in his list. That is why he did not write, "fourthly miracles, fifthly gifts of healings, etc." Rather, he wrote, "after that miracles, then gifts of healings, helps, governments, diversities of tongues" [I Cor. 12:28]. The ministries in this list which follow the words "after that" are not spiritual leadership ministries.

Concerning this list of ministries, you may ask, "Why aren't the evangelist and pastor included?" It may be that the pastor and the evangelist are not in this list simply because Paul did not intend to offer a complete list of ministries, but was simply giving examples of different ministries. It could also be that Paul referred only to the ministries of the apostle, prophet, and teacher because they were the ministries most familiar to the Corinthian believers.

Some believe that the pastor is in Paul's list under the designation "governments." They think that because pastors usually oversee local churches, the word "governments" could be referring to him. The pastor is not, however, an "after that" ministry and would not follow the ministry of helps in a list where the Holy Spirit purposely used numbers to set the spiritual leadership ministries apart.

Why is the evangelist missing from this list of ministries? Perhaps Paul excluded the evangelist because he was referring to ministries that function primarily in the local church. The evangelist, although he does have responsibility to teach and lead in the church, does not have as primary a role as the other ministries. Perhaps the elevated role of the evangelist in reaching outside the church influenced Paul to exclude this office from this list.

I do not believe, as do some, that the ministry of the evangelist is in this list, but called "working of miracles" or "gifts of healings." As with the pastor, the evangelist is not an "after that" ministry. Although some evangelists may work miracles and have healing ministries, not all will. If Paul had wanted the evangelist in this list, he would have simply used the designation "evangelist" and included it with the other spiritual leadership ministries.

Looking Forward

The specific terms apostle, prophet, evangelist, pastor, and teacher narrowly designate each of the five spiritual leadership offices. There are many other general terms, however, like elder, bishop, overseer, steward, laborer, servant, ruler, shepherd, father, and parent, which indicate the shared responsibilities of all the spiritual leadership ministries. It is very important to understand that although each of the five spiritual leadership ministries have unique qualities and responsibilities, they share many qualities and responsibilities. Before we study the unique attributes of each spiritual leadership office, let's learn about some of the responsibilities they share.

25

The Primary Responsibilities of Spiritual Leaders

There are basic responsibilities that all five spiritual leadership ministries share. No spiritual leader is permitted to ignore these basic, clearly taught responsibilities and focus narrowly on the things that belong more specifically to their office. If they do, the church will not prosper under their leadership and the will of God will be diminished. It is critical to the well-being of the church and the ongoing purposes of God that spiritual leaders comprehend, embrace, and fulfill their shared responsibilities. Let's briefly examine these shared responsibilities.

They Lead the Way in Spiritual Life

Anyone called to one of the five spiritual leadership offices is called and graced to lead the church in right paths; paths which are the will of God. This responsibility is clearly expressed in these words Paul wrote to the believers in Thessalonica,

> *"And we beseech you, brethren, to know them which labour among you, and are over you in the Lord, and admonish you; And to esteem them very highly in love for their work's sake."*
>
> I Thessalonians 5:12-13

Paul exhorted these believers to know them who were "over" them in the Lord. The word "over" he used is the Greek *proistemi*. It means, "to place before, to superintend, to care for, or to give attention to." In general, *proistemi* means, "to lead the way as a leader, by example and oversight." In I Thessalonians 5:12, *proistemi* describes the work that the spiritual leaders in Thessalonica were already doing.

In his instructions to Timothy about the essential requirements for one who desired to be a spiritual leader, Paul said that man must be,

> *"One that ruleth well his own house, having his children in subjection with all gravity; For if a man know not how to rule his own house, how shall he take care of the church of God?"*
>
> I Timothy 3:4-5

The word "rule" Paul used in presenting this essential requirement of a spiritual leader is the same word *proistemi* he used in I Thessalonians 5:12. If a man "know not how" to *proistemi* — lead the way — in his own small home, especially where his children were concerned, he certainly would not know how to take care of the larger and more significant house of God; the church. In God's design, someone desiring to be a spiritual leader in His great house must have already demonstrated the know how and the will to lead in their own small house.

The writer of Hebrews exhorted believers concerning their relationship with spiritual leaders with these profound words,

> *"Remember them which have the rule over you, who have spoken unto you the word of God: whose faith follow, considering the end of their conversation...Obey them that have the rule over you, and submit yourselves: for they watch for your souls, as they that must give account, that they may do it with joy, and not with grief: for that is unprofitable for you."*
>
> Hebrews 13:7, 17

The words "have the rule" used in these verses come from the Greek *hegeomai*. This word was used in Bible times of those who did the work of governing, of being a chief, or of commanding. *Hegeomai* means, "to lead the way by laying hold of, to lead with one's self, to guide and direct, or to lead to a particular destination." *Hegeomai* accurately expresses the significant responsibility of spiritual leaders to lay hold of other believers, especially those immediately under their care, and to skillfully lead them forward in sound spiritual life.

This exercise of leading the way is uniquely expressed by the author of the Hebrew epistle. Following every short section of teaching, he exhorted believers to walk in the light of what he taught. His exhortations, interestingly, always began with the words, "Let us." For example, he said, "Let us hold fast the profession of our faith without wavering" and "Let us offer the sacrifice of praise to God continually" and "let us consider one another to provoke unto love and to good works" [Heb. 10:23-24; 13:15]. The oft repeated "Let us" accurately expresses proper spiritual leadership. First, a spiritual leader must know the truth himself. Then he must walk in the light of the truth he knows. Then he must teach that truth to other believers. Finally, he must exhort those believers to walk with him, leading them forward in the truth he is walking in.

There is a significant difference between "You should" and "Let us" — between "pointing the way" and "leading the way." Through preaching and teaching, spiritual leaders point the way. But they have not fulfilled their responsibility to lead the way if they are not living what they are teaching, showing others their life, and diligently leading others forward in the walk of faith.

They Oversee the Flock of God

The apostle Peter instructed spiritual leaders to take oversight of the God's flock when he wrote,

> *"Feed the flock of God which is among you, taking the oversight thereof..."*
>
> *I Peter 5:1-2*

The words "taking the oversight" come from the Greek verb *episkopeo* which means, "to inspect, to carefully oversee, and to take care of." *Episkopeo* not only implies being given a responsibility, but points to the execution and fulfilling of that responsibility. "Taking the oversight" is not a matter of taking a title or assuming a position, but is a matter of discharging the duties of the task assigned.

Paul confirmed Peter's instructions to spiritual leaders in his final address to the elders from Ephesus when he said,

> *"Take heed therefore unto yourselves, and to all the flock, over the which the Holy Ghost hath made you overseers..."*
>
> Acts 20:28

The elders from Ephesus had been made "overseers" by the Holy Ghost. The word "overseers" comes from the Greek *episkopos* and refers to those individuals who are responsible to be guardians or superintendents over others. *Episkopos* is often translated "bishop."

Paul exhorted the elders/overseers from Ephesus to "take heed... to all the flock." The words "take heed" come from the Greek *prosecho* and mean, "to care for, to provide for, to give attention to, or to devote thought and effort to." These men who had been made overseers by the Holy Spirit were reminded to fulfill their responsibility by watching over, caring for, providing for, and, in every way, paying attention to the flock.

Paul also exhorted these spiritual leaders to "watch" [Acts 20:31]. "Watch" comes from the Greek *gregoreuo* and means, "to give strict attention, to be cautious, and to be active." One aspect of watching these spiritual leaders were to engage in was guarding the flock from dangerous wolves [Acts 20:29]. Wolves are men with ungodly motivations and destructive intents. When wolves attempt to penetrate healthy flocks, spiritual leaders are not supposed to pray about the situation or seek unity by looking for areas of common ground. They are supposed to run the wolves off or kill them. All true and skilled shepherds know how to kill!

Paul informed the Colossian believers that he was watching over them when he wrote,

> *"For though I be absent in the flesh, yet am I with you in the spirit,*

joying and beholding your order, and the stedfastness of your faith in Christ."

Colossians 2:5

To "behold" means, "to discern, to look upon, or to have the power to see." Paul was fulfilling his responsibility as a spiritual leader by watching over the Colossians believers in the spirit, even when he was physically absent from them.

In his very important instructions to Timothy about the required character of a man who desired to function in spiritual oversight, Paul said,

"This is a true saying, If a man desire the office of a bishop, he desireth a good work."

I Timothy 3:1

The words "office of a bishop" Paul used in this verse comes from the single Greek verb *episkopeo.* This word refers not to the office or title of bishop, but to the function of bishoping — the function of overseeing. In this important opening to his significant instructions about the qualifications for spiritual leadership, Paul did not remark that it was admirable if a man aspired to a title or position, but that it was admirable if a man desired to labor in an oversight role in the church.

In Revelation two and three, Jesus addressed the seven spiritual leaders of the seven churches in Asia minor. He referred to each spiritual leader as the "angel of the church of." The word "angel" comes from the Greek *angelos* and is often translated "messenger" in the New Testament [Mt. 11:10; II Cor. 12:7; Phil. 2:25]. The "angel" of each of these churches was not a heavenly being sent to protect that church, but was the human spiritual leader entrusted with the oversight of that church. That these seven spiritual leaders were depicted as seven stars in Jesus' right hand reveals that they were under the direct authority of the Head of the church [Rev. 1:16, 20].

Although all the members of all seven churches were to hear what the Spirit was saying to them, Jesus' words were first directed "unto the angel of the church." Jesus addressed the spiritual leader of each church because the condition of each church was directly associated with the quality of oversight being rendered by its spiritual leader. His specific words to each "angel" reveal that some had exercised oversight in ways that could be praised, but that others had failed in oversight and, therefore, the church under their care had suffered. To one of the spiritual leaders, Jesus said, "I have something against you" [Rev. 2:4]. To two of the spiritual leaders, Jesus said, "I have a few things against you" [Rev. 2:14, 20]. The words of the Head of the church to several of these spiritual leaders were negative and very stout.

If the spiritual leader in Thyatira had fulfilled his responsibility, the false prophetess Jezebel would not have secured a place in that church. It could have maintained its spiritual strength and moral purity and fulfilled the will of God. Because the spiritual leader failed in his responsibility, Jesus had to deal with Jezebel Himself. Damage had already been done, however, to the place where Jesus could not give the untainted part of this church any further assignment, but exhorted them to "hold fast" to what they had [Rev. 2:18-24].

Spiritual leaders are responsible to watch over the church. Like a good school superintendent, they must promote an atmosphere of order, discipline, love, and kindness. Like a good parent, they must give needed encouragement and support, but also, at times, inform believers that their behavior is unacceptable and bring necessary correction. Like a good shepherd, they must feed the flock with truth, but also protect the flock from unsound and false spiritual leaders. Because believers need a safe and healthy environment where they can learn, grow, fail, and practice their Christian lives, God puts "overseers" in place.

They Provide Pasture

In his first epistle, the apostle Peter exhorted spiritual leaders with these challenging words,

"The elders which are among you I exhort...Feed the flock of God

which is among you, taking the oversight thereof, not by constraint,
but willingly; not for filthy lucre, but of a ready mind..."

I Peter 5:1-2

These elders were to, "Feed the flock of God." The word "feed" comes from the Greek *poimaino* and means, "to furnish pasture, to nourish, to rule or govern, to serve the body, or to supply the requisites for the soul's need." In a rich, expansive, and challenging way the word *poimaino* describes one of the profound responsibilities of those called and graced to be spiritual leaders.

Peter's exhortation to these elders may have been inspired by his own conversation with Jesus in John 21. Three times in that conversation Jesus asked Peter whether or not he loved Him. Three times Peter responded, "Yes." Each time Peter responded that he loved Him, Jesus told him to "feed my sheep" [Jn. 21:15-17]. Twice Jesus used the Greek *bosko* which simply means "feed" and once He used the word *poimaino*. The third time Jesus asked Peter if he loved Him, Peter became very sorrowful; most likely reminded of the three times he had denied his Lord. Again Peter answered "Yes" to Jesus and again Jesus instructed Peter, "feed My sheep." Jesus' thrice uttered instruction to "feed my sheep" was, no doubt, branded on Peter's conscience. Perhaps it was out of this soul impacting exchange with Jesus that Peter boldly exhorted other elders to "feed the flock of God."

The responsibility to *poimaino* the flock of God is much more expansive than simply preaching a good Sunday morning sermon. It includes teaching the full counsel of God's Word, bringing encouragement and correction, creating an atmosphere where the Holy Spirit can speak, guiding believers to safe and healthy spiritual places, and fully setting the spiritual table for the people of God.

Paul confirmed Peter's exhortation when he used *poimaino* in his exhortation to the elders from Ephesus concerning their responsibility as bishop/elders. He told them,

"Take heed therefore unto yourselves, and to all the flock, over the

*which the Holy Ghost hath made you overseers, to feed [poimaino]
the church of God..."*

Acts 20:28

The work of "providing pasture" is perfectly modeled by the Chief Shepherd in Psalm 23. In that Psalm, the Shepherd leads His flock in green pastures and causes them to lay down beside quiet waters. He restores the souls of those under His care and leads them in right and righteous paths. He guides, corrects, and brings comfort with His rod and staff. He anoints the heads of the sheep, protecting them from irritating insects. In the midst of daily danger and in the presence of life threatening enemies, the Shepherd prepares a table for their nourishment. Even in the valley of the shadow of death, He is present and ministering.

Because of the Chief Shepherd's commitment to the owner of the sheep, His heart of compassion for the sheep, and His carefully honed skills in providing pasture, the sheep who follow Him have no wants. This is the high standard of providing pasture that those called and graced to be spiritual leaders must strive after.

They Teach and Maintain Sound Doctrine

Spiritual leaders are responsible to establish believers in the faith, never turning away from teaching them the full counsel of God [Col. 2:7; Acts 20:27]. Although the very significant responsibility to teach doctrine and establish believers in the faith is generally understood by ministers and the church alike, there is substantial room for improvement in this area.

In the Old Testament, God promised to provide shepherds who would feed His people with knowledge and understanding [Jer. 3:15]. In Hebrews 13:7, those called to lead the way in the church were referred to as those who "have spoken unto you the word of God." In I Thessalonians 5:12, spiritual leaders were referred to as those who "admonish you." Because churches and believers cannot prosper without truth and because Christianity as God intends cannot survive apart from truth, teaching sound doctrine is an indispensable part of the work of spiritual leaders. Basics of the faith must be declared and reiterated often till believers lay hold of them and become grounded and settled and "established in the faith as [they] have been taught" [Col. 2:7].

Immediately following the conversion of 3000 people on the day of Pentecost, "They continued steadfastly in the apostles doctrine" [Acts 2:42]. The apostles continued to "teach in the name of Jesus" [Acts 4:18] and "entered into the temple early in the morning, and taught" [Acts 5:21].

Paul is an exceptional example of the important ministry of teaching. He and Barnabas taught new believers in Antioch for a whole year [Acts 11:26]. In Corinth, Paul continued "a year and six months, teaching the Word of God among them" [Acts 18:1]. In Ephesus, Paul did not shun to declare the whole counsel of God, but taught "publicly, and from house to house" for three years [Acts 20:20, 27].

In his letter to the Colossians, Paul declared that he taught every man in all wisdom in order to present every man fully matured in Christ [Col. 1:28]. He exhorted believers to become "established in the faith, as ye have been taught" [Col. 2:7]. Paul was a consummate teacher because he was deeply conscious of his responsibility as a spiritual leader to bring new converts and young churches to steadfast faith, spiritual maturity, and readiness for service.

Paul spoke of his teaching as a striving and agonizing according to God's working in him [Col. 1:29]. In his first letter to the Corinthians, he said that he taught the same truths the Holy Ghost taught and used the same words the Holy Ghost used, comparing spiritual things with spiritual, so that believers would know what had been freely given to them from God [I Cor. 2:10-13].

In I Timothy 5:17-18, Paul described the teaching ministry of elders as "labor in the word and doctrine." He described the one who taught as an "ox that treadeth out the corn" and as a "labourer worthy of his reward." Spiritual leaders must spend time treading out the corn of God's Word through study, prayer, and teaching.

In his important letters to Timothy and Titus, Paul made it very clear that any believer who had aspirations to function in spiritual leadership must be a skilled teacher. He wrote,

> *"A bishop then must be...apt to teach...And the servant of the Lord must not strive...apt to teach...Holding fast the faithful word as he hath been taught, that he may be able by sound doctrine both to exhort and to convince the gainsayers."*
>
> I Timothy 3:2; II Timothy 2:24; Titus 1:9

The Amplified Bible clearly states the necessity of spiritual leaders being skilled teachers with these words,

> *"Now a bishop must be...a capable and qualified teacher...he must be a skilled and suitable teacher..."*
>
> I Timothy 3:2; II Timothy 2:24 Amp

Paul exhorted Timothy to gain God's approval by rightly dividing the word of truth [II Tim. 2:15]. Timothy was also exhorted to "preach the word" with all longsuffering and doctrine because some believers would not endure sound doctrine, but would gather to themselves unsound teachers [II Tim. 4:1-4].

Paul wrote these profound words concerning himself and his fellow ministers,

> *"Let a man so account of us, as of the ministers of Christ, and stewards of the mysteries of God. Moreover it is required in stewards that a man be found faithful."*
>
> I Corinthians 4:1-2

Those who are called to spiritual leadership are "stewards of the mysteries of God." A "steward" is one who faithfully keeps and carefully administers what belongs to another. Spiritual leaders are called to the very significant responsibility of safe-keeping the Word of God. They must keep doctrine pure. They must have the highest regard for the words of God. They cannot add their opinions, twist scriptures to support cute sermons, mangle the Word of God by improperly applying it, or ignore any of its important truths. True spiritual leaders will also rise to the occasion when less than careful men, regardless of whether their motivations are pure or not, misquote, misinterpret, or misapply the Word of God. If any man speaks, he must speak as if it were God Himself speaking [I Pet 4:11].

Regardless of their preferences to preach something exciting, to deliver a "new word," or to be on the "cutting edge of God's new move," spiritual leaders must teach sound doctrine. It is unhealthy for the church when ministers feel compelled to search for or create something new. True and developed spiritual leaders are not moved by emotions, by concerns of falling behind national ministries, or by fears that believers will think they are unspiritual if they don't say something profound every week. They are, rather, serious students of the Word of God, careful dividers of that Word, and skilled deliverers of that Word. God's people don't need carefully crafted ear candy; they need heavenly manna!

They Guard Against Unsound Doctrine

Defending the church against unsound doctrine is a basic responsibility of all spiritual leaders. Unfortunately, this responsibility often goes unfulfilled. Some who declare they are "called to preach" have little or no idea at all what their responsibilities are. Some called but not well-developed spiritual leaders not only fail to defend the church against unsound teaching; they actually contribute to the winds of doctrine that destabilize believers and local churches by promoting "exciting new revelations" that impress people and bring applause.

Paul often warned local churches and spiritual leaders about unsound doctrine and unsound teachers. He was willing to expose by name men who were teaching unsound doctrine, such as Hymenaeus and Philetus [II Tim. 2:17]. He engaged in strong and vigorous contention with the Judaizers who wanted to promote their unsound doctrine in the church at Antioch [Acts 15:1-2]. He declared that he was not like many "which corrupt the word of God" [II Cor. 2:17]. And when he heard about the false teaching being peddled in the churches of Galatia, he wrote a very strong, scathing, and confrontational epistle to expose and debunk that dangerous doctrine and expose the unsound teachers promoting it.

Before leaving Ephesus, Paul called the spiritual leaders together and exhorted them to defend God's flock against unsound ministers and their unsound doctrines [Acts 20:17-32]. When instructing Timothy and Titus concerning their ministry responsibilities, he emphasized the necessity of defending against unsound doctrine and unsound ministers. In fact, he charged Titus with the responsibility of sharply rebuking unsound teachers [Tit. 1:9-13]. The word "rebuke" he used was the Greek *elegcho*. This word describes the activity of showing someone their fault and demanding an explanation. Titus was to rebuke unsound teachers "sharply" [Tit. 1:13]. Paul also told Titus that when a man had been warned two times concerning his unsound doctrine and still refused to change, he was to be regarded as a heretic and rejected [Tit. 3:10].

Paul told Timothy that the "servant of the lord" must humbly instruct "them that oppose themselves" [II Tim. 2:25]. As with Titus and the elders from Ephesus, Paul conferred upon Timothy the responsibility of charging false teachers to desist in their activities when he said,

> *"...charge some that they teach no other doctrine"*
> *I Timothy 1:3*

The church in Pergamos had been leavened with unsound doctrine because of the incompetence of the spiritual leader there [Rev. 2:12-17]. That is why Jesus told him, "I have a few things against you." Concerning the unsound doctrine that had infiltrated that church, Jesus said, "which doctrine I hate." Jesus planned to come to that church Himself and fight against the unsound doctrine with the sword of His mouth; the Word of God. That church was in doctrinal trouble and, therefore, in spiritual trouble, because the spiritual leader of that church had failed in his responsibility. True spiritual leaders must be willing to expose and expel unsound spiritual leaders from the church body.

They Correct and Discipline

Spiritual leaders will be required, at times, to exercise their God-given responsibility and their God-granted authority to bring discipline to the church. As an apostle to Corinth, Paul engaged in the unpleasant task of removing a young man from the church who was committing incest with his father's wife [I Cor. 5:1-7]. This action was necessary, said Paul, to, "Purge out...the old leaven" [I Cor. 5:7]. In taking this action, Paul not only brought correction to one individual; the whole church in Corinth "sorrowed to repentance" and approved themselves [II Cor. 7:8-13]. Understanding that he had been granted authority for the benefit of God and the church, he wrote,

> *"For though I should boast somewhat more of our authority, which the Lord hath given us for edification, and not for your destruction, I should not be ashamed."*
>
> *II Cor. 10:8*

Sometimes believers and local churches must be corrected or even rebuked. In his second epistle to the Thessalonians, Paul sounded out a warning to believers there who were unwilling to work. He corrected their busybody, out of order lifestyle by stating that if they did not work, they could not eat. He commanded them to work quietly and eat their own bread [II Thess. 5:11-12].

In his familiar instructions to Timothy, Paul charged him with the responsibility of bringing correction through preaching. He wrote,

> *"I charge [thee] therefore before God, and the Lord Jesus Christ, who shall judge the quick and the dead at his appearing and his kingdom; Preach the word; be instant in season, out of season; reprove, rebuke, exhort with all longsuffering and doctrine."*
>
> *II Timothy 4:1-2*

Timothy was to "reprove" and "rebuke." Both of these words carry the idea of speaking in a way that brings strong conviction or even a censure. They can mean, "to call one to account or to show one his fault." The work of exhorting, teaching, and commending is often enjoyable for those who are spiritual leaders. But showing believers their error, their faults, their shortcomings, and their sins is also a necessary part of the spiritual leader's work. To fulfill this important aspect of ministry, a spiritual leader must be familiar with the lives of those he leads.

At times true spiritual leaders will also be required to bring public correction to other called and, perhaps, otherwise good spiritual leaders, who have fallen into error or sin. Paul penned these clear, but challenging words to Timothy,

> *"Against an elder receive not an accusation, but before two or three witnesses. Them that sin rebuke before all, that others also may fear."*
>
> *I Timothy 5:19-20*

Too often spiritual leaders fail to follow the clear principles of God's Word because they fear the potential fallout of doing so. Rather than trusting that God is wise and acting in agreement with His principles, they project into the future, assume what the fallout of a decision might be, and then come back to the present moment and make decisions based on the assumed outcome. This is no way for spiritual leaders to make decisions. Just as they take God at His Word where promises are concerned, ministers must also take God at His Word where principles are concerned. They must embrace and follow His principles in love and humility and let the chips fall where they fall; trusting, of course, that God's wisdom will always produce the best results in the end. A few years ago the Lord said to me, "You must have as much faith in My principles as you have in My promises."

Paul told Timothy that no accusation against an elder should be brought or heard without the substantiating word of two or three witnesses. The reason for this is that an accusation, even if false, can derail a man's ministry and greatly decrease his influence in the church. An accusation against a minister must not be lightly brought.

On the other hand, if a spiritual leader sins, he should be rebuked publicly. This is God's wisdom for helping to maintain health in the ministry and health in the body of Christ. When the sin of ministers is hidden or swept under the rug, other ministers and the church at large "learn" that sin is not so bad and that there are no consequences for disobeying God. This is not a message most ministers would preach from the pulpit in their Sunday morning sermon, but this message is preached by precept all throughout the modern church world. And the results, as could be predicted, and as they always are when God's wisdom is ignored, are not good.

Paul said that the errant elder should be "rebuked" before all. This word comes from the Greek *elegcho* and means, "to convict, to bring to the light, to expose, to chide, to bring shame." The action of public rebuke does not seem very loving or merciful. It is, however, loving and merciful for several reasons. First, it brings needed correction and consequence to the spiritual leader who has erred, saving him, perhaps, from even further error in the future. Second, it sets an example and sounds a warning for other spiritual leaders and potential spiritual leaders so that they do not live their lives carelessly or take their ministries too lightly. Third, it sets an example for the whole church about what God expects. It is never wise to disregard the wisdom of God, even if it seems very difficult.

In bringing discipline, spiritual leaders must pursue a balance between correction and encouragement. They must also be careful to correct in ways that are appropriate to the situation and to the spiritual age of those being corrected. A moderate position between mercy and judgement will provide believers or spiritual leaders the opportunity to grow through correction without becoming completely discouraged. In this way, younger believers and spiritual leaders will not be overwhelmed by trying to achieve maturity in too short a time.

They Build Strong Churches

It is very critical to God's ongoing work that the church and local churches be firmly established in the faith and properly constructed in the pattern which He has supplied. Paul exhorted the Colossian believers to be "rooted and built up and established in the faith as you have been taught" [Col. 2:7]. Paul's words, though written to believers in general, are a very good guide to spiritual leaders about their work. Believers and churches must be rooted, built up and established. This can only happen when spiritual leaders fulfill their responsibility to teach and build.

The critical work of building strong churches is significantly different from the activity of having "Breakthrough meetings" or "Fresh Touch meetings" or any other kinds of meetings designed to provide believers with temporary relief from chronic problems. Too many ministers, totally unaware of their responsibilities, have never even ventured into the arena of church building. They are too busy preaching cutting edge messages, getting current revelation, stirring up believers, meeting immediate needs, promoting new ventures, and expanding their own ministries. It is one thing to get believers stirred up, fired up, and engaged in exciting activities. It is another thing altogether to build believers and local churches according to God's blueprint; bringing them to full spiritual stature, strong and stable life, and effective, fruitful service.

In the Old Testament, God instructed Moses to build a tabernacle according to the pattern which was shown to him on the mount [Ex. 25:9, 40]. More than once God admonished Moses to make "all things according to the pattern shewed to thee in the mount" [Heb. 8:5]. The tabernacle would be the place on earth that God inhabited and the means by which He would both dwell among His people and manifest to the world. It could not, therefore, be built on the whims of man, but had to be built according to the pattern God gave. When Moses finished all the work of constructing the tabernacle according to God's pattern, God filled the tabernacle with His glory. We read,

> *"So Moses finished the work. Then a cloud covered the tent of the congregation, and the glory of the LORD filled the tabernacle. And Moses was not able to enter into the tent of the congregation, because the cloud abode thereon, and the glory of the LORD filled the tabernacle."*
>
> *Exodus 40:33-35*

Later in Israel's history, David desired to build a permanent temple for God. God told David that because he had blood on his hands through warfare, he could not build the temple, but that his son Solomon would build it [I Chron. 28:2-5]. When David commissioned Solomon to build the temple, he admonished him to build it according to the pattern given to him by the Spirit of God. Notice David's words,

> *"Take heed now; for the LORD hath chosen thee to build an house for the sanctuary: be strong, and do [it]. Then David gave to Solomon his son the pattern...of all that he had by the spirit...All this, said David, the LORD made me understand in writing by [his] hand upon me, [even] all the works of this pattern."*
>
> *I Chronicles 28:10-12,19*

David transmitted to Solomon the blueprint which had been transmitted to him by the Spirit of God. He exhorted Solomon to follow that pattern and he did so. When Solomon finished the temple according to the pattern God had given, God filled the temple with His glory [II Chron. 4:11-14]. His glory was so strong that the priests could not even stand to minister.

In the book of Ezekiel we find a profound vision that Ezekiel had of the heavenly temple. At the beginning of this vision an angel told Ezekiel,

> *"Behold with thine eyes, and hear with thine ears, and set thine heart upon all that I shall shew thee; for to the intent that I might shew them unto thee art thou brought hither: declare all that thou seest to the house of Israel."*
>
> *Ezekiel 41:4*

Beginning at Ezekiel chapter forty and continuing all the way through chapter forty two, a man of brass with a measuring line measured every part of the heavenly temple. He measured the doors, the thickness of the walls, the entry of gates, the posts, the windows, and everything else. This man of brass was measuring the temple to determine if it was in the pattern.

At the end of chapter forty two, the man of brass finished his work of measuring. Immediately following, Ezekiel saw the glory of God come from the east and fill the temple. Just as with the tabernacle of Moses and the temple of Solomon, when this temple was found to be in the pattern, God filled it with His glory. After filling the temple with his glory, God spoke out of the temple and said to Ezekiel,

> *"Thou son of man, shew the house to the house of Israel, that they may be ashamed of their iniquities: and let them measure the pattern."*
>
> Ezekiel 43:10

God was angry at Israel because they were in violation of the pattern He had ordained for them. He wanted Ezekiel to communicate His displeasure by showing Israel the pattern of His heavenly temple and telling them to adjust themselves to fit His pattern. One thing God said to Ezekiel along these lines was,

> *"In their setting of their threshold by my thresholds, and their post by my posts, and the wall between me and them, they have even defiled my holy name by their abominations that they have committed: wherefore I have consumed them in mine anger."*
>
> Ezekiel 43:8

Rather than following God's pattern, Israel had set "their threshold by [God's] threshold, and their posts by [His] posts." They had introduced their own ways into God's design and God did not like it.

Perhaps the most profound part of Ezekiel's vision occurred in chapter forty seven. There Ezekiel saw waters begin to issue out of the sanctuary and run into the desert. This "temple stream" grew and grew until it was a mighty river that could not be crossed over. Everywhere this river went there was healing, fish, trees, and fruit. This mighty healing water only began to flow out of the temple after God had filled the temple with His glory. But God only filled the temple with His glory after it had been carefully measured and found to be in the pattern.

God's New Testament temple, the church, must also be properly built in the pattern He has given. When it is, He will fill the living temple with His glory. The in-filling of God's glory in the properly built church will eventually become that mighty out-flowing river of Divine virtue to a dry and needy world. Although many believers, including ministers, do not understand this very important spiritual concept, this is how God has designed to bring His rivers of Life to the world.

The New Testament church is called the temple of God [I Cor. 3:16]. It is to be "fitly framed together" as Paul said, and grow into a holy temple in the Lord [Eph. 2:20-22]. The spiritual work of laying foundations, fitly framing the church together, and constructing a strong, stable, and beautiful temple that God can inhabit by His glory is a significant part of the work of spiritual leaders and should not be ignored.

Jesus foretold His intent to build this kind of a church with these words,

> *"And I say also unto thee, That thou art Peter, and upon this rock I will build my church; and the gates of hell shall not prevail against it."*
>
> *Matthew 16:18*

It is the will of God the Father and of the will of the Head of the church, Jesus, that the church be so well built that the gates of hell cannot prevail against it.

Because Paul understood his critical responsibility to build the church, he regarded himself a builder and identified himself as a "wise masterbuilder." He wrote,

> *"According to the grace of God which is given unto me, as a wise masterbuilder, I have laid the foundation, and another buildeth thereon."*
>
> *I Corinthians 3:10*

The word "masterbuilder" is the Greek *architekton*. This word comes from *arche* which means "rule or beginning" and *tekton* which means "an artificer." This word was used figuratively by Paul in 1 Cor-inthians 3:10 of his spiritual work of laying the foundation of the local church in Corinth.

Several things are absolutely essential to the building of strong, enduring, and effective local churches. First, there must be a proper foundation. Jesus Christ, of course, is the only foundation of the church and of every local church. "For other foundation can no man lay than that is laid, which is Jesus Christ," said Paul [I Cor. 3:11].

Second, upon the foundation of Jesus Christ the church must be built in the pattern which God has provided. This is why the written Word of God is so important. Upon the foundation of Jesus Christ, ministers must lay first principles and teach primary foundational doctrines. Chiding believers who had not grown as they should have, the writer of Hebrews wrote,

> *"For when for the time ye ought to be teachers, ye have need that one teach you again which be the first principles of the oracles of God...Therefore leaving the principles of the doctrine of Christ, let us go on unto perfection; not laying again the foundation..."*
>
> *Hebrews 5:12; 6:1*

After declaring that he had properly laid the foundation of Jesus Christ, Paul warned other men to be careful how they built on that foundation when he said,

> *"...another buildeth thereon. But let every man take heed how he buildeth thereupon."*
>
> *I Corinthians 3:11*

I have heard ministers say, "If the foundation of the house is wrong, the whole house will be wrong." That saying is true. It can also be true, however, that the foundation of a house is right, but upon that foundation things are built wrong and, therefore, the whole house is wrong. Many local churches have the right foundation of Jesus Christ, but upon that right foundation many things are out of order and, thus, that church is not fit for God's glory or able to execute His will.

Third, right materials must be used in building the church. Again, Paul wrote,

> *"Now if any man build upon this foundation gold, silver, precious stones, wood, hay, stubble...Every man's work shall be made manifest."*
>
> *I Corinthians 3:12-13*

Both in Moses' tabernacle and Solomon's temple, the proper materials for the house were essential. God was very specific on this matter. This reality is also true concerning the New Testament temple; the church. Wood, hay, and stubble are useless materials for building the glorious temple of God. A temple built of these materials will burn and disappear. Gold, silver, and precious stones, on the other hand, are strong, enduring, and even beautiful. A house built of these materials will stand, flourish, and function. Ministers must very carefully consider what kind and what quality of materials they are using when they are building the church.

Whenever there is a void in spiritual leadership, the "temple" will be in disrepair. This will be true even though God has a plan, is on the throne, and Jesus is Head of the Church. Only when true, strong, sound, and skilled spiritual leaders are on the scene doing their work effectively will the church be built as it should be built; strong, solid, unshakable, beautiful, and effective upon the foundation of Jesus Christ and the solid rock of God's Word.

They Model the Christian Life

Another primary responsibility of spiritual leaders is to model, or to be an example of, the Christian life. In I Timothy 1:16, Paul wrote,

> *"Howbeit for this cause I obtained mercy, that in me first Jesus Christ might shew forth all longsuffering, for a pattern to them which should hereafter believe on him."*
>
> *I Timothy 1:16*

Paul described himself as a "pattern" for others who would believe. The Greek word for "pattern" is *hupotuposis* which means, "an outline, sketch, brief and summary exposition, the pattern to which something must be conformed." Paul was not to be imitated in every detail of his personal life, but, as a spiritual leader, he was to be a basic model of the Christian life. He was to be a pattern to which others could conform.

In II Thessalonians, Paul informed believers that although he could have required their financial support, he worked "to make [himself] an ensample unto you to follow [imitate]" [II Thess. 3:9]. He told the Philippians,

> *"Brethren, be followers together of me, and mark them which walk so as ye have us for an ensample."*
>
> *Philippians 3:17*

The Greek word for "ensample" is *tupos*. This word means, "a type, or an example to be imitated," and was used to refer to those kind of men who were worthy of being imitated. Paul employed the word *tupos* when he wrote this exhortation to Timothy,

> *"Let no man despise thy youth; but be thou an example [tupos] of the believers, in word, in conversation, in charity, in spirit, in faith, in purity."*
>
> *I Timothy 4:12*

Paul also used *tupos* when he exhorted Titus to be a "pattern." He wrote,

> *"In all things shewing thyself a pattern [tupos] of good works..."*
>
> *Titus 2:7*

In I Corinthians, Paul exhorted believers with these words,

> *"Be ye followers of me, even as I also am of Christ."*
>
> *I Corinthians 1:11*

In this scripture, Paul used the Greek *mimetes* which means "to imitate." Recognizing the important responsibility of modeling the spiritual life, Paul grew to maturity and then boldly challenged the believers in Corinth to imitate his life.

The writer of Hebrews exhorted believers with these words,

> *"Remember them which have the rule over you, who have spoken unto you the word of God: whose faith follow, considering the end of their conversation."*
>
> *Hebrews 13:17*

The word "follow" in the above verse comes from the Greek *mimeomai* which means "to imitate." The Hebrew believers were to imitate those who were leading them [Heb. 13:7]. It is very interesting that although spiritual leaders were described in this verse as those who have "spoken unto you the word of God," believers were not encouraged to follow their teachings, but to imitate their lives. If believers are exhorted by the Spirit of God through the Word of God to follow the example of spiritual leaders, it is obvious that spiritual leaders must live lives that can be emulated!

Willing to be Known

When ministers speak from the pulpit, they are expressing their ministry gifts. This is important and necessary, but it is not enough. Believers need more than well crafted sermons; they need living examples. They need to see the Word made flesh. This is a primary reason God has ordained spiritual leadership in the church.

Paul exhorted the Thessalonians believers to "know them which labour among you" [I Thess. 5:12]. The word "know" comes from the Greek *eido* and means, "to perceive, to discern or know, or to discover." One meaning of this word is "to interview." Anyone who considers themselves a spiritual leader must be willing to be known. If spiritual leaders refuse to permit others to know them, it reveals that they are ignorant concerning ministry, that they are selfish, that they have things to hide, or all of the above.

One requirement Paul gave to Timothy concerning those who could be an elder/bishop was hospitality [I Tim. 3:2]. Hospitality refers to being willing to entertain in one's home. Some modern day ministers squirm at this thought and exempt themselves from this requirement by stating that "familiarity breeds contempt." The Holy Spirit said to me one time, "Familiarity only breeds contempt if you are contemptible." If a minister lives in a way that is not harmonious with his own preaching and teaching, people will feel contempt toward him. If a minister is properly developed and mature, on the other hand, the message of his life and the message of his message will be congruent and he will make a double impact upon the lives of those he serves.

Spiritual leaders should let people see how they behave with their wives and children. They should let people see them live in the market place of life. They should allow believers to listen to them pray and watch them worship. They should permit believers to see how they treat other people; saved or unsaved. They should allow believers to observe how they deal with the difficulties of everyday life.

"But," you might say, "won't a minister's anointing be bothered if he fellowships too much with other believers?" There is, of course, a proper balance in this area. Like all people, ministers need privacy and a private life. But ministers who run away from people because it "disturbs their anointing" are either ignorant or selfish. They are operating on false pretenses by presenting themselves as ultra-spiritual when they are actually failing in one of the primary responsibilities of spiritual leadership; the responsibility of being an example. Jesus could minister with children on His lap. Ministers are supposed to follow His example.

After ministering recently at a local church, the pastor, church leaders, and myself went to a special room in the church to have lunch. A believer with no recognized position in the church found their way to that room and entered to thank me for my teaching. I stood up from the table, shook their hand, had a brief conversation with them, and thanked them for their words of appreciation. Later, the pastor and several of the church leaders commented to me about the gracious way

I had treated that person. I realized again how much the simple modeling of Christian character can impact the lives of others.

It is profound that in the lists of qualifications for spiritual leadership Paul gave to Timothy and Titus, there is no mention of calling, gifting, or vision. There is, however, a long list of character qualifications. God is well aware of the substantial impact a spiritual leader's personal life will make upon those who follow him. Knowing the impact of modeling, God requires that spiritual leaders attain and maintain a standard of maturity that can be observed and imitated.

They Prepare the Saints for Service

Another basic responsibility of spiritual leaders is stated in Ephesians 4:12,

"For the perfecting of the saints, for the work of the ministry, for the edifying of the body of Christ..."

Ephesians 4:12

Spiritual leaders are responsible for "perfecting" the saints. This word comes from the Greek *katartismos* and means, "complete furnishing or equipping, to arrange, to put in order, to mature, to make a fitted limb." *Katartismos* can also mean, "to mend, to repair, or to restore."

The word *katartismos* was used in Jesus' day of mending fishing nets [Mt. 4:21]. After returning from fishing each night the fishermen would spread their nets on the shore and examine them. If the nets were weak or broken, the fishermen made necessary repairs. If the nets were full of weeds, they were cleaned up. If the nets were tangled, they were patiently untangled. If there were holes in the nets, they were repaired. By examining, repairing, and restoring, the fishermen put their nets in good working order for the next evening of work.

Many people come into the body of Christ broken, weak, and tangled up. Some, because of their upbringing and past life, are very much out of order and need to be re-arranged. Many have wrong thinking.

Some are missing important character traits. Some need much encouragement while others need to be admonished and corrected. Many need help in getting properly placed in the body. Every believer needs help in some area of life in order to become what they ought to be. And that is a primary reason God calls, graces, and employs spiritual leaders.

The apostle Paul understood this significant responsibility and diligently sought opportunities to fulfill it. Writing to the Thessalonians, he said,

> *"Night and day praying exceedingly that we might see your face, and might perfect that which is lacking in your faith? Now God himself and our Father, and our Lord Jesus Christ, direct our way unto you."*
>
> *I Thessalonians 3:10*

Paul strongly desired to be with the Thessalonian believers so that he could "perfect" what was "lacking" in their faith. The verb "perfect" Paul used is the Greek *katartizo* which means, "to arrange, to complete, to make fit, to put in order." The word "lacking," from the Greek *husterema*, means, "deficient, poverty, or behind." There were areas of spiritual life where the Thessalonian believers were deficient. Their spiritual deficiencies would not only leave them weak and immature themselves; their deficiencies would also keep them from being as useful to God as they should be. Paul, a knowledgeable and competent spiritual leader, was desirous to rectify their deficiencies and, by so doing, make them fit for both life and service.

Spiritual leaders are responsible for the perfecting of the saints. When they fulfill this responsibility, believers will be strong and healthy, will function effectively, and will fulfill their own God-ordained ministries. If spiritual leaders do not fulfill their responsibility to perfect the saints, many called, placed, and graced members will be nothing more than dead weight in the body of Christ. They will not contribute to its fitness or to its capacity to perform service for God.

They Pray for the Church

One of the notable passions of the apostle Paul was his life of prayer. It is apparent from his letters, especially to the Ephesians, Colossians, and Philippians, that praying for believers and for the church was one of his primary focuses.

In his letter to the Galatian churches, Paul declared, "I travail in birth again until Christ be formed in you" [Gal. 4:19]. To the Ephesians, he wrote that he gave thanks for them without ceasing and made mention of them in his prayers [Eph. 1:15]. To the Colossians, he wrote,

> *"We give thanks to God and the Father of our Lord Jesus Christ, praying always for you...For this cause we also, since the day we heard it, do not cease to pray for you..."*
>
> *Colossians 1:3, 9*

Another spiritual leader who prayed much for believers was Epaphras. Paul wrote concerning him,

> *"Epaphras, who is one of you, a servant of Christ, saluteth you, always labouring fervently for you in prayers, that ye may stand perfect and complete in all the will of God."*
>
> *Colossians 4:12*

In spiritual leadership, no ignored responsibility can be made up for by doing something else. Leading does not take the place of teaching. Teaching does not take the place of modeling. Modeling does not take the place of prayer. When those called to lead the church fail to pray, nothing can make up for it; not even other important spiritual activities. Praying is one of the primary ways spiritual leaders are called to serve God and the church.

It is important that modern day spiritual leaders note the example that Paul and other early spiritual leaders set in that they prayed regularly and prayed earnestly for the church. It is also important to note what the early spiritual leaders prayed.

For the Ephesian church, Paul prayed that God would grant them a spirit of wisdom and revelation, that their spiritual eyes would be opened, and that they would know [Eph. 1:17-19]. He also prayed that they would be "strengthened with might by [God's] Spirit in the inner man" [Eph. 3:16]. For the Colossian church, Paul prayed that they would be filled with the knowledge of God's will in all wisdom and spiritual understanding so that they could live powerfully and bear fruit [Col. 1:9-10]. For the Philippian church, Paul prayed that their love would abound in knowledge and judgement, that they would be able to sense what was vital and prize what was excellent, and that they would live a life that God approved [Phil. 1:9-11]. For the Colossian believers, Epaphras prayed that they would stand perfect and complete in all the will of God [Col. 4:12]. For the Galatians, Paul prayed that Christ would be formed in them [Gal. 4:19].

The spiritual leaders of the early church prayed at the very foundation and core of sound spiritual life and effective service. The answer to their prayers would mean that believers would be enriched in truth and in the wisdom of God. It would mean that believers would understand who they were in Christ and know God's will for them. It would mean that believers would grow to full maturity in faith, love, grace, patience, and strength and bear much fruit as they labored in the will of God. If modern day spiritual leaders would simply embrace the themes of prayer that Paul and other early spiritual leaders embraced and pray consistently and fervently, the spiritual growth of the church would accelerate and the effectiveness of the church would improve.

The Heart of a True Spiritual Leader

Spiritual leaders must genuinely care for God's people and labor among them with a willing heart. Peter said, "not by constraint, but willingly." They should not serve in ministry because they are constrained by God or persuaded by others. They should not enter into relationships with God's people to make financial gain or to make a name for themselves. Their care of God's flock must be willing, heartfelt, and genuine.

Paul told the church at Corinth that he would gladly spend and be spent for them [II Cor. 12:15]. And he wrote these words to the church at Thessalonica,

> *"But we were gentle among you, even as a nurse cherisheth her children: So being affectionately desirous of you, we were willing to have imparted unto you, not the gospel of God only, but also our own souls, because ye were dear unto us...As ye know how we exhorted and comforted and charged every one of you, as a father doth his children."*
>
> *I Thessalonians 1:8, 11*

The heart of a true spiritual leader is portrayed in these words. Paul had a deep and fatherly affection for the Thessalonians. He was willing not only to pour out the truth of God's Word to them, but also his very own life. His deep feelings of compassion would likely be foreign to many modern-day ministers.

Good spiritual leaders are fully committed to the health, strength, stability, and success of those under their care. They lay down their lives for the sheep. They gladly spend and are spent. A minister who does not genuinely care for God's people is either not a true spiritual leader or, as we sometimes say, "doesn't have a clue."

A Full Time Occupation

Spiritual leadership ministries are most often full time vocations. Typically, they are financially supported by the church body so that they can fully engage in all the responsibilities of ministry we have just studied [I Cor. 9:14]. Spiritual leaders do not go to war at their own expense, but live from their ministry work and from the support of others [I Cor. 9:7]. They are permitted to eat the fruit of their labor and drink the milk of the flock [I Cor. 9:7]. Like the apostles in Jerusalem, they are free from other work so that they can give themselves fully to the work of prayer and the ministry of the Word [Acts 6:4, 6].

Paul taught that "God has ordained that those who preach the gospel should live by the gospel" [I Cor. 9:14]. He also penned the only "Thou shalt not" in the New Testament when he wrote,

"Thou shalt not muzzle the mouth of the ox that treadeth out the corn."

I Corinthians 8:9

"But," you might say, "Paul worked for his own support." Yes, sometimes he did. But Paul, by his own testimony, was an exception to the New Testament principle God clearly ordained [I Cor. 9:1-18]. For the sake of the purity of the gospel, for the sake of presenting a pattern of Christian life, and for his own dignity and reward, Paul did not always exercise his right to be financially supported [I Tim. 1:16; II Thess. 3:9].

The basic New Testament principle concerning spiritual leadership ministries is that their full time occupation is the ministry they are called to and graced for. This does not mean, of course, that spiritual leaders cannot work or that there will never be a time in their life when they might have to work. God has ordained, however, that spiritual leaders live by the gospel, not by secular work [I Cor. 9:14; Gal. 6:6]. This is the principle to strive toward.

Now that we have learned a little about the shared responsibilities of the five spiritual leadership ministries, let's learn about the unique aspects of each of these ministries.

26

The Apostle

Some members of the body of Christ are called and graced to be apostles. The word "apostle" comes from the Greek *apostolos* and means, "sent one," or, "one sent to an appointed place." Although all believers are "sent ones" there are some whose full time ministry is to go to certain places and certain people groups to preach the gospel, teach the Word, and establish and oversee works for God.

Some Christians are tentative about the ministry of the apostle. Some think the office of the apostle is no longer valid. They consent that apostles operated in the early church, but conclude that they are not needed in the modern church and have been replaced by pastors and teachers. Not understanding that the present dispensation of grace and the church age extends from the day of Pentecost till the second coming of Christ, they fail to realize that the commission, the ministries, the equipment, and the design of the church remains the same as it was in the book of Acts.

There are more modern day apostles than most Christians think. Because the ministry of the apostle is often esteemed in a completely different way than the ministry of the pastor, teacher, and evangelist, unBiblical ways of thinking concerning apostles have emerged. If someone were to say, "I am a pastor," most believers would comment, "Praise God." If, however, someone said, "I am apostle," many believers would say, "Who does that person think he is?" This shows that Christians often think and believe in ways that have no basis in God's written Word.

Along with the twelve apostles, a number of other believers during Bible times were apostles. Paul was an apostle as was Barnabas [Acts 14:4, 14]. James, the Lord's brother, was called an apostle [Gal. 1:19] as were Silas and Timothy [I Thess. 1:1; 2:6]. Andronicus and Junia are mentioned as "of note among the apostles" [Rom. 16:7].

On the other hand, only one person in the New Testament was called an evangelist. That was Philip [Acts 21:8]. And no person in the New Testament was specifically called a pastor. Although most Bible scholars agree that James was the pastor of the church in Jerusalem, he was never specifically called a pastor. And though it seems clear that both Timothy and Titus functioned as pastors, neither was specifically designated a pastor.

Different Kinds of Apostles

Not all apostles are the same in calling, gracing, and function. As with other ministries, there are different varieties, diverse measures of gifting, and different levels of responsibility and authority in the apostolic office.

Completely unique among all apostles were the twelve apostles Jesus chose. We often call them the apostles of the Lamb. Not only were they selected to work with Jesus and to preach and do miracles in conjunction with His ministry; they were also eye witnesses of His works and of His death and resurrection. When these apostles had to choose a replacement because of the abdication of Judas Iscariot, Peter stated that they must choose someone who had been with them from the beginning of Jesus' baptism right up to the time of His resurrection [Acts 1:16-26].

Among the twelve apostles of the Lamb there was diversity. Peter, James, and John were at the forefront of leadership among the twelve and were noted by Paul as pillars in the Jerusalem church. James was most likely the pastor and primary overseer there. John often accompanied Peter, but did no miracles that we know of. Peter was clearly a main speaker and leader among the twelve and was specially noted for his miracles.

Concerning other apostles of the Lamb, we don't know as much. There is almost no Bible record, for example, of the ministry activity of Andrew, even though he was Peter's brother and was called by Jesus at the same time as Peter. We know that by the hands of the apostles many mighty miracles were done [Acts 2:43; 5:5, 12], but we never read that Nathaniel, Matthew, or other apostles did mighty works. It is interesting that we know more about Philip, Stephen, Apollos, and Epaphras than we know about some apostles of the Lamb.

Among the apostles of the early church, Paul and Peter held places of preeminence; they were chief apostles. Peter was specially commissioned and endowed to go the Jews while Paul was specially commissioned and endowed to go to the Gentiles [Gal. 2:8-9]. These two men had more expanded commissions, higher levels of responsibility, and made greater impacts than other apostles.

An interesting example of diversity in function between apostles that worked together can be noted in Paul and Barnabas. These two men were commissioned and sent out as a ministry team by the Holy Spirit [Acts 13:2, 4]. Although they worked together in ministry [Acts 13:5, 6, 46, 50], Paul was clearly the primary speaker as evidenced by this scripture,

"And they called Barnabas, Jupiter; and Paul, Mercurius, because he was the chief speaker."

Acts 14:12

Paul was not only the primary speaker on this apostolic team of two; he was also more well known than Barnabas because of his unique and notable miracles.

Some apostles of Bible days hold a unique place in that they were used by God to bring forth revelation that is now part of the New Testament. Paul is the most well-known apostle used by God for this purpose. He wrote these words concerning his and other apostles' part in this work,

"How that by revelation he made known unto me the mystery... Which in other ages was not made known unto the sons of men,

as it is now revealed unto his holy apostles and prophets by the Spirit..."

Ephesians 3:2-5

According to Paul, truths about the New Covenant were made known to him and other apostles and prophets which were not known in former ages. These truths came by unique revelation and were transmitted to the church in writing. Many of these truths, written as epistles, are now part of the canon of Scripture believers embrace as God-inspired truth. In this matter, the apostles Paul, Peter, John, and James hold a unique place.

Some modern day ministers who call themselves missionaries might actually be apostles. As you may know, the word "missionary" is never used in the Bible to designate a spiritual leadership office. Not all missionaries, of course, are apostles. Some might be teachers, pastors, evangelists, or prophets. Some could be other ministry gifts — helpers, exhorters, showers of mercy — that have a special passion to reach out to nations and people groups other than their own.

First Apostles

In Ephesians four, Paul placed the ministry of the apostle first when he wrote,

"When [Christ] ascended up on high, he...gave gifts unto men... And he gave some, apostles..."

Ephesians 4:8,11

In I Corinthians twelve, Paul stated that the ministry of the apostle was first. He wrote,

"And God hath set some in the church, first apostles..."

I Corinthians 12:28

Paul did not state why he placed the apostle first in Ephesians 4:11 or why he clearly designated the apostle as first in I Corinthians 12:28. There could be several reasons that he did so.

The apostle could be noted as first because apostles often go first to open doors and lay the groundwork for future spiritual work in new geographic territories and among new people groups. Other ministers come later and "build upon this foundation" [I Cor. 3:12]. The Holy Spirit once said to me, "The apostolic gifting opens the doors to nations."

The apostle Paul said that he did not want to preach where another man had preached or build upon another man's foundation [Rom. 15:20]. He informed the church at Rome that he was planning a journey to Spain because he had fully preached the territory he was presently in [Rom. 15:23]. The desire to plow in virgin fields is often a characteristic of those graced to be apostles.

The apostle may also be noted as first because apostles often function in evangelistic work. They preach the gospel of salvation knowing that it is the power of God unto salvation [Rom. 1:16]. They preach by the power of the Spirit and tear down the philosophies and strong beliefs of cities, people groups, and even whole nations [II Cor. 10:3-5]. When the apostle Paul went to Corinth the first time, he purposely determined, "not to know any thing among you, save Jesus Christ, and him crucified" [I Cor. 2:2]. The apostle's evangelistic fervor and Holy Ghost power in preaching is the spiritual activity of laying Jesus Christ as the foundation for new churches and works of God.

The apostolic ministry might also have been placed first because it holds a pre-eminent place of authority in the church. This authority, as Paul wrote of himself, is not for tearing down, but for building the church and the kingdom of God [II Cor. 10:8; 13:10]. In holding a place of spiritual authority in the church and among other ministries, the apostle does not act as a dictator, but as an older brother, helping the Lord Jesus oversee the church.

An example of how apostolic ministry functions can be seen in Acts eleven. Although unnamed dispersed believers preached the Word and won converts to Christ in Antioch [Acts 11:20-21] it was Barnabas and Paul who laid the spiritual foundation of that church. Later, prophets came from Jerusalem to teach and to give guidance and direction. In time, there were prophets and teachers in the church at Antioch [Acts 13:1]. For a season, this church was Paul's home church. He often returned there to rehearse his apostolic endeavors.

Paul also established the church in Ephesus. After twelve men were filled with the Holy Spirit, he taught for at least two years in the school of Tyrannus [Acts 19:7-10]. He taught both publicly and from house to house [Acts 20:20]. He oversaw the church there for three years before turning it over to Holy Ghost appointed elders [Acts 20:28-31]. During that time, he shared the whole counsel of God and warned the elders of potential future problems [Acts 20:27-31]. When his season in Ephesus was ended, he moved forward in new plans [Acts 19:21]. He continued to watch over this church, however, even placing Timothy there to help him as he exercised spiritual oversight [I Tim. 1:3-4].

Apostles are not usually apostles to the whole world or even to a whole nation. Apostles are only apostles to the people they are sent to. Paul, for example, was an apostle to the Gentiles [Eph. 3:2]. He declared to the church at Corinth that he was an apostle to them if to no others [II Cor. 10:13-15]. Peter, on the other hand, was an apostle to the Jews [Gal. 2:8].

Some apostles have strong callings to particular nations or ethnic groups and may establish churches, open Bible training schools, or even establish ministry headquarters in certain nations. Some apostles may spend their whole ministry life in one particular nation.

Apostles are not only pioneers to certain geographic places and people groups, but are sometimes used by God to re-open the way to lost truths. I can think of several men I consider apostles who have re-introduced truths to the church that were almost lost. Now many others are teaching these re-introduced truths.

Other apostles have re-opened ways into certain methods of ministry. They went first [and often suffered for it] and many have followed. Oral Roberts and Kenneth Hagin helped to re-introduce the ministry of laying hands on the sick in public meetings and the laying on of hands for believers to be filled with the Spirit. Other men pioneered ministries like Youth For Christ, Young Life, and Youth With A Mission that were directed toward teens. Others have re-introduced worship and music to the church.

Works of an Apostle

Because of their commission and grace, apostles not only pioneer new works, but often oversee local churches. Paul told the church at Colossi that although he was absent from them in the flesh, he was with them in spirit. He said,

> *"...I am with you in the spirit, joying, and beholding your order, and the stedfastness of your faith in Christ."*
>
> *Colossians 2:5*

Paul watched in prayer over the churches he had established to be sure they remained sound in the faith and in divine order. He often re-visited churches he had founded. Acts 15:41 says that Paul traveled "confirming the churches." In Acts 15:36, he said to Barnabas, "Let us go again and visit our brethren in every city where we have preached the word of the Lord, and see how they do."

Paul wrote often to the churches he established. Several times he declared to the church at Corinth that he was their apostle and had authority from God to build into their lives [I Cor. 13:10]. He set this church in order both through epistle and through personal visits [I Cor. 11:17-34].

Paul wrote a scathing epistle to the Galatian churches to arrest their attention lest they fall back into Judaism. He called them foolish and asked who had bewitched them [Gal. 3:1]. He spoke a curse over those who had promoted false teaching [Gal. 1:8-9]. Paul exercised his authority and fulfilled his responsibility as an apostle to the Galatian believers by bringing strong correction.

Paul also exercised his apostolic grace for the benefit of the church in Rome even though he did not establish that church and had never visited them. Because he was graced as an apostle to the Gentiles, however, he was bold to point the way for that church. He wrote,

> "Nevertheless, brethren, I have written the more boldly unto you...
> because of the grace that is given to me of God, That I should be the
> minister of Jesus Christ to the Gentiles..."
>
> *Romans 15:15-16*

Because of their unique grace to pioneer, build, and oversee God's
church, apostles often have a father-heart and a father-role in the body
of Christ. Sometimes this includes helping oversee other spiritual leaders. The apostle Peter wrote to other spiritual leaders to guide them in
their ministries. He declared himself to be an elder as they were, but
obviously had a place over them in the spirit [I Pet. 5:1-4].

The apostle Paul had a deep affection and a strong sense of responsibility for the younger ministers Timothy and Titus. He watched
over them in prayer and carefully instructed them concerning their
personal lives and ministry responsibilities. Some ministers who oversee other ministers and ministries and call themselves "bishops" may
actually be apostles.

Signs of an Apostle

Visions, supernatural encounters, and special miracles seem to
be more present in the lives of apostles than of other spiritual leadership ministries. Perhaps the difficult nature of the apostolic ministry in
plowing, building, and overseeing the church requires a more certain
calling. I have read after several apostles who were called to ministry
through heavenly visions. In II Corinthians 12:12, Paul wrote,

> "Truly the signs of an apostle were wrought among you in all pa-
> tience, in signs, and wonders, and mighty deeds."
>
> *II Corinthians 12:12*

When Jesus selected the twelve original apostles in Matthew ten,
He gave them power to do mighty works. Notice this scripture,

> "Then he called his twelve disciples together, and gave them pow-

er and authority over all devils, and to cure diseases. And he sent
them to preach the kingdom of God, and to heal the sick...And they
departed, and went through the towns, preaching the gospel, and
healing everywhere...And the apostles, when they were returned,
told him all that they had done."

Luke 9:1-2, 6, 10

The book of Acts confirms that in the early days of the church the apostles did most of the mighty works. Note these scriptures,

"...and many wonders and signs were done by the apostles...And
by the hands of the apostles were many signs and wonders wrought
among the people."

Acts 2:43; 5:12

From all the cities around Jerusalem, people brought those who were sick or vexed with unclean spirits to the apostles, and they were healed [Acts 5:16].

Proper Estimation

Those who believe they are called to be apostles must be careful to properly estimate themselves. Even if one is called to be an apostle, it may not yet be his season to operate in that office. Paul was called to be an apostle to the Gentiles on the road to Damascus [Acts 26:14-18]. He did not begin to operate immediately in his apostolic ministry, however. In the early years of his ministry, he primarily preached the gospel to the Jews in the synagogues, functioning as an evangelist and preacher. It was not till several years after his conversion that the Holy Ghost declared it was time for him to travel together with Barnabas and minister to the Gentiles [Acts 13:1-4]. And even more time passed before Paul turned to the Gentile world and began founding and over-seeing Gentile churches as an apostle [Acts 14:44-48].

To be skillful as an apostle can take years of preparation. One may start in ministry as a preacher of the gospel, but the higher aspects of apostolic ministry, which can include oversight of churches and other ministers, may not fully manifest till some years of seasoning have passed. I have met individuals who believed they were called to be apostles to cities or geographic regions who did not even have success in keeping a small local church in order. They overestimated their calling and, consequently, had trouble themselves and made trouble for others. It would have been better if they had submitted to a sound spiritual leader who could have helped them estimate themselves more accurately.

We are living in a season of time in church history when the ministry of the apostle is again being recognized and embraced. The reception by the church of this office not only re-opens doors of service for those truly called to this office, however. It also opens doors for "would-be" apostles. Just because a person calls himself an apostle is no guarantee that he is, in fact, an apostle. He could simply be an overzealous, ignorant believer. He could be someone called to spiritual leadership, but not to the office of the apostle. He could be a wrongly motivated believer taking advantage of the opportunity to be embraced by the church's open arms toward the apostolic office.

Paul strongly contended against so called "super apostles" who had gained a foothold in the Corinthian church. He called them "false apostles, deceitful workers" [II Cor. 11:13]. Believers must be careful of those who call themselves apostles and claim that the plans of God cannot be accomplished unless all the future life and work of the church is built on them. This over-expanded presentation of the role of the apostolic office will produce error, unsoundness, and potential future trouble for the church, just as any out of balance and out of context teaching does.

Jesus commended the believers in Ephesus because they judged as liars some who called themselves apostles, but were not [Rev. 2:2]. By refusing to embrace self-declared, but not true apostles, this local body escaped the error and trouble which always follows the embracing of unsound spiritual leaders.

27

The Prophet

Some members of the body of Christ are called and graced to be prophets. In Ephesians 4:12, Paul listed the ministry of the prophet second. In I Corinthians 12:28, he specifically stated that the prophet's ministry was second. Like the other four spiritual leadership ministries, the primary responsibilities of the prophet are to oversee the church, teach and establish doctrine, prepare believers for works of service, and guide the church in the will of God. Like other spiritual leaders, prophets accomplish their ministry by teaching the Word of God, by speaking under the inspiration of the Holy Spirit, by modeling the Christian life, and by watching over the saints in prayer.

The ministry of the prophet is a spiritual leadership ministry. Those who hold this office will be occupied in full time ministry either leading a church, traveling to churches, or reaching out to the world at large. They will be teaching regularly, will be overseeing believers' lives, and will have a place of governance in the church.

Believers are often tentative about the office of the prophet just as they are tentative about the office of the apostle. The image of the Old Testament prophet often weighs in their minds and makes it hard for them to believe that anyone could function as a prophet in the New Testament. It is interesting to note, however, that more believers were specifically referred to as prophets in the New Testament than as teachers or pastors.

The Function of the Prophet

The word "prophet" comes from the Greek *prophetes*. This word is composed of two parts which mean, "to forthtell, or one who speaks forth." To prophesy means, "to bubble up," or, "to be inspired." In Greek writings a prophet was an interpreter of hidden things. In God's economy a prophet was considered one who spoke by the Spirit of God; speaking what he had received by revelation, both things concerning the future and things related to the kingdom of God. Though not all prophets will foretell the future, there will usually be an element of special inspiration in what a prophet speaks. Even their teaching will have a different "flavor" than the teaching of a pastor or teacher.

Along with teaching and leading, the prophet will speak forth by the immediate inspiration of the Holy Spirit. He may bring forth a particular truth that is needed at the moment — a word in season. He may reveal the affairs of someone's life. He might give direction to individuals and local churches. He may even reveal future events as did the prophet Agabus. Although prophesying is a part of the prophet's ministry, not every prophet will prophesy about the same things, in the same way, or in the same measure. As with the other spiritual leadership offices there can be varieties and diverse measures of grace-gifting in the prophetic office.

From the book of Acts, we learn that some prophets were part of local assemblies and functioned as spiritual leaders. We know, for example, that there were prophets in the church in Jerusalem. Some of them travelled to Antioch after the church there had been in existence for about a year [Acts 11:27]. Later, we read that there were "certain" prophets and teachers in the Antioch church [Acts 13:1]. These prophets and teachers were known by name and were likely part of the spiritual leadership there. It may have been one of these prophets that spoke by the Holy Spirit to Barnabas and Paul concerning their future direction in ministry [Acts 13:1-4].

In Acts chapter fifteen a company of believers traveled from Jerusalem to Antioch to deliver the apostles' decision concerning the dispute over circumcision. In this company were two men named Judas and Silas. They were noted as being "chief among the brethren" and were prophets [Acts 15:22, 32]. After the message from Jerusalem was read to the church, Judas and Silas "exhorted the brethren with many words, and confirmed them" [Acts 15:32]. Although these men were prophets, they did not prophesy on that occasion, but exhorted and taught. Later, Judas returned to Jerusalem. Silas remained in Antioch and was Paul's choice as a companion in ministry after he and Barnabas separated [Acts 15:33-34, 40].

Agabus was another prophet who travelled with the company of believers from Jerusalem to Antioch. While he was in Antioch, he "signified by the spirit that there should be a great dearth throughout all the world." His prophetic prediction was accurate [Acts 11:28]. Later, Agabus travelled from Judea to Caesarea and prophesied to Paul concerning what would befall him in Jerusalem [Acts 21:10-11]. Agabus clearly had a ministry of foretelling.

There were also prophets in the church at Corinth. Paul explained how they should function for the edification of the church when he wrote,

> *"Let the prophets speak two or three, and let the other judge. If any thing be revealed to another that sitteth by, let the first hold his peace. For ye may all prophesy one by one, that all may learn, and all may be comforted. And the spirits of the prophets are subject to the prophets."*
>
> I Corinthians 14:29-32

Paul guided the church in Corinth with spiritual understanding so that the prophets would function decently in their ministries. He taught that if something was suddenly revealed to a prophet who was not speaking, the prophet who was speaking should hold his words and let the other prophet give forth [I Cor. 14:30]. The prophets were to judge one another's words. The result of the prophets ministering harmoniously and in order was that "all may learn, and all may be comforted" [I Cor. 14:31].

Some use Paul's teaching in I Corinthians 14:31 that, "ye may all prophesy one by one," as proof that every believer can prophesy. This scripture must be understood in its proper context, however. In verses 29-32, Paul was speaking concerning the prophet's ministry, not the believer's ministry. His statement that "ye may all prophesy one by one" was part of his instructions about how the prophets should flow together in ministry in the local church body.

It is not true, of course, that only prophets can prophesy. Other believers can prophesy by the manifestation of the Spirit on special occasions [I Cor. 12:10]. And some believers are graced to prophesy [Rom. 12:6].

Prophecy or the Office of the Prophet

There is a significant difference between being called and graced to be a prophet and being called and graced to prophesy. The office of the prophet is the second highest office in the church. It is a place of significant responsibility. Believers called to and graced for this office will labor full time in ministry, just as do the other spiritual leadership ministries.

It is important to understand that just because a believer prophesies, even if regularly, that does not certify him as a prophet. He may simply be graced to prophesy [Rom. 12:6] or may prophesy occasionally by the manifestation of the Spirit [I Cor. 12:10]. Being aware of this difference will keep believers from pushing beyond their callings and help the church to remain sound.

In my own ministry, I prophesy occasionally. And I often minister messages that are a "word in season." That does not make me a prophet, however. Sometimes I say about myself that there is a often a prophetic flavor in my teaching. I do my best to follow the leading of the Holy Spirit both in teaching God's Word and in being available to be used by the Holy Spirit in the manifestation of the Spirit.

Some over zealous local churches open their doors too quickly to those who claim to be prophets delivering a "not to be missed" word from God. Some of these so-called prophets have a word for every person in every meeting. I have seen some people take so seriously what a self-proclaimed prophet prophesied that they modified the course of their life. Others have made significant changes because they were not taught that the word they received, even if right, may be for a later season.

Those who claim to be prophets and desire to prophesy must be careful. They should offer proper instruction to the people they minister to. If a believer mis-steps because of a word from a self-proclaimed prophet, that self-proclaimed prophet bears a significant measure of the responsibility. All ministers, including prophets, are accountable to God and responsible for people.

What About Prophetesses?

The Bible records that Philip the evangelist had four daughters who prophesied [Acts 21:8-9]. They may have been prophetesses, but we cannot be sure. We do know, however, that the prophetess is a valid New Testament ministry. This fact is confirmed by Jesus' words to the local church in Thyatira [Rev. 2:18-29]. In that church, a woman named Jezebel, one who called herself a prophetess, was wielding ungodly influence. When Jesus corrected this church, He did not say, "Didn't you know that there are no prophetesses in the New Testament?" Rather, He exposed Jezebel as a false prophetess and foretold her terrible future.

The fact that Jesus did not discredit the office of the prophetess indicates that there can be New Testament prophetesses. Jesus expected, however, that the leadership and the believers in Thyatira would be more accurate in their assessment of who was truly called to that office. He expects the same today.

I Wish I Were a Prophet

Throughout my years of ministry, I have met believers who were not prophets, but believed they were. Some of them thought they were prophets because they sometimes prophesied in church services or other special meetings. Some of these believers were graced to prophesy or were being used by the Holy Spirit in the gift of prophecy, but were not called and graced for the office of the prophet.

Some believers think they are prophets because they sense things in their spirits. The privilege of knowing things by the Holy Spirit, however, belongs to all believers because the Holy Spirit indwells all believers. I often sense things about local churches, individuals, and even the future. And I am usually accurate. I don't know things because I am a prophet, however, but because I listen to the Holy Spirit.

I have met some women who were convinced they were prophetesses. Some were working full time jobs and had no place of leadership in the church. Some of them could not have even qualified for practical service on the basis of the standards established by the early church [Acts 6:1-7]. Some were so unstable in their own lives that they needed serious help.

I remember speaking with one woman a few years ago who thought she was a prophetess. I asked her why she thought she was. She told me that another prophetess had prophesied to her that she was a prophetess. I knew the woman she was referring to who had prophesied to her. I told this woman, "Actually, neither you or the woman who prophesied to you are called to the prophetic office." Needless to say, she was offended. This poor woman's life was out of order and so was the woman's life who had prophesied to her. These women just wanted desperately to be something in ministry and so they pretended they were. Sometimes true spiritual leaders have to take their place and help others who are sincerely wrong or are playing spiritual games.

A few years ago, I was ministering at a church in a particular nation. After one meeting the pastor asked to speak privately with me. He said, "Brother Guy, I have a problem in my church that I would like to ask you about." Before he could say anything more, I said, "Don't say a word. I will tell you what the problem is. You have a woman in your church who is divorced, over forty, bitter, and thinks she is a prophetess." He was shocked at my words and probably thought I was a prophet! He asked me how I knew what was going on in his church.

I answered, "I have seen this same problem in many places." Then I asked him, "Is this woman part of a group of women who pray for you?" He answered, "Yes." I told him to have them stop because they were probably trying to pray him out of the church. His eyes opened wide and he said, "That might be why I have been feeling such oppression lately."

Some people are desperate to be spiritual. Some people need to be needed. Some people desire to be extra special in God's kingdom. And some people have vivid imaginations! These kinds of individuals often need a true spiritual leader to speak into their lives, pop their spiritual bubbles, and help them get back on course.

28

The Evangelist

Some members of the body of Christ are called and graced to be evangelists. The word "evangelist" comes from the Greek *euangelistes*. This word literally means, "a messenger of good," and signified those who were bringers of the good tidings of the Gospel.

Evangelists are, by the very meaning of the word, proclaimers. They proclaim the gospel of salvation through faith in Jesus Christ. They pray for, preach for, and live for the reaping of souls. The heart of the evangelist is well portrayed in Jesus' request to his disciples that they pray for laborers to be thrust forth into the harvest [Mt. 9:37-38]. The harvest of sinners is the heartbeat of the evangelist. The lost are his great concern and his highest joy is to bring them into God's kingdom.

The work of the evangelist is described by Paul in his first letter to the church at Corinth. He wrote,

"For the preaching of the cross...is the power of God...it pleased God by the foolishness of preaching to save them that believe...But we preach Christ crucified...For I determined not to know any thing among you, save Jesus Christ, and him crucified."
I Corinthians 1:18, 21, 23; 2:2

The evangelist is not so much an explainer or an expounder of truth as he is a declarer and a preacher. He is a sower of the incorruptible seed of God's Word. He boldly proclaims the message of salvation through the substitutionary death of Jesus Christ and expects men's hearts to be pricked by the power of the Spirit [Acts 2:37]. Although the evangelist's message may seem simple or even foolish, it is, in fact, the power of God unto salvation [Rom. 1:16]. Paul himself, a greatly enlightened and knowledgeable minister, determined to know nothing among the Corinthians during his first visit except the message of Jesus Christ crucified [I Cor. 2:1-4].

I remember teaching a minister's conference several years ago. After my teaching, one of the pastors asked me, "Do you think it is important to make the gospel message relevant to the people?" I heard myself say, "No, we do not make the message relevant to the people. We preach the simple truth of God's salvation and, by the power of the Word and Spirit, make people relevant to the message!" I have never forgotten that important spiritual reality concerning the message of salvation through faith in Jesus Christ. Methods of evangelizing may change from decade to decade, but the gospel message remains the same.

Evangelists, although they may not declare as large a scope of truth as other spiritual leaders, should know just as much of God and His Word as others do. They should not allow the fact that a primary aspect of their work is to preach the simple gospel to keep them from understanding the full counsel of God themselves.

Like the other spiritual leadership ministries, evangelists may be drawn to certain places or certain people groups. Some may feel called to particular nations. Some may feel drawn to a particular age group. Some may feel called to the down and out. Others may feel called to reach into the political world.

Philip the Evangelist

Philip is the only believer specifically designated an evangelist in New Testament [Acts 21:8]. In Acts 8:5, we read this concerning his ministry,

> *"Then Philip went down to the city of Samaria, and preached Christ unto them. And the people with one accord gave heed unto those things which Philip spake, hearing and seeing the miracles which he did."*
>
> *Acts 8:5-6*

Because of Philip's clear preaching of Christ and the accompanying demonstration of miracles, deliverance, and healings, the whole city of Samaria turned to God. It is interesting to note that although Philip led sinners in Samaria to Christ, he did not minister the baptism in the Holy Spirit to them. Instead, Peter and John were sent from Jerusalem to minister to these new converts. Through prayer and the laying on of hands, the new converts were filled with the Holy Ghost [Acts 8:14-18]. Philip was careful to stay within his own calling and grace. That is not to say that evangelists cannot minister the infilling of the Holy Spirit. Apparently, however, Philip did not believe that particular aspect of ministry belonged to him.

An evangelist may minister, as did Philip, in the working of miracles, deliverance, and other mighty works. We must not make this a requirement or a necessary distinguishing mark of the evangelist's office, however, because the Word of God does not make it so.

Along with preaching the gospel to the lost, evangelists should be involved in maturing the saints and preparing them for ministry [Eph. 4:11-12]. It would be profitable for the church if pastors and Bible school deans invited true evangelists to exhort, teach, and train believers to be effective as witnesses. When evangelists minister to the church, other believers called to that ministry will recognize their calling, answer it, and begin to prepare themselves. Believers not called to be evangelists will develop a heart for the lost and learn how to reach out as witnesses and reconcilers.

Cautions for the Evangelist

Those who are called and graced as evangelists must not allow the fact that they preach the simple message of Christ to bother them. Unfortunately, some evangelists desire to be recognized as educated and sophisticated; they don't want to be perceived as simple men with a simple message. Any evangelist who thinks this way must abandon his unspiritual thinking and get in his place and in his grace. Untold thousands are waiting for his clear and strong message of salvation through Christ.

Evangelists must be careful not become angry if other believers or other spiritual leaders don't have the same strong burden for the lost that they have. They must remember that their calling and grace includes a motivation toward the lost which is unique to their office. Certainly, all Christians should care about the lost. Not all, however, will burn with passion like the evangelist.

Evangelists must beware of the temptation to leave their evangelistic office and try to pastor a local church so that they can enjoy the comfort of a home and the assurance of a certain income. They must remember that they are not, in fact, pastors or teachers. If a believer is called and graced as an evangelist, but hiding in a church pulpit pretending to be a pastor, he should resign his false post, report to the Lord, and get out in the harvest. Certainly, it is possible that he will not have as much financial security as when he was pastoring a church. God, however, will supply every need. The precious fruit of the earth is important. The harvest is waiting. Evangelists, like all other believers, must take their place and remain in their grace.

Evangelists should understand that they do not have to be shouters or theatrical. Just because some evangelists preach loud doesn't mean that all evangelists should preach loud. It is not the volume of the evangelist's voice that will bring impact, but the weight of his words. Volume is no substitute for content or utterance in the Holy Spirit.

Local churches should follow the strong exhortation of Jesus and pray for the thrusting forth of evangelists [Mt. 9:37-38]. The Lord of the harvest needs men to stand in this office and preach Christ in such a way that, as was the case with Philip, whole cities will repent and turn to God.

29

The Pastor

Some members of the body of Christ are called and graced to be pastors. In many ways the ministry of the pastor and the ministry of the teacher are similar. Perhaps that is why, when expressing the unique spiritual leadership ministries in Ephesians four, Paul did not separate the pastor and teacher as he did with the other offices, but said,

> *"And he gave some, apostles; and some, prophets; and some, evangelists; and some, pastors and teachers."*
>
> Ephesians 4:12

The English word "pastor" in Ephesians 4:12 comes from the Greek *poimen*. The pastor is "a herdsman, a shepherd, one who tends the flock; not merely one who feeds them." In the King James Bible, *poimen* is only translated "pastor" in Ephesians four. All other places it is translated "shepherd" and is often used of Jesus.

During Bible times the task of a shepherd was to lead and feed the sheep, to defend the sheep from attackers, to heal wounded and sick sheep, to find lost sheep, and to live among and earn the quiet confidence of the sheep they were shepherding. These responsibilities characterize the work of all five spiritual leadership ministries, but especially highlight what the pastor should do. Pastors could read Psalm 23 and the words Jesus spoke about the "good shepherd" and be wonderfully guided and challenged in their ministry work.

The use of the word "shepherd" for this spiritual leadership office profoundly connects those who are called to this ministry to a "flock." Pastors typically function in the oversight of one local body while the other spiritual leadership ministries may minister to a larger portion of the body of Christ. Local churches are usually, although not exclusively, the primary responsibility of a pastor [or pastors] who has been made an overseer of that flock by the Holy Ghost. Some pastors may oversee a single congregation for the entirety of their ministry.

The pastor is called to be the good shepherd who gives his life for the sheep entrusted to his care. He does not use the sheep to fulfill his vision. He does not abuse the sheep as an overlord. And he does not take a place of leadership over the sheep because he wants them to support his personal lifestyle or ministry vision. The true pastor's greatest vision is to passionately and skillfully care for the flock God has set him over [Acts 20:28].

Unlike a teacher or prophet who may only visit a congregation on occasion, the pastor has an ongoing responsibility for the same sheep. Daily, he must watch over the flock he has been set over. Like other spiritual leaders, he will give an account to God for his work [Heb. 13:17].

The pastor, along with the other spiritual leaders, is responsible to bring believers to spiritual maturity. The pastor, however, provides more "hands on" care. This daily task can be daunting. Some believers are very independent and will run to another church if they are corrected or challenged. This does not, however, alter the fact that the pastor has been entrusted with the responsibility to teach, train, and discipline the flock under his care. Uncles, aunts, and baby-sitters can have occasional fun with children and then leave to do their own thing. Parents, on the other hand, have the ongoing and difficult task of raising their own children. So it is with pastors. They must not shrink back from the duty of watching over the souls entrusted to their care.

It is usually the responsibility of the pastor to locate the vision of God for the local body he serves. He should not imitate another pastor or borrow his direction from other spiritual leaders unless the Head of the Church so directs. As the spiritual leader of a particular flock, he must locate the general vision and the specific strategy entrusted to that church.

Like the other spiritual leadership ministries, there can be variety in the pastoral office. Some pastors are skilled administrators, some are strong teachers, some are evangelistic, and some are prophetic. Because of variety in the office of the pastor, local churches tend to differ in spiritual personality. Some churches are like teaching centers, some like worship centers, and others are like evangelistic centers or prayer centers. Although these differences between churches cannot be completely avoided, pastors should be careful to lead their churches into the full pasture of God's counsel and not only into their favorite parts.

If pastors would build primarily from the pattern of the Word of God, by the help of the Holy Spirit, and under the direction of the Head of the church, our local churches would not be so different. The significant differences in strengths, weaknesses, styles, and personalities between churches is primarily the result of differences in the personalities, preferences, opinions, and emphases of different pastors; not a result of Jesus directing churches in different ways.

Cautions for Pastors

Those who are called to be pastors must be careful not to wander outside their grace. It is certainly possible, of course, that just as Peter was sent on a special mission to the house of Cornelius a pastor may be sent on a special mission to a foreign country or another local church. Sometimes it is refreshing and even healthy for pastors to have a break from their own sheep and be used by God to minister to other sheep in other places. Pastors must be careful, however, not to leave their flocks unattended and vulnerable while they reach out to others.

At this time in church history it can be especially tempting for pastors to try to expand their ministry activity beyond their true calling, grace, and commission. The possibility of becoming well know and attaining "nationally recognized" status can be exciting and tempting. But, as always in the economy of God, obedience is the first principle. Pastors must be content, if God does not ask more of them, to stay in their grace, stay in their place, and care for the sheep entrusted to their care. Like all other believers, they should stay within the limits of their commission [II Cor. 10:12-15].

More than any other spiritual leadership ministry, the pastor must be well established and confident in his calling and grace. Because he is most often with his own "family" and in his own "country" he is the ministry gift which can most easily be examined and most likely be underrated. He may have to face resistance from those who cannot perceive that he is a divinely placed and divinely graced ministry gift. Jesus said that no prophet is without welcome except by those who know him too well in the natural [Mk 6:4]. Jesus was not just speaking about the office of the prophet, but about those who have been called to speak for God and are doing so. Although a pastor should never present himself as "God's gift to the world" he must, sometimes through his words, but certainly by his daily carriage, earn a place among his own flock as a heaven sent grace-gift.

30

The Teacher

Some members of the body of Christ are called and graced to be teachers. According to Ephesians 4:11 and I Corinthians 12:28, teachers are spiritual leaders in the church. They have a significant responsibility to establish doctrine, train believers for works of service, and help guide the affairs of the church.

The word "teacher" comes from the Greek *didaskalos*. It is also translated master and doctor in the New Testament. A teacher was one who was considered qualified and skillful in teaching the things of God. The fact that *didaskalos* is often translated doctor and master shows that one who was called a teacher was considered to be, or at least expected to be, an expert in knowledge.

Teachers are, perhaps more than the other ministry gifts, builders. They should not be primarily interested in getting out their latest revelation, but should have a deep concern for the strength, soundness, blessedness, and effectiveness of the church. They should build upon the foundation of Jesus Christ with the sound doctrines of the Word of God. They should aspire to lay gold, silver, and precious stones upon the foundation of believers' faith.

Like the other spiritual leadership ministries, teachers must speak by the inspiration of the Holy Spirit and by divine utterance, not just by carefully crafted notes. The eloquent delivery of a well crafted sermon is no substitute for the accurate delivery of Spirit-inspired Truth. The revelation teachers deliver should be divine impartations of truth which establish believers in the will of God.

The doctrine of teachers must be uncorrupt, sound, weighty, and sincere. They must teach truth which cannot be refuted or even argued against [Tit. 2:7-8]. Because I am a teacher and have a passion for building strong local churches, I am often concerned at the weightlessness and sometimes frivolous and questionable doctrines of teachers and other spiritual leaders. Too often, they touch on what they should teach on, teach on what they should touch on, and espouse personal opinions and cute phrases as if they were fundamental Bible doctrines.

Whether or not people feel blessed by a teacher's teaching is not an accurate assessment of a teacher's effectiveness. The proof of good teaching is not the amount of applause or the level of people's emotional barometers during the teaching, but the quality of fruit which comes forth and remains in the weeks, months, and years which follow.

Apollos

Apollos is a good example of a New Testament teacher. Paul wrote this of him,

> *"I have planted, Apollos watered..."*
>
> *I Corinthians 3:6*

In the natural realm a seed is only planted once. It is watered, however, month after month and year after year, until it grows into a full plant and produces all its fruit. The ministries of the apostle and the evangelist are often planting ministries. The ministry of the teacher is a watering ministry. Teachers water believers with truth from God's Word till they grow strong, become established, and bring forth all their fruit. Preaching the gospel produces the new birth. Teaching the full counsel of God's Word produces full age and complete spiritual stature.

The Bible says that Apollos was "an eloquent man, and mighty in the scriptures" [Acts 18:24]. Obviously, he was motivated toward study and graced with strong revelation of the Word of God. When he went to Corinth and taught, he "helped them much which had believed" [Acts 18:27].

Some teachers are like Apollos was before Aquilla and Priscilla helped him; they are fervent in spirit, but not fully instructed in God's counsel themselves [Acts 18:26]. Apollos had the right motivation and was in the right ministry, but he lacked knowledge. Because he allowed himself to be helped, he became more effective in his ministry. Some fervent teachers need more instruction themselves so that they can become effective teachers.

Like the other four spiritual leadership ministries, teachers should be able to teach the full counsel of God's Word and teach each area of doctrine comprehensively. If they need to teach from carefully scripted notes in the early years of their ministry, that is acceptable. A true teacher, however, who has properly developed himself, will be able to fully and accurately expound the many essential doctrines of the Word of God without even opening his Bible.

If the Lord strongly impresses a teacher to emphasize one or two main subjects, they should obey and do so. In my opinion, however, it is a rare thing for God to direct any spiritual leader to focus on only one or two subjects. Even if this were to happen, it is still required of them to have comprehensive understanding of the whole counsel of God's Word. If they don't, they will not be able to teach their specific subjects in proper Biblical context.

After I ministered one Sunday in a local church, a gentleman approached me and said, "Wow. That was fantastic teaching. I was so blessed and enriched." Then he added, "Of course, I suppose after you have taught a message so many times, you really get good at it." I smiled at him and said, "Actually, today was the first time I ministered that message." The poor man was embarrassed. Apparently, he had learned by observation that many teachers had only one or two messages and taught those messages everywhere they traveled.

Sometimes believers and even other ministers make a grave mistake concerning the office of the teacher. They view teachers as those who approach things from a very academic perspective and are, therefore, boring in their presentation of the Word of God. They think teachers always have well constructed notes. I have often heard teachers described as "those who love to dig into Bible concordances and make outlines." Unfortunately, this silly thinking often becomes self-fulfilling prophecy.

The spiritual leadership office of the teacher should not be compared to the vocation of the school teacher. True teachers are those who are called and graced to teach the revelation of God's Word and love God and His people enough to lay down their lives in study, prayer, and teaching.

Some pastors need to correct their thinking about the office of the teacher. Too often they think of and refer to teachers as "guest speakers" or "itinerants." These terms are not Biblical. There is no such ministry as "guest speaker" or "itinerant." If teachers are perceived and received as "guest speakers" the churches where they minister will not receive the fullness of what the teacher can deliver. If, on the other hand, teachers are perceived and received as spiritual leaders, they will be able to impart truth, deliver revelation, and build effectively into believers' lives. Those who are called, placed, graced, and prepared to stand in and deliver from the office of the teacher can be a tremendous boon to the body of Christ when they are properly received.

Cautions for Teachers

Teachers must not feel insignificant because their calling and grace is to teach. Like all other ministry gifts, they meet a significant need in the church. Often, when I visit a church for the first time, pastors ask me how I want to minister to the sick or do my altar call. I usually tell them that unless the Spirit of God leads me in a special way, I will not pray for the sick, give an altar call, or minister to people to be filled with the Holy Spirit. Because I am called, graced, and gifted to teach, I give my time, attention, and energy to teaching. Sometimes, of course, the Holy Spirit may direct me to minister in other ways.

Teachers must be careful not to yield to the pressure to deliver messages that pastors will approve, congregations will applaud, and believers will pay for. That is being led in the wrong way. Teachers must get their doctrine from the scriptures and their leading from the

Head of the Church and from the Holy Spirit. They should not allow themselves to be heaped by immature believers with itching ears [II Tim. 4:3]. If this happens, the direction of the church will be determined by the least developed believers instead of by those called and graced by God to lead.

Variety

As with all other ministries there can be varieties and measures in the office of the teacher. Some teachers may be called and graced to teach in one country. Others may travel to many different countries. Some teachers may be called to teach in many different local churches. Others may be called and graced to teach in one local church, working in tandem with a pastor or with other spiritual leaders. Others may be called and graced to teach in Bible schools, Christian colleges, or seminaries. Some teachers will teach with greater revelation and greater authority than others. Although this may be a result of study and commitment, it can also be a consequence of the measure of teaching grace stewarded to them.

Like all other members of the body of Christ, I have been endowed with a grace-gift for service in God's kingdom. I am a teacher who has been assigned the task of establishing believers in doctrine and preparing them for service in the body. Because I am called to the office of the teacher, I have been endowed with a special ability to learn and to teach. You could say I have an endowment to extract and to impart truth. In the early years of my ministry it was the consistent experience of being able to draw out and effectively deliver the truths of God's Word that helped convince me I was called to the office of the teacher.

Whereas some traveling teachers cannot afford to stay too long in one place, I feel that I cannot, for the sake of the church, afford to go somewhere for just one service. Occasionally, I will consent to speak just one Sunday morning or one Wednesday night in a local church. I accomplish far more, however, when I stay in one place and build over a period of four or five days or even a week.

Within my grace to teach is a more specific grace. I have always been motivated to minister messages that fit specific people in specific places at specific times. Because I have endeavored to follow this grace-motivation, pastors regularly inform me that what I minister in their churches is precisely what was needed at the time. Often, I ministered the same truths they had been recently emphasizing. I have even had pastors tell me that I taught their sermon notes from the prior week point by point. Recently, two pastors told me that what I had ministered in their churches answered very specific questions they had prayed about just days before I came.

Why does this happen? This happens because I am graced this way. Because I am graced this way, I am motivated this way. Because I am motivated this way, I pray this way, prepare this way, and strive to minister in this way. I always ask the Head of the church and the Holy Spirit to inspire my heart with the words that will best minister to the people where I am teaching.

Section Five

After That

Ministries

After that miracles, then gifts of healings
Helps, governments, diversities of tongues
Are all workers of miracles? Have all the gifts of healing?
Do all speak with tongues? Do all interpret?

31

After That Ministries

Although the spiritual leadership ministries have a lead role in the life of the church, there are many other valid and important New Testament ministries that meet other valid and important needs. I describe these ministries as "after that ministries." I borrowed this term from Paul's first epistle to the Corinthians. After stating in I Corinthians 12:28 that "God hath set some in the church" and listing by number three spiritual leadership ministries — first apostles, second prophets, and third teachers — he said "after that" and listed other ministries. He wrote,

> *"...after that miracles, then gifts of healings, helps, governments, diversities of tongues...are all workers of miracles? Have all the gifts of healing? do all speak with tongues? do all interpret?"*
>
> *I Corinthians 12:28-30*

In the above scripture, Paul mentioned six "after that" ministries; each designed to meet serious needs in the church and among the unsaved. Gifts of healings is a ministry designed to meet the needs of those who are sick. Helps is a ministry which provides "hands on" assistance in the church. Diversity of tongues is a ministry which works together with interpretation of tongues to bring edification and direction to the church or to individual believers. And Paul listed three other ministries.

Paul was not attempting, in the above verses, to set out a complete list of New Testament ministries. His purpose, rather, was to underscore his previous teaching about the diversity of ministries which

God has designed to function within the one body of Christ.

In Romans 12:6, Paul offered another list of non-spiritual leadership ministries. He wrote,

> *"...whether prophecy, let us prophesy...Or ministry, let us wait on our ministering: or he that teacheth, on teaching; Or he that exhorteth, on exhortation: he that giveth, let him do it with simplicity; he that ruleth, with diligence; he that sheweth mercy, with cheerfulness."*
>
> *Romans 12:6-8*

Again, Paul was not setting out a complete list of New Testament ministries, but, as with his epistle to the Corinthians, was supporting his teaching that there are many different ministries God has designed for the one body of Christ. By giving this sampling of ministries, Paul not only laid a foundation of understanding for these believers, but delivered a word of motivation to help all believers move toward their unique and important ministries.

In the next few chapters, we will briefly examine the "after that" ministries Paul listed in I Corinthians 12:28-30 and Romans 12:6-8 as well as several other ministries that are generally recognized as valid New Testament ministries.

32

Graced to Prophesy

According to Romans 12:6, some believers are graced to prophesy. This means that on a consistent basis they will bring forth specially inspired words of exhortation, edification, comfort and, perhaps, personal direction and foretelling. A word of prophecy may be given to the church in general, to a local church, or to individual believers.

In his first epistle to the Corinthians, Paul revealed how the ministry of prophecy can bring edification to the church and encouraged believers to desire this ministry. He wrote,

> *"But he that prophesieth speaketh unto men to edification, and exhortation, and comfort...he that prophesieth edifieth the church... but rather that ye prophesied: for greater is he that prophesieth than he that speaketh with tongues, except he interpret, that the church may receive edifying...prophesy...that all may learn, and all may be comforted."*
>
> I Corinthians 14:3-5, 31

God desires that the church grow spiritually. And He wants the church to be encouraged and to walk in His perfect will. The ministry of prophecy can aid in these important areas.

Varieties of Prophecies

Depending upon the variety and measure of prophetic grace stewarded, believers will prophesy in different ways, about different things, and on different levels. Some may prophesy to the church in general. Some may prophesy direction or correction. Some may prophesy revelation of the Word. Some may exhort by special inspiration. The range of prophecy can be very broad. Believers graced to prophesy must understand this fact so that they don't try to fit too narrow a definition.

A prophecy may edify or build up. It may be the revelation a believer or local church needs to be strengthened or encouraged in a difficult time. Some prophecy can be inspired revelation. Some prophecy might exhort. To "exhort" means to say words to put people on a proper path for the future. A prophecy, then, could direct someone's feet off one path and onto another. It might also assist someone in making a right decision by confirming what God has already spoken to their heart.

On one occasion, I prophesied this simple word to a young couple in a church where I was ministering: "It is time to have your own roots and bear your own fruits." This prophecy confirmed what the Lord had been speaking to them for several months and gave them courage to make a decision about their future life and ministry. It helped them to literally move to another place and pioneer a church which has now become a wonderful blessing in that community.

Another time I prophesied these words to a brother in the Lord in a special meeting: "If you don't slow down, you are going to get in trouble." This brother told me that I was the third person in one month to give him those specific words. He knew exactly what the Lord was saying to him. Several years after I spoke this word, I met this brother again. He said that the word of prophecy I gave him had saved him from trouble and set the course of his life for several years.

A prophecy can bring comfort. The word "comfort" comes from the Greek *paramuthia*. This word refers to any speaking which is intended to persuade, to stimulate, or to console. A prophecy of comfort could be based on a Bible verse or be an "I am with you" from the Lord. Often this kind of prophecy reminds believers of what they already know and encourages them to hold fast in times of trouble.

It can also be within the scope of prophecy to testify or preach by special inspiration. In this variety of prophecy a person may bring forth a revelation, a truth, or even a word in season for another person or for a local church. This type of prophecy may be a declaration of what the Lord is inspiring at that moment.

Sometimes a prophecy can reveal a secret concerning one's personal life. Paul said that if someone in the church prophesied and an unsaved or unlearned person was in the assembly, the secrets of his heart would be exposed and he would be convinced that God was real. People can be turned from sin and turned to God by a word of prophecy [I Cor. 14:24-25].

A prophecy can also foretell the future. It seems to me, however, that the foretelling of future events belongs more specially to the office of the prophet than to one who is graced to prophesy.

Cautions in Prophecy

In Romans 12:6, Paul instructed those who were graced to prophesy to do so "according to the proportion of faith." There must be harmony between what God has stewarded to a believer in terms of a grace to prophesy and the measure and variety of prophecy a believer functions in. Those who are graced to prophesy should not think of themselves too highly and go beyond what has been measured to them.

Not all believers are graced to prophesy. If gifts differ according to the grace given and some are graced to prophesy, then it is obvious that not all are graced to prophesy. Certainly, because all believers have the Holy Spirit, they can perceive things. Near the time that Paul was going up to Jerusalem, he traveled through many different cities. In every city the Holy Ghost witnessed that bonds and afflictions awaited him [Acts 20:23; 21:4]. All the believers knew what was ahead for Paul. That did not mean, however, that they were all graced to prophesy. They were just sensitive to the witness of the Holy Spirit.

It is important to remember that being graced to prophesy is not the same as being graced for the spiritual leadership office of the prophet. Even if a believer prophesies on a consistent basis, it does not mean he is a spiritual leader. Philip had four daughters who prophesied, but there is no evidence that they were spiritual leaders [Acts 21:9]. Prophecy is a wonderful vocal gift and can certainly assist, bless, and edify others, but it is not a spiritual leadership office. Although prophets will prophesy, not all who prophesy are prophets.

33

Graced to Teach

According to Romans 12:7, some believers are graced to teach. This means that they have been stewarded a special spiritual talent to bring forth truths from God's Word in a clear and understandable fashion. In one sense, of course, all believers can and should teach. The writer of Hebrews wrote,

"For when for the time ye ought to be teachers..."
Hebrews 5:12

After being saved for a while, believers should be established in the elementary principles of the doctrine of Christ and able to transmit those doctrines to younger disciples. Paul reminded the believers in Rome that they were able to teach one another [Rom. 15:14]. He also stated that believers could teach one another in psalms, hymns, and spiritual songs [Col. 3:16]. Although every Christian can teach at some level, not every Christian has a special calling and grace to teach.

In his first letter to Timothy, Paul associated the ministry of teaching with the role of some elders. The elders who ruled well, he said, should be considered worthy of double pay; especially those who labored in the word and in doctrine [I Tim. 5:17]. Apparently, some ruling elders did not teach and some ruling elders did teach. The ruling elders who did teach were exemplifying Paul's exhortation in Romans twelve. Being graced to teach, they taught according to their proportion of faith. The ruling elders who did not teach were also following Paul's exhortation in Romans twelve. They did not teach because although they were graced to rule, they were not graced to teach. No matter how much some believers desire to teach, they can not do the ministry of teaching if no teaching grace has been stewarded to them.

Paul may have been referring to the grace ministry of teaching when he wrote these words to Timothy,

> *"And the things that thou hast heard of me...the same commit thou to faithful men, who shall be able to teach others also."*
>
> *II Timothy 2:2*

A spiritual leader himself, Timothy was to commit Paul's teachings to faithful men who were "able to teach others also." Paul's words imply that some faithful men would be able to teach, but others may not be. Why would some faithful men be able to teach when other faithful men would not be able to teach? The answer is in the word "able." From the Greek *hikanos*, this word means, "enough, or sufficient in ability." Some faithful men were sufficient in ability to teach because a teaching grace had been stewarded to them.

In his letter to Titus, Paul instructed him to ordain elders in every city [Tit. 1:5]. These men were to hold fast to the faithful word and "be able by sound doctrine both to exhort and to convince the gainsayers" [Tit. 1:9]. It cannot be said for certain that the men Titus was to ordain would hold one of the spiritual leadership offices. It can be said for certain, however, that they were required to be spiritually mature and able to teach. They would only be able to teach sound doctrine in a convincing way if God had stewarded to them some measure of teaching grace and they had been faithful to develop it.

Teaching and the Office of the Teacher

There is a significant difference between being graced to teach the Word of God and being called to and graced for the spiritual leadership office of the teacher. The ministry of teaching does not include the responsibility of oversight or the exercising of authority and governance in the church that belongs to the office of the teacher.

Along these lines, the Holy Spirit spoke to me one time and said,

"There is a great difference between a Bible teacher and a spiritual leader." What the Lord was trying to get across to me at the time was that I was, in fact, called to the spiritual leadership office of the teacher and, therefore, had responsibility in teaching, leading, modeling, perfecting believers, and exercising spiritual oversight in the church. Those who are called to the office of the teacher are not fulfilling their ministries if they only teach the Word, but fail to lead and govern.

Some who are graced to teach might be Sunday school teachers or Bible study leaders in home cell groups. Some who are graced to teach might teach the youth or children. Some who are graced to teach might even teach in a local church while the pastor is on vacation or ministering in some other place. Pastors should help develop and give opportunity to believers who are graced with teaching gifts. It could be very profitable for them to have believers in their churches who were mature, graced to teach, and developed enough in their giftings that they could teach the flock while he was gone.

Some who are called and graced to teach are currently sitting undeveloped and unemployed in local churches. The whole body suffers when called, placed, and graced believers are unemployed because the church and its spiritual leaders are ignorant of spirituals.

34

Graced to Rule

According to Paul's teaching in Romans 12:8, some believers are graced to rule. The word "rule" comes from the Greek *proistemi* and means, "to stand before, to lead, to superintend, or to attend to something with care and diligence." In Romans 12:8 and other places in the New Testament *proistemi* refers to the ministry believers do who are graced to lead in the church.

The grace ministry of ruling listed in Romans 12:8 is akin to the ministry of governments that Paul included in his list of ministries in I Corinthians 12:28. The word "governments" comes from the Greek *kubernesis* which denotes governing, steering, or piloting. A closely related form of this word is translated "master" [helmsman or pilot] in Acts 27:11 and "shipmaster" in Revelation 18:17.

Believers graced to rule are God-equipped with an ability to help guide the affairs of the church at some level. They may assist in the oversight and administration of a local church. They may "take the helm" for a pastor so that he can rest or give special time to prayer and study. They may oversee a Sunday School program, cell groups, or other special ministries in a local church. Some who are graced to rule may administrate the ministry of a traveling teacher, an evangelist, or a Christian organization. Some who are graced both to rule and to teach may minister in the pulpit.

Elders/Bishops

Throughout the New Testament, believers functioning in the ministry Paul referred to in Romans twelve as "ruling" and in I Corinthians twelve as "governments" were described as elders and/or bishops.

The Greek word for elder is *presbuteros*. *Presbuteros* was used in Bible times of men who managed public affairs and administered justice. *Presbuteros* was used among Christians of those who presided over local assemblies. In the church, the word "elder" denoted a man who was older spiritually.

The Greek word for bishop is *episkopos*. This word means, "an overseer, a guardian, or a superintendent." A bishop was a man charged with the duty of making sure that the things being done by others were being done properly. The word "bishop" highlights the function of the person rendering the service more than the title, office, or age of the person rendering the service.

In I Timothy 3:1, Paul wrote about those who desired "the office of a bishop." The words "the office of a bishop" in this verse actually come from the single Greek verb *episkope*. This word describes the function of bishoping, not the office or title of bishop. *Episkope* is the work of watching over what others are doing, confirming that what is being done is being done properly, and bringing correction to what is being done improperly.

The terms "elder" and "bishop" were often used in the same context to describe the same man or group of men. For example, Paul called for the elders [plural] of the church in Ephesus to meet him in Miletus [Acts 20:17]. When they arrived, he charged them to fulfill their stewardship with these words,

> *"Take heed therefore unto yourselves, and to all the flock, over the which the Holy Ghost hath made you overseers..."*
>
> *Acts 20:28*

Paul referred to the elders from Ephesus as those whom the Holy Spirit had made overseers [bishops]. These elders/bishops, set into ministry by the Holy Spirit, were responsible to lead, feed, oversee, and protect that local church. We cannot say for certain that these elders were called and graced for one of the five spiritual leadership offices. We do know for certain, however, that they were called to and responsible to oversee the church faithfully just as those who are graced to rule are instructed to do so with diligence [Rom. 12:8].

In his epistle to Titus, Paul instructed him to ordain elders/bishops in each city. He wrote,

> *"For this cause left I thee in Crete, that thou shouldest...ordain elders in every city, as I had appointed thee...For a bishop must be blameless..."*
>
> Titus 1:5, 7

Again, Paul used the designations elder and bishop interchangeably. Titus was to ordain elders in every city [vs. 5] and these bishops [vs. 7] had to meet certain requirements. In the early days of the church, many local churches did not have their own spiritual leaders. Men like Paul, Timothy, and Titus often had the primary oversight of these churches. Because they could not be everywhere at one time, they appointed other mature and faithful men who were graced and able to rule — to lead and to attend to — these churches in their absence.

Ruling Elders/Bishops

The connection between the grace ministry of ruling and the ministry of the elder/bishop is clear in Paul's teaching. For example, when he listed the qualifications for the bishop in his first letter to Timothy, he said that a potential bishop had to first "rule" well in his own house. The word "rule" he used in these verses is the same word *proistemi* that he used in Romans 12:8 when he taught that some are graced to "rule." Paul said that before an elder could be permitted a ruling "position" in God's house, he had to first demonstrate an ability to rule in his own home.

Paul was also referring to the grace of ruling when he instructed Timothy concerning the financial compensation of elders. He wrote,

> *"Let the elders that rule well be counted worthy of double honour, especially they who labour in the word and doctrine."*
>
> I Timothy 5:17

The word "rule" Paul used here is, again, the Greek *proistemi* which means, "to stand before, to lead, to superintend." The word "well" is the Greek *kalos* which means, "excellently, rightly, with no room for blame, or nobly." According to Paul, the elders who were doing an excellent job of ruling were to be considered worthy of double financial remuneration. Paul's words strongly suggest that when those who are graced to rule do so excellently, they are a significant benefit to the church.

Some of the ruling elders Paul referred to in the above scripture may have been spiritual leaders — apostles, prophets, pastors, evangelists, or teachers. Some of the men he referred to, however, were ruling, but not teaching doctrine. These could not have been in one of the five spiritual leadership ministries since all spiritual leaders must be able to teach. All of the five spiritual leadership ministries are graced to rule, but not all believers who are graced to rule are called to and graced for one of the five spiritual leadership offices.

Understanding the Bishop

In his salutation to the Philippian church, Paul specifically addressed the bishops. He wrote,

> *"Paul...to the saints in Christ Jesus which are at Philippi, with the bishops and deacons..."*
>
> *Philippians 1:1*

The believers functioning as bishops in Philippi were addressed by Paul as distinct members of that local body. Notice that Paul spoke of bishops, plural, rather than one bishop over the church in Philippi. Clearly, Paul and the early churches recognized the ministry of the bishop.

Some Christians think that the designation bishop always refers to the spiritual leadership office of the pastor. It is clear from God's Word, however, that a bishop is not always a pastor. Other Christians think that bishops are higher-up spiritual leaders who oversee other spiritual leaders, oversee several local churches, or who are heads of ministerial organizations. This also does not agree, however, with the use of the word bishop in the New Testament.

Believers who are graced to rule are sometimes called elders/ bishops. They are enabled to help oversee, administrate, govern, and rule in the affairs of local churches. Some of them will also be graced to teach the Word of God [I Tim. 5:17]. If they are faithful and meet the requirements of Titus 1:6-9 and I Timothy 3:1-7, they will fulfill a very important ministry in the church. Functioning in the ministry of ruling, they can be a tremendous asset to the church and to those who are functioning as spiritual leaders.

The significant role in the church for the grace-gift of ruling/governing is not well understood and, therefore, often remains not filled. If the grace ministry of ruling was taught properly, those graced for this ministry could grow into their place, labor in their grace, and be a great benefit to local churches, to the church at large, and to the kingdom of God.

It could be Biblical, for example, and even advantageous, to have local churches which are primarily overseen by spiritual leaders, to be aided, even taught and guided, by other believers who are called and graced by God to rule. These rulers/elders/bishops would, of course, be spiritually mature and would have already qualified themselves by virtue of their character. Knowing how to rule, administrate, and superintend their own lives and homes, they would also be able to rule in the church. The planting and proper development of new local churches could flourish under this Biblical model. And those called to spiritual leadership offices would have a much greater freedom to develop other aspects of their ministries.

Rule Diligently

In Romans 12:8, Paul exhorted the believers who were graced to rule to do so with diligence. The word "diligence" comes from the Greek *spoude* and means, "earnestness in accomplishing or striving after anything." Those who are graced to rule should do so with energy and seriousness. When they serve with an earnest motivation, they will minister excellently.

35

Graced to Serve

According to Romans 12:7, some members of the body of Christ are graced to serve. Concerning this ministry, Paul wrote,

"Or ministry, let us wait on our ministering..."

Romans 12:7

The word "ministry" in this verse is the Greek *diakonia* from which we derive our English word "deacon." The Amplified Bible renders *diakonia*" as practical service" and says,

"[He whose gift] is practical service, let him give himself to serving..."

Romans 12:7 Amp

Serving is a unique ministry. It is distinct from prophecy, teaching, giving, exhortation, ruling, and showing mercy. Those who are called to *diakonia* are specially motivated and specially gifted to serve in practical, natural ways.

The modern and more narrow understanding of deacons as those who collect and count money was not present in the New Testament. Although the work of a deacon could include administering finances, the ministry of serving refers to any kind of practical work. It can include running errands, ushering, mowing someone's lawn, straightening chairs, assisting spiritual leaders, or doing any other natural task that would qualify as "practical service." Believers called and graced to serve imitate Jesus' ministry of washing His disciples' feet.

In the salutation of his letter to the Philippians, Paul specifically addressed servers/deacons when he wrote,

> *"Paul...to the saints in Christ Jesus which are at Philippi, with the bishops and deacons..."*
>
> *Philippians 1:1*

In I Timothy 3:8-13, Paul instructed Timothy about the qualifications for servers/deacons. He did not detail the function of the deacon, but by his words we know that this ministry was recognized and understood by the early church and filled by certain believers.

Helps Ministry

According to I Corinthians 12:28, God calls and graces some believers to serve in the ministry of "helps." The word "helps" comes from the Greek *antilepsis*. This word is made up of *anti*, which means, "in place of," and *lambano* which means, "to lay hold of, to render assistance, or to support." Basically, *antilepsis* means, "to give aid or to help someone else with their task." It includes the sense of being able to perceive what is needed. The word *antilepsis* was used of supporting the weak in Acts 20:35 and described the practical work of the house of Stephanas in ministering to the saints [I Cor. 16:15]. Those who serve in this ministry perceive where help is needed and then render that help.

Aaron and Hur are good Old Testament types of the ministry of helps. Notice this interesting scripture,

> *"And it came to pass, when Moses held up his hand, that Israel prevailed: and when he let down his hand, Amalek prevailed. But Moses' hands were heavy; and they took a stone, and put it under him, and he sat thereon; and Aaron and Hur stayed up his hands, the one on the one side, and the other on the other side; and his hands were steady until the going down of the sun."*
>
> *Exodus 17:11-12*

By holding up Moses' hands when he was tired, these men not only assisted Moses, but enabled Israel to achieve a great victory. Because of their help, Moses' "hands were steady" and God was glorified.

Deacons in Jerusalem

A good example of the ministry of serving is found in Acts six. In the church at Jerusalem certain widows were being neglected in the daily serving of food. The apostles exhorted the church to select seven men to "appoint over this business." The men chosen to do this ministry would "serve tables" [Acts 6:2]. The words "serve tables" come from the Greek *diakoni,* or deacon. Those who could be considered for this ministry had to have a good report and be full of wisdom, faith, and the Holy Ghost [Acts 6:3, 5].

Seven men were chosen for this ministry. After they were chosen, they were,

> *"...set before the apostles: and when they had prayed, they laid their hands on them."*
>
> *Acts 6:6*

The approach the apostles took in selecting and setting apart men to help in this area of need makes it clear that they esteemed the ministry of serving not only as genuine, but as necessary. They saw this ministry as so vital that they set apart a special time of prayer and the laying on of hands for those selected to be deacons.

When the seven deacons in Jerusalem fulfilled their ministry of serving food the apostles were able to give themselves to their ministry of prayer and preaching the Word. When believers graced for the ministry of serving fulfill their ministries, they free up others, including those called to spiritual leadership offices, to fulfill their ministries.

Epaphroditus

In his letter to the church at Philippi, Paul referred to a man named Epaphroditus with these words,

"...Epaphroditus...ministered to my wants...for the work of Christ he was nigh unto death, not regarding his life, to supply your lack of service toward me."

Philippians 2:25, 30

Paul stated that Epaphroditus "ministered" to his wants. "Ministered" comes from the Greek *leitourgos* and describes a person who is busy with holy things. Epaphroditus was, in fact, busy with holy things because he was meeting the needs of a fellow believer and minister. Later, Paul said that Epaphroditus supplied something that was lacking in the service of the Philippians. The word "service" he used was, again, the Greek *leitourgos*.

What did Epaphroditus do that caused Paul to highlight his service? Basically, he helped Paul in practical matters. Some who observed his activity may have said, "Epaphroditus certainly is a nice Christian man." Paul and the Holy Spirit, however, described his service as "the work of Christ." Epaphroditus was one of the "every man" who had received grace for ministry. He was one of the "joints" and the "every parts" of Ephesians 4:16 who was effective and supplied something from Christ to another part of the body. Epaphroditus didn't just do kind deeds because he was a Christian; he did the work of Christ because he was God graced!

Other Bible Servers

Other individuals in the New Testament were also cited as servers. John Mark was a servant to Paul and Barnabas [Acts 13:5]. The English Bible describes him as a "minister." This word comes from the Greek *huperetes* which means, "one who works with the hands, an assistant, or one who aids another in any work."

A little known woman from the book of Acts was also well known for her ministry of practical service. She "was full of good works and alms deeds" [Acts 9:36]. Tabitha was esteemed as so vital to the church that when she died the disciples called for Peter to come and raise her from the dead. When he came, the disciples showed him all the coats and garments she had made. Peter proceeded to raise this woman from the dead so that she could continue her ministry of good works [Acts 9:36-41].

Many other believers assisted in practical ways in the early church. In his letter to the Romans, Paul referred to Phebe as a servant [or deaconess] of the church in Cenchrea [Rom. 16:1]. He also spoke of "Mary, who bestowed much labour on us" and "Urbane, our helper in Christ" [Rom. 16:6, 9]. In his letter to the Corinthians, Paul mentioned his appreciation of Stephanus, Fortunatus, and Achaicus because they had supplied to him what the church at Corinth had been deficient in supplying [I Cor. 16:17].

Modern Day Servers

Those who are graced to serve might clean the church, maintain ministry equipment, or duplicate tapes. They may plan or oversee special events. Some may help their pastor and his family with daily tasks. Others may assist missionaries in foreign countries. Basically, servers take care of whatever practical affairs need to be taken care of in order for the church to function effectively and fulfill its God-given vision.

I know several churches that are blessed with successful businessmen who function in the ministry of serving. Yes, these men are skilled in business and know how to make money. It is also evident, however, that they are graced to serve in practical ways. Thank God that in some churches both the pastor and his congregation are well enough educated in the Word of God to know that a man who is successful in business may also be called and graced to serve.

In December of 1995, while ministering at a church in St. Petersburg, Russia, I enjoyed an afternoon snack with some of the church staff. We were served tea in a wonderful, careful, and heartfelt way by a man who seemed to be about fifty years old. One of the ladies of the church told me that this man, a recent convert, had never had a family. One of his constant hopes and lifetime dreams was to have a family of his own to serve. Soon after he was saved, he migrated into the ministry of serving, giving himself completely to it. I don't think I have ever seen anyone serve with such grace and with such a spirit of joy! When this man employed his grace-gifting and poured the tea, it was an enriching experience for all.

Is Serving Important?

Some might think that the ministry of serving is unimportant. But consider this: If a person is hungry, what do they need from God? Do they need healing? No. Do they need a prophetic word? No. Do they need a demon cast out? No. What do they need? They need food! Their need will be met when a server brings food to their home.

Like other believers called to other ministries, those graced to do practical service should give themselves to their ministry. They should not become weary in well doing or wish they were more spectacular. They should not esteem their "labor of love in the Lord" as vain, but realize that they will be fairly rewarded. Note the Holy Spirit's important words in Hebrews 6:10,

> *"For God is not unrighteous to forget your work and labour of love, which ye have shown toward his name, in that ye have ministered to the saints, and do minister."*
>
> *Hebrew 6:10*

According to Hebrews 6:10, believers, by doing practical labors of love, have "shown" something. The word "shown" comes from the Greek *endeiknumi* which can mean, "to manifest, display, or put forth." What do some believers show by their deeds of practical service? They show the manifold grace of God!

In the above scripture, the word "ministered" and the word "minister" both come from the Greek *diakoneo*, which, as we have already learned, is the English word "deacon." Those who labor in practical ways to meet the needs of the saints are fulfilling the important ministry of the deacon and, as the above scripture says, will not be forgotten by God.

Paul confirmed the reward of those who do practical service with these words,

"For they that have used the office of a deacon well purchase to themselves a good degree, and great boldness in the faith which is in Christ Jesus."

I Timothy 3:13

Paul stated that those who "used the office of a deacon well" purchase to themselves a "good degree" and boldness by being faithful stewards of the grace entrusted to them. The words "well" and the word "good" that Paul used both come from the Greek *kalos* which means, "beautiful" or "excellent." The word degree means, "a level of dignity or wholesome influence." The words "good degree" mean, then, "to reach an excellent and wonderful level of wholesome influence." Those servers who do their ministries well, bring dignity to the church and to themselves and are a godly and wholesome influence.

36

Graced to Exhort

According to Romans 12:8, some members of the body of Christ are graced to exhort. The word "exhort" comes from the Greek *parakaleo* and is often interpreted "console." It means, "to encourage, to strengthen, and to entreat." Believers graced to exhort are specially motivated and specially enabled to speak words of encouragement to the discouraged. Their words help others to not faint in times of trouble and encourage them to not grow weary when their race seems too long. Exhorters stir others to proper action and steer them toward good paths for the future.

A word of exhortation is what discouraged people need. They seldom need to be rebuked or corrected. A rebuke, in fact, could be the final blow to the hope of one who is discouraged. They need to be reminded that God is with them and that they can prevail. They need to be encouraged to continue. They need to be told, "You can do it!" They need to hear, "Keep pressing on. Never give up. You will overcome!" They need a word like Paul gave to the Galatians when he wrote,

> "...let us not be weary in well doing: for in due season we shall reap, if we faint not."
>
> *Galatians 6:9*

Exhortation could be called spiritual cheerleading. It provides support to those who are faltering and an extra push to those who are doing fine, but could do even better with a little encouragement. An exhortation is a simple message that says, "You can do it; just keep going!"

God is an Exhorter

Seventy years after Israel was taken captive into Babylon, God charged them to return to Jerusalem and rebuild the temple of Solomon. Many Jews returned to Jerusalem to labor in this vision. After laying the foundation of the temple, they met with strong resistance, became discouraged, and ceased working for sixteen years. To encourage His people to return to their work, God sent the prophets Haggai and Zechariah. These prophets encouraged God's people with these simple words of exhortation,

> "...I am with you, saith the Lord."
>
> *Haggai 1:13*

They also said,

> "...be strong, O Zerubbabel, saith the Lord...and be strong, all ye people of the land, saith the Lord, and work: for I am with you, saith the Lord of hosts..."
>
> *Haggai 2:4*

These words were not teaching, direction, or correction; they were exhortation. They encouraged God's people to continue with the work which they already knew was His will.

Jesus' Ministry of Exhortation

In Isaiah, we find these prophetic words about Jesus,

> "The Lord hath given me the tongue of the learned, that I should know how to speak a word in season to him that is weary..."
>
> *Isaiah 50:4*

The word "weary" in the above scripture means, "to be fatigued or to faint." Those who are exhausted from the difficulties of life and at risk for fainting need to be encouraged by someone who can speak for God. Because God gave Jesus the tongue of the learned, He was able to speak to the weary. His ability to encourage was part of His endowment. Jesus not only knew what word to speak. He also knew how to speak that word in the right season. Notice that Jesus knew how to speak "a word." When people are ready to faint, they usually do not need a lengthy teaching. They just need a word.

Tychicus

In his letters to the Ephesians and the Colossians, Paul referred to a man named Tychicus. This man was a "beloved brother" to Paul and a "faithful minister in the Lord" [Eph. 6:21; Col. 4:7]. Paul told the Ephesians that he had sent Tychicus to them "that he might comfort your hearts" [Eph. 6:22]. According to the Amplified Bible, Tychicus was sent to "console and cheer and encourage and strengthen." Paul also sent this man who was effective in the ministry of encouragement to the Colossians. He wrote,

> *"Whom [Tychicus] I have sent to you for the same purpose; that he might...comfort your hearts."*
>
> *Colossians 4:8*

The Amplified Bible says,

> *"I have sent him to you for this very purpose...that he may comfort and cheer and encourage your hearts."*
>
> *Colossians 4:8 Amp*

A Word of Encouragement

People can be bruised by life or become discouraged because of difficult circumstances or difficult people. In these hard times, their bright fires may begin to wane and they may lose hope. Nothing re-kindles flames and re-energizes hope like a Holy Spirit inspired, grace-filled word from an exhorter.

Those who are graced to exhort should realize that their ministry not only keeps the discouraged from quitting, but can also help those who are doing well to stand stronger, run faster, and be more effectual.

There are many in the body of Christ who are steady in their races, but could win first place with a few more "shouts" of encouragement!

I have profited from the grace of the exhorter myself. In the midst of difficult times, exhorters have encouraged me to press forward in my ministry of teaching. They validated my work, confirmed my years of study and effort, and motivated me to excel in and fulfill my ministry. If they had not spoken to me, I would not have fallen apart or quit. I would, however, have missed the extra energy and enthusiasm which results from words of encouragement.

In the book of Proverbs, we find this beautiful word picture,

"A word fitly spoken is like apples of gold in pictures of silver."
Proverbs 25:11

The right word rightly spoken is precious to the hearer. It can be as valuable and beautiful as apples of gold framed in pictures of silver.

Speak Up

If you are graced to exhort, then exhort. There may be a person waiting for you right now who is in a critical situation and on the verge of giving up. That person does not need a long teaching. They do not need to be healed. They do not need a word of prophecy. They do not need to be evangelized. They just need a simple, God-empowered word of exhortation. If you are an exhorter, you can supply that hope-giving word to them!

37

Graced to Give

According to Romans 12:7, some members of the body of Christ are graced to give. This means that God has stewarded to them a special wisdom to attain wealth for the benefit of the body of Christ and the world. Those who are called and graced to give are granted a special ability to know what to do and when to do it in the business realm. Gaining money for the sake of God's kingdom is their strong motivation. Their ability to prosper is not just a manifestation of a "business head." It is also the manifestation of a heavenly grace.

Each grace-gift in the body of Christ meets a particular need. The body of Christ needs knowledge. To meet that need some are called and graced to teach. Believers need comfort and encouragement. To meet that need, some are called and graced to show mercy or to exhort. The kingdom of God, the church body, and those who are called to spiritual leadership have financial needs. To meet that need, some are called and graced to give.

Just as those who are graced to teach have a special ability to gain and give revelation of the Word of God, so those who are graced to give have a special ability to gain and to give money. Just as Balazeel and Aholiab were endowed by God with wisdom to craft and to work in design, so some believers are endued by God with ability to be crafty in business. Just as those who are called to be spiritual leaders are endowed with wisdom to build the church, so those who are called to give are endowed with wisdom to build financial wealth.

Just as the revelation a teacher gains is not only for himself, so the money a giver gains is not only for himself. Givers, like all other members of the body, have been stewarded a special ability so that others can be blessed. Those who are graced to give are responsible to supply finances to others according to the grace stewarded to them.

We know, of course, that every member of the body of Christ should give of their finances into the work of God. Every believer should sow seed. Every believer should give to the poor. Every believer should return natural things to ministers who have supplied spiritual things to them. All believers should give liberally to every good work [II Cor. 9:8].

As much as it is true that every believer is responsible to give something of their finances, it is also true that some believers are specially graced to give. That will be their strong motivation and in that area of ministry they will have special ability. Their giving of finances will not only meet the needs of others, but will bring them joy as they fulfill their calling.

Givers Should Give

Paul taught that those who are graced to give should do so with simplicity. In Romans twelve, he wrote,

> *"...he that giveth, let him do it with simplicity..."*
>
> *Romans 12:7*

The word "giveth" is the Greek *metadidomi* which is translated either "giveth" or "impart." Givers impart money to others. The word "simplicity" comes from the Greek *haplotes* and can mean, "singleness, simplicity, sincerity, without hypocrisy, or generosity." Givers should give with simplicity. They should not make a big deal out of their giving, but do it humbly and quietly. Givers should give with singleness of mind and without hypocrisy, motivated by a sincere desire to serve God by fulfilling their ministry. Givers should give generously, not holding back more for themselves than is proper, realizing that their ability to get wealth is, in part, a result of their unique grace endowment.

One of the important things that can occur when givers fulfill their ministry is that those who are graced to be spiritual leaders are liberated to function in their ministries. The financial supply from a giver can free them from the restriction of the "muzzle" of lack [I Tim. 5:18]. If no one supports spiritual leaders, they are required to meet their own needs either by faith and prayer or by working a natural job. The effort and energy they should be putting into study, prayer, teaching, and leading is diverted and spent as they attempt to meet their own needs.

When givers fulfill their ministry, their own financial "pot" will never run dry. Because they are graced by God to develop and impart wealth and because they have an attending wisdom to manage that wealth, they will never deplete their supply. When givers minister according to their grace, finances will flow steadily just as the widow's oil flowed continuously from her earthen pots.

Kings and Priests?

In the recent past, a teaching surfaced in the body of Christ that categorizes believers as either "priests" — those called to serve God in full time ministry — or "kings" — those called to serve God by financially supporting the priests. Unfortunately, the Bible words "kings" and "priests" have been improperly used in this teaching. Although it is true that some believers are called to full time spiritual leadership ministries and some believers are called to supply finances, the "Kings and Priests" teaching is not accurate.

The New Testament teaches that all believers are both kings and priests [I Pet. 2:9; Rev. 1:6]. All believers are kings in that they have authority through Jesus Christ over sin and death, over Satan and his demons, and over sickness and disease. All believers are priests in that they are called of God and cleansed by the blood of Jesus so that they can bring the spiritual sacrifice of worship and praise.

I'm sure that the teaching of "Kings and Priests" helped some believers locate what kind of service they should render to the Lord. It is more Biblical and accurate to teach, however, as Paul did in Romans 12:7, that some believers are called and grace-endowed to give.

My Father's Grace to Give

My father is a partner in a family business called Duininck Companies. All the partners in this family business recognize and acknowledge that a part of their calling and grace in the body of Christ is to supply finances. Their vision is to function skillfully in business, create wealth, and invest some of that wealth in the kingdom of God.

At one time my father wrestled with his calling and grace. He wondered if what he was doing in business was important in the kingdom of God. Should he do something different? Should he be more involved in the practical functioning of a local church? Was a lack of desire to serve in the nursery at church wrong? Was he being disobedient or selfish?

It became evident to my father that he alone was responsible to settle the matter of his calling regardless of what any other person thought or said. Over time, he became settled in the fact that a part of his calling and grace was to work in business and supply finances to the church. He determined that he was God-gifted to administrate in business, create wealth, and supply finances into the kingdom of God.

As my father and the other partners of Duininck Companies have followed the direction of God for their lives and labored diligently according to their calling and grace, their business has prospered, they have operated in wisdom and favor, and wealth has been created to invest in the kingdom of God. If my father or any of the other partners would have abandoned their business, they would have abandoned their unique commission and special grace. As a result, the body of Christ would have suffered from a lack of supply in the financial realm.

Cautions for the Giver

Sometimes those who are graced to give are yielded places of leadership in the church. Money makes a place for them. And sometimes those who are called and graced by God to make money desire to get involved in the leadership of the church at a level they are not graced for. Those who are graced to give, according to Paul and the

Holy Spirit, should give and do so liberally and with simplicity. Paul did not teach that those who are graced to give should teach, rule, or lead.

This does not mean, of course, that no businessmen and no givers can lead in the church. If givers are grace-gifted in other ways, they should serve in those way. Givers might also be graced to teach, to exhort, to administrate, or even to work miracles. Like all other believers, givers must soberly evaluate their calling and grace so that they can serve properly and effectively in the body of Christ.

38

Graced to Show Mercy

According to Romans 12:8, some members of the body of Christ are graced to show mercy. The words "show mercy" come from the Greek *eleeo* which means, "to have mercy on, to help one afflicted or seeking aid, to bring help to the wretched." Showing mercy always begins with feelings of compassion and finishes in deeds of kindness.

Those who are showers of mercy are specially motivated and gifted to administer the mercy of God to the broken, bruised, lonely, and hurting. Their ministry is important because it touches the souls of people. Just as gifts of healing bring the power of God to bear upon the human body, so showing mercy brings the compassion of God to bear upon the human heart.

The shower of mercy meets the need of the broken hearted. Those who are broken hearted do not need an evangelist, a miracle worker, or a server. They need someone who is graced to administer mercy. When someone has lost a loved one, they do not need a teaching, a healing, or a prophetic word. They need a warm embrace or a strong and loving arm around their shoulder.

Jesus was a Shower of Mercy

Like all other grace ministries, those who show mercy do a part of the ministry of Jesus. Isaiah prophesied about the mercy ministry of Jesus when he said,

> *"A bruised reed shall he not break, and the smoking flax shall he not quench..."*

> Isaiah 42:3

To be "bruised" means to be crushed, oppressed, or broken. A "smoking flax" was the wick on a lamp that had gone dull and was almost extinguished. The "bruised reed" and "smoking flax" of Isaiah depict those who have been crushed or oppressed and whose lights are growing dim. When Jesus ministered the mercy of God to people in these conditions, He brought comfort, strength, restoration, and hope.

When Jesus introduced His ministry in Luke four, He spoke these words,

"The Spirit of the Lord is upon me, because he hath anointed me...
he hath sent me to heal the brokenhearted..."

Luke 4:18

Jesus was not only anointed to preach the gospel, heal the sick in body, work miracles, and cast out devils. He was also anointed to heal the broken hearted. The church continues Jesus' ministry and brings healing to the broken hearted when those who are graced to show mercy fulfill their ministry.

A Valuable Ministry

We know that showing mercy is important because Jesus referred to it in His teaching. He said that those who had given a cup of cold water, visited prisoners, clothed the naked, and fed the poor had actually ministered to Him. He characterized those who showed mercy as those who had done works that God was pleased with [Mt. 25:31-46]. According to Jesus, believers who show mercy will receive a hearty welcome into glory from the King as he says,

"...Come, ye blessed of my Father, inherit the kingdom prepared for
you from the foundation of the world..."

Matthew 25:34

James echoed Jesus' teaching when he wrote,

"Pure religion and undefiled before God and the Father is this, to
visit the fatherless and widows in their affliction..."

James 1:27

The word "pure" James used comes from the Greek *katharos* and means, "free from corrupt desire, sincere and genuine, free from every admixture of what is false." Sometimes believers are motivated toward the more supernatural and spectacular ministries because of the possibility of applause, recognition, and financial recompense. Serving in the way James suggested, on the other hand, holds little possibility of applause, recognition, and financial remuneration and, therefore, usually comes from hearts untainted by impure motivations.

How to Administer Mercy

The administering of mercy can be through words, through works, through touch, through special visits, or through times of prayer. It could include visiting those in prison, clothing the naked, or visiting the fatherless and widows as James taught. Showing mercy could include comforting those who have lost friends and families through death or other reasons.

Paul instructed showers of mercy to do so with cheerfulness [Rom. 12:8]. One reason showers of mercy must maintain a cheerful attitude is because working with those who are hurting and broken-hearted can be emotionally draining. Another reason that showers of mercy must maintain a cheerful attitude is because their ministry is not spectacular and may go unnoticed. Because those who show mercy often do so without recognition and affirmation, they must be careful not to become discouraged themselves.

If you are called and graced to show mercy, be sure to minister out of your grace and not out of your emotions. Give out of your gift, not out of yourself. Minister, as Peter said, with the ability which God has given you [I Pet. 4:11]. And be careful to maintain an attitude of cheerfulness.

39

Graced to Heal

According to I Corinthians 12:28 and 30, some members of the body of Christ are set in the church and graced to minister in the gifts of healings. These believers have the power of God adapted to them to meet physical needs. God is a healer of physical bodies. Jesus was a healer of physical bodies. And some members of the body of Christ will be healers of physical bodies.

When the ministry of healing is manifested among sinners, they realize that God is good and are drawn toward Him. When the ministry of healing is manifested among saints, they are repaired and maintained so that they can continue running their races for God. The Lord is for the body [I Cor. 6:13]. He will heal. Sometimes He will heal directly. Sometimes He will heal through believers who lay their hands on others by faith. Sometimes He will heal through the manifestation of the Spirit called gifts of healing. And sometimes He will heal through the members of the body of Christ who are specially called and graced with gifts of healings.

In one sense, all believers can minister healing. According to Jesus, healing the sick is one of the signs that follows believers [Mk. 16:18]. There are believers, however, specifically called and uniquely endowed with ability to heal the sick. When those who are thus endowed function in their ministries, they will manifest this ministry on a regular basis and at an effective level. Not all believers are called and specially endowed to minister healing to the sick, but some are.

We know from the book of Acts that the apostle Peter had a ministry of healing. His reputation for healing was so profound that people tried to get into his shadow [Acts 5:15]. The book of Acts does not record that people tried to get in John's shadow, in Nathaniel's shadow, or in Matthew's shadow. Apparently, these apostles were not as well known for having healing ministries. Peter ministered more in healing than other apostles because of his calling and grace.

Recently, I was speaking with a minister who is graced with gifts of healings. He told me that when he was filled with the Holy Spirit, he began immediately to operate in the healing ministry. He said that he was often laying hands on people and that they were often healed. I asked him if he was confident in this ministry. He said, "Yes, I know that I can minister in this way at any time and people will be healed." It was apparent that this man had been dealt a gift of grace and a measure of faith in the area of healing.

This man told me that he was once in a church meeting where another minister was teaching. When the minister who was teaching came to the end of his message, he sensed that the Lord wanted to heal people, but not through him. He began to ask other ministers who were present if they felt a special anointing of healing on them. Two or three responded in the negative. Then the minister asked this man if he felt a special anointing for healing. He replied, "The ministry of healing is always with me. I can always minister in this gift and get results." He stepped to the front of the church, called people forward, and laid hands on them. Every person he laid hands on was healed!

Had this man acted in an arrogant manner? No. Had he taken a step of blind faith? No. Had he sensed a special healing anointing? No. He simply stepped out on the basis of his grace-gift and in his proper proportion of faith. He knew his grace-gift, was confident in it, and manifested it for the benefit of the sick.

Often when I minister in churches, pastors ask me if I plan to minister to the sick when I am finished teaching. Although I believe it is God's will to heal and believe that the healing power of God can be transmitted through the laying on of hands, I seldom minister to the sick. Because I know that my primary calling and grace is to teach, I primarily teach. If I sense a special leading of the Holy Spirit to minister to the sick, I will do so. Otherwise there is no more reason for me to lay hands on the sick than any other believer. I concentrate on my primary ministry of teaching, but remain open to the manifestation of the Spirit.

Sometimes those who are graced for spiritual leadership ministries are also graced with gifts of healings. The apostle Peter, for example, had a profound healing ministry. The apostle Paul was endowed by God to work such special healings that when handkerchiefs or aprons from his body were laid upon the sick, diseases went out of them [Acts 19:11-12]. Philip was an evangelist who also had a healing ministry and a miracle ministry. Just because someone is graced for a spiritual leadership ministry, however, does not mean they are graced with gifts of healing.

Diversity in the Gifts of Healings

During His earth ministry, Jesus often ministered to the sick. Because He had the Spirit without measure, He was able to heal every sickness and all manner of disease. In Matthew, we read,

"And Jesus went about all Galilee, teaching in their synagogues, and preaching the gospel of the kingdom, and healing all manner of sickness and all manner of disease among the people."
Matthew 4:23

Perhaps you noticed that concerning this ministry called gifts of healings, both "gifts" and "healings" are in the plural. The reason there are gifts of healings is because there are many different kinds of physical sicknesses and diseases that need to be dealt with.

One person graced with gifts of healings may have good success with cancers, but not with deaf ears. Another may have good results with skin diseases, but never have a blind eye opened. Another may have unusual results with the deaf. One minister I know has significant results ministering to those who have been injured in accidents.

We learn from Acts 8:7 that palsied and lame individuals were healed by Philip the evangelist. It is interesting that the two diseases specifically mentioned concerning his healing ministry were leg problems. It is possible that Philip's gift of healing was in the area of damaged legs.

If you are called and graced to minister healing, realize that you may be more effective in ministering to one area of sickness than another. This will keep you from being frustrated or confused if you have better results with some physical problems than with others. Discover what areas of sickness and disease you are more equipped to deal with and concentrate in those areas.

Cautions for Those with Healing Ministries

Those who are graced with the gifts of healings are not necessarily called and graced to teach and lead in the church. Gifts of healings is not a spiritual leadership ministry and is not a teaching office. Gifts of healings is an "after that," non-leadership ministry [I Cor. 12:28]. Although gifts of healings is an important ministry, it does not establish doctrine, produce spiritual growth, train believers for ministry, or give correction and direction. Trouble has sometimes been caused in the church because individuals who were graced with healing and miracle ministries, but not called and graced for one of the spiritual leadership ministries have taken or have been given places of spiritual leadership.

Believers often have silly ways of thinking. Sometimes those who are called and graced to teach hunger after healing and miracle ministries. Why do they do this? Because they don't want to be perceived as ministers without power. On the other hand, those who are called and graced with healing and miracle ministries sometimes want to have teaching and leadership ministries. Why do they want this? Because they don't want to be perceived as ignorant.

For those graced with gifts of healings the same principle applies that applies to all other ministries. Locate your grace, stay in your place, and minister by the special ability God has stewarded to you!

40

Graced to Work Miracles

According to I Corinthians 12:28, some members of the body of Christ are called and graced to work miracles. This means that God has measured to them a special power to effect changes in the natural realm. Physical disease, demons, nature, matter, and even death can be effected by the working of miracles. This ministry can benefit the church, but it primarily blesses and impresses the unsaved. When miracles occur, men are drawn toward God "seeing" His goodness and power.

Like all other ministries, workers of miracles can operate in their ministry consistently. Concerning this fact, you might say, "Brother Guy, believers can't just work miracles. Working of miracles is a gift of the Spirit. Miracles can only be worked as the Spirit wills." Actually, you are both right and wrong.

It is true that working of miracles is one of the nine manifestations of the Spirit. In this manifestation of the Spirit any believer could be used by the Spirit on a special occasion to work a miracle. The manifestation of the Spirit is as the Spirit wills and cannot be pre-planned or manufactured.

There is also, however, a grace ministry of working of miracles. Concerning this ministry, Paul did not ask, "Could anyone be used by the Spirit of God to work miracles?" He asked, "Are all workers of miracles" [I Cor. 12:29]. This is a significant distinction. Just as he asked, "Are all apostles? are all prophets? are all teachers?" so he asked, "are all workers of miracles." Apostles, prophets, and teachers are not manifestations of the Spirit. They are New Testament ministries. So, too, working of miracles is a New Testament ministry.

Some believers are called, placed in the body, and specially en-dowed with power to be workers of miracles. In this ministry, they are not used occasionally in the manifestation of the Spirit called working of miracles; they are a worker of miracles. Some believers can say, then, "I am a miracle worker."

When a miracle is needed, the worker of miracles will be able, by the power of God, to provide a miracle. When they work miracles, they are manifesting the grace-gift stewarded to them. Most miracle workers will not work miracles every day. They will, however, work miracles regularly. Like all believers, they must be submitted to God and do only what they see the Father doing.

Again, you might say, "Brother Guy, I know that an administrator can administrate when he wants to and a helper can labor in the helps ministry at will. I know a teacher can say that at 7:00 P.M. he will teach and be confident that he has the ability from God do so. But a believer could never say that they were going to start working miracles at 7:00 P. M. and actually do it. Working of miracles is only as the Spirit wills."

I have a question for you, "Aren't the various members of the body of Christ entrusted with the various aspects of Jesus' ministry and the various measures of His gifting?" Jesus was anointed by the Father to teach. When there was a need for teaching and the Father was direct-ing Him to teach, He taught. So too, some believers are called to teach and can teach as the Father directs them.

Jesus was also empowered by God to work miracles; He was a miracle worker. When a miracle was needed, He worked one. When His mother asked him to turn water to wine, He did it. He did not fast and pray about it. In fact, He did not even want to do that particular miracle [Jn. 2:1-11]. He could perform that miracle, however, because He had the power to do so. When the wind was about to sink the dis-ciples' boat, Jesus commanded it to be still and it obeyed Him [Mt. 8:23-27]. When the multitudes were hungry, Jesus multiplied the fishes and the loaves [Mk. 8:1-9].

One reason we don't see working of miracles manifested more

in the body of Christ is because the teaching about this ministry has been incomplete and sometimes wrong. After the body of Christ began to understand that some believers were called to be teachers, some believers began functioning in that ministry. After the body of Christ learned that some believers were called to healing ministries, some believers began functioning in that ministry. When the body of Christ is taught properly about working of miracles, some believers will begin to function in that ministry.

Another reason the working of miracles has not been more in operation is because the success of any ministry gift is somewhat dependent upon how people perceive and receive that ministry gift. If believers do not receive a teacher as a teacher, it is difficult for the teacher to manifest his ministry. If believers do not receive a miracle worker as a miracle worker, the miracle worker will be hindered. In fact, this very thing happened to Jesus in His own home town [Mt. 13:53-58]. Was Jesus a miracle worker? Yes. Did He work any mighty miracles in Nazareth? No. Why not? Because the people did not receive Him as a miracle worker. When miracle workers are developed in spiritual stature, submitted to God, functioning in their ministries, and properly received by people, they will work miracles.

New Testament Examples

Peter was a worker of miracles. His healing of the lame man at the gate called Beautiful was described in the Word of God as a "miracle of healing" [Acts 4:22]. When Tabitha died the disciples sent word to Lydda and asked Peter to come and raise her from the dead [Acts 9:36-42]. Why didn't they raise Tabitha from the dead themselves? They had authority in Jesus' name, didn't they? Why didn't they use their faith? And why didn't they send for Matthew, John, or Andrew? The disciples in Joppa sent for Peter because Peter was recognized as a worker of miracles.

Stephen, one of the seven men in Jerusalem who had been selected to minister to the Grecian widows as a deacon, was also noted as a worker of miracles. The Bible reports of him that,

"Stephen, full of faith and power, did great wonders and miracles among the people."

Acts 9:8

Philip the evangelist, another one of the seven men selected to minister to the widows in Jerusalem, was later noted as a miracle worker. The Bible says,

"And the people with one accord gave heed unto those things which Philip spake, hearing and seeing the miracles which he did...."

Acts 8:6-7

Paul was also known for his miracles. In Acts nineteen we read,

"And God wrought special miracles by the hands of Paul: So that from his body were brought unto the sick handkerchiefs or aprons, and the diseases departed from them, and the evil spirits went out of them."

Acts 19:11-12

It is very likely, also, that Barnabas worked miracles because we read that he and Paul testified in Jerusalem that miracles and wonders had been wrought among the Gentiles by them [Acts 15:12].

In the early church, many who had miracle ministries held spiritual leadership offices. Paul was an apostle who worked miracles. Philip was an evangelist who worked miracles. We are not sure if Stephen held a spiritual leadership office, but we are sure that he worked miracles. And Acts 5:12 says that, "by the hands of the apostles were many signs and wonders wrought among the people." It is important to acknowledge, however, that believers not called to one of the five spiritual leadership offices can be called and graced to work miracles.

Casting Out Demons

Two places in the book of Acts the casting out of demons is described as a miracle. In Acts eight, we read this concerning Philip's ministry,

"And the people with one accord gave heed unto those things which Philip spake, hearing and seeing the miracles which he did. For unclean spirits, crying with loud voice, came out of many that were possessed..."

Acts 8:6-7

Notice in this scripture that the word "For" connects miracles with the ousting of demons. Casting out demons was a part of the miracles Philip worked.

Paul also worked miracles by casting out demons. In Acts nineteen, we read,

"And God wrought special miracles by the hands of Paul: So that from his body were brought unto the sick handkerchiefs or aprons, and the diseases departed from them, and the evil spirits went out of them."

Acts 19:11-12

Jesus also associated the casting out of demons with the working of miracles. In Mark nine, we read,

"And John answered him, saying, Master, we saw one casting out devils in thy name, and he followeth not us: and we forbad him, because he followeth not us. But Jesus said, Forbid him not: for there is no man which shall do a miracle in my name, that can lightly speak evil of me."

Mark 9:38-39

Some believers will cast out demons. This ministry was not only a significant part of Jesus' ministry, but was listed by Him as the first sign that would follow the disciples as they carried on His ministry [Mk. 16:17]. This ministry was manifested often in the book of Acts; although primarily through the apostles.

Those who are called to the ministry of deliverance may also experience the manifestation of the Spirit called discerning of spirits [I Cor. 12:10]. This special ability to "see" will enable them to know who is truly demonized so that they can exercise authority over the spirit causing the problem. This is important because if a person is possessed by an evil spirit, they will not be whole till the demon is cast out.

On one occasion a man who was blind and dumb was brought to Jesus. If Jesus had only been able to see in the natural realm, He may have laid hands on the man for healing. In this case, however, the man's physical problem was the result of being demonized [Mt. 12:22]. Jesus cast the demon out and the man became well. So, too, the bowed together woman that Jesus healed in the synagogue was possessed by a spirit of infirmity [Lk. 13:11]. The discerning of spirits is important in the ministry of deliverance because it enables a believer to determine if the cause of someone's problem is demonic.

Demons are cast out by the exercise of authority in Jesus' name and by the use of God's power. Those who are called to this ministry need not war in the flesh, travail, do special kinds of prayer, plead the blood, or employ other spiritual gimmicks. They must simply exercise their authority in Jesus' name, use the power entrusted to them, and the demons will obey.

It is true that all believers can cast out demons. Through faith in Jesus' name and the exercise of authority, they can achieve some results. As is true with all other ministries, however, some believers will be specially graced for this ministry.

Areas of Caution for the Miracle Worker

Those who are graced to be workers of miracles must be careful not to think more highly of themselves than they ought. They are not more special to God or more spiritual because they have been graced with miracle working power. Like all other believers, they are stewards of a particular variety and measure of the ability of Christ. The way they are gifted is a result of God's purpose and grace [II Tim. 1:9].

Those who are graced as workers of miracles must not take advantage of people financially. When people are desperate for a miracle, they will pay. Although people are permitted to financially bless a worker of miracles or any other ministry gift for that matter, workers of miracles are not permitted to minister in their endowment for the purpose of financial gain. They must not demand payment for their heavenly gifts. When Elisha healed Naaman of leprosy, Naaman wanted to pay him. Elisha, however, refused payment [II Kings 5:15-16]. He did not permit himself to start down the dangerous road of being personally benefitted by the administration of his heavenly endowment.

41

Graced to Minister in Diverse Tongues

According to I Corinthians 12:28 and 30, some members of the body of Christ are called and graced to minister in diverse tongues. On a consistent basis, though not necessarily every day or in every believers' meeting, they will speak by inspiration in an unknown tongue and then they or another believer will interpret the unknown tongue into a known tongue. This ministry takes place primarily in the church and in believers' meetings.

You might say to me, "But, brother Guy, all believers can be filled with the Spirit and speak in other tongues." You are right. You must realize, however, that speaking in other tongues serves two distinct purposes. One purpose of speaking in other tongues is personal and devotional. When believers pray in other tongues, they are primarily speaking mysteries with God, edifying themselves, or worshipping God [I Cor. 14:2, 4].They might also be praying for others [Rom. 8:26; Eph. 6:18]. This kind of speaking in tongues is prayer and the direction is from believers to God [I Cor. 14:2, 14, 15].

Another purpose of speaking in tongues is the ministry of speaking in diverse tongues. This ministry occurs when a believer is inspired by God to speak a message from Him to others in an unknown language. This kind of speaking in tongues is ministry and the direction is from God, through a member of the body of Christ, to the people. When this ministry is actuated and the unknown tongue is interpreted, either by the one who uttered it or by an interpreter, the diverse tongue and its interpretation is equal to prophecy. Paul taught this truth when he wrote,

> *"...for greater is he that prophesieth than he that speaketh with tongues, except he interpret, that the church may receive edifying."*
> I Corinthians 14:3-5

When those graced to minister in diverse tongues do so and their tongues are interpreted, the church will hear from God and be edified [I Cor. 14:5, 16-17].

Although all believers can be filled with the Spirit and pray in other tongues to God, not all believers are set in the church and graced to function in the ministry of diverse tongues. That is why Paul asked, "do all speak with tongues?" [I Cor. 12:30]. The implied answer to his question is "No." What Paul meant is that not all believers are graced to speak by inspiration in those diverse tongues which must then be interpreted into a known language for the edification of the church. The ministry of speaking in diverse tongues delivers the first half of an inspired message from God.

You might respond, "But, brother Guy, the ministry of speaking in tongues is a gift of the Spirit and occurs only as the Spirit wills." You are both right and wrong. Yes, diverse tongues is one of the nine manifestations of the Spirit listed in I Corinthians twelve. The Holy Spirit could manifest Himself through any believer, inspiring them to bring forth a diverse tongue which could be interpreted to edify the church. A believer could be used by the Spirit of God this way one time and never be used this way again. Or a believer might be used in this manifestation of the Spirit occasionally. Some believers will never be used by the Spirit to minister in diverse tongues.

Some believers, however, are set in the church and grace-gifted to give messages in diverse tongues. That is their ministry, or one of their ministries, and they will operate in it consistently. Bringing forth messages in diverse tongues will not be a one time occurrence or even a rare occurrence for these believers, but will be part and parcel of their spiritual service.

In September of 1997, my youngest brother Kelly and his wife Pattie opened a Bible School in Western Samoa in the South Pacific. In October of that same year, I was privileged to travel there and minister to the first year students. Before the start of class one morning, I had the impression that the Holy Spirit wanted to move in some special way. So rather than starting with teaching, I started with worship.

After leading a few songs of worship, I knew God wanted to speak. I asked if anyone had something from the Lord. Someone took the microphone and began to speak in other tongues. Their message in other tongues went on for about a minute. When they finished, I took the microphone and began to interpret into English what the Holy Spirit was saying.

After the morning classes were over, my brother told me that what was said through tongues and interpretation of tongues very accurately confirmed what he had on his heart concerning the purpose of the Bible school. In this case, tongues and interpretation of tongues confirmed the plan of the Lord in a precise and encouraging way.

The ministry of speaking in tongues and its companion gift, interpretation of tongues, is an important ministry in the church. Because tongues and interpretation of tongues is equivalent to prophecy, this ministry can bring much needed encouragement, revelation, and direction.

42

Graced to Interpret Tongues

According to I Corinthians 12:30 and I Corinthians 14:28, some believers are set in the church by God and graced to interpret diverse tongues. Do all believers interpret tongues? No, but some do.

The ministry of interpreting tongues is not, as some teach, an acquired ability to translate words from one known language into another known language. When I travel to foreign countries to teach, I always use an interpreter to translate my teaching from English into the native language of that country. This translation is not, however, the ministry of interpreting tongues.

The ministry of interpreting tongues is a supernatural ability to interpret the meaning of an inspired diverse, unknown tongue so that those who are present can know what God is saying. When diverse tongues are interpreted into a known language the message is equivalent to prophecy.

Interpreting tongues was an acknowledged ministry in Paul's day. In fact, Paul instructed the believers in Corinth that no one should speak out a message in tongues in their meetings unless an interpreter was present. He wrote,

> *"If any man speak in an unknown tongue, let it be by two, or at the most by three, and that by course; and let one interpret. But if there be no interpreter, let him keep silence in the church; and let him speak to himself and to God."*
>
> *I Corinthians 14:27-28*

Apparently, the believers in Corinth knew who were interpreters of tongues among them. If an interpreter was present, a believer could exercise liberty in giving a tongue. They would not have to hope and pray that the Holy Spirit would give someone the interpretation. The present interpreter would be able to interpret because he was called and equipped by God for that ministry. If no interpreter was present and a believer could not interpret his own utterance in tongues, he was to keep silent. There would be no reason to speak in tongues because without an interpretation the church would not be edified.

Paul made it clear in both I Corinthians 12:28-30 and in I Corinthians 14:27-28 that some believers are interpreters. Those graced to interpret other tongues will not just interpret on rare occasions by a special manifestation of the Spirit. They are interpreters.

You may say, "But interpreting tongues can only happen as the Spirit wills because interpreting tongues is a manifestation of the Spirit as Paul taught in I Corinthians 12:10." Yes, in one aspect you are right. Interpreting tongues is, in fact, one of the nine manifestations of the Spirit. Any believer could be used to interpret a tongue as the Spirit willed for a special occasion. Interpreting tongues is also, however, a New Testament ministry. According to Paul, some believers are interpreters.

43

Graced to Minister in Music

Although there is no mention of the music ministry in the New Testament, we do find the office of the musician present and well described in the Old Testament. Because all believers are "priests unto God" and because the church is a "spiritual house, an holy priesthood, to offer up spiritual sacrifices," I have included the music ministry as a valid New Testament ministry.

The music ministry is often categorized as a ministry of helps. In my opinion, this is a mistake. The music ministry, although not one of the five spiritual leadership ministries, is more connected to teaching, leading, prophecy, and the moving of the Holy Spirit than it is to practical service. It is, in fact, a vocal ministry and a leadership activity. Classifying musicians and worship leaders as helps ministers misrepresents their function and underestimates the extremely significant calling of the church to worship God as a royal priesthood.

When the music ministry is improperly valued, some who are called to it may not give themselves to their calling as they should and will not, therefore, develop to their full potential in natural or spiritual skill. Consequently, the church will forfeit excellence in its ministry of worship. Since worship to God is one of the primary ministries of the church, we must accurately classify those who lead us in that ministry.

Music and the Move of the Spirit

Music is connected to the manifestations of the Holy Spirit, to the glory of God, and to the prophetic voice of God. When the prophet

Elisha agreed to prophesy to three kings, he called for a minstrel because he understood that there was a connection between music and the moving of the Holy Spirit. When the minstrel played, the Spirit of God came upon him and he prophesied the plan of God [II Kings 3:15].

When Saul was tormented by an evil spirit, his servants suggested that he seek out a cunning player on the harp. They knew that when a skilled musician played the evil spirits would depart and the afflicted person would be comforted. David was the skilled musician chosen to play for Saul [I Sam. 17:16-18]. When he played the presence of God came and the evil spirits left.

At a later time in Israel's history, when Jehosophat was king, three enemy nations came against them. After all the people waited upon God in prayer the Spirit of God spoke through a man named Jehaziel and gave prophetic direction for the whole nation. Jehaziel was a priestly musician; a descendent of Asaph [II Chron. 20:14]. There is a connection between music and the prophetic voice.

After Solomon finished building the temple of the Lord, the whole nation came together to dedicate it. When the musicians and singers worshipped in unity the glory of God filled the temple in such a profound way that the priests could not stand to perform their service [II Chron. 5:13-14].

In Acts 13, we read that as the teachers and prophets in Antioch ministered to the Lord, the Holy Ghost spoke [Acts 13:1-4]. We cannot say for sure that music was part of their worship, but it may have been. In Acts 16, we read that Paul and Silas prayed and sang praises in prison. After they sang, a great earthquake shook the foundations and all the prisoners were freed. There is a connection between music and the manifested glory of God.

The Levitical Musicians

Not long after Israel's deliverance from Egypt, God instructed Moses to separate the tribe of Levi from the rest of Israel to be priests unto Him. The Levites were responsible for the service of sacrifice in the temple. From the time of Moses till David, they fulfilled that ministry by offering burnt sacrifices to the Lord in the holy place.

When David became king of Israel, he took the chief men of the Levitical priests and ordained them into full time music ministry [I Chron. 15:16; II Chron. 23:18]. Evidently, David knew that the offering of animals was not sufficient worship for God. He understood that God did not really desire the sacrifice of bulls and goats, but the sacrifice of praise which proceeds from men's hearts.

Some of the Levitical musicians David ordained were instrumentalists, some were singers, and some were leaders. These musicians were responsible to sing, to play instruments, and to minister unto the Lord night and day in the temple. This was their full time work [I Chron. 9:33]. David wrote psalms for these musicians and invented musical instruments for them to play [I Chron. 16:7; 23:5]. After the temple of Solomon was built and dedicated, these musicians ministered "by course."

There was clear order among the Levitical musicians. Some sang melody, some sang harmony, and some played instruments [I Chron. 15:16-24]. There was also a structure of authority among the musicians. Men like Asaph, Heman, and Ethan were leaders in their time [I Chron. 15:17]. One man, Chenaniah, "instructed about the song, because he was skillful" [I Chron. 15:22]. The Levitical musicians were instructed in "songs of the Lord" [I Chron. 25:7]. They were skillful in ministering to the Lord and leading the nation of Israel in worship. They did not use the phrase, "make a joyful noise," as an excuse for a lack of excellence.

Some musicians were said to "prophesy with harps, with psalteries, and with cymbals" [I Chron. 25:1]. Heman, one of the original Levitical musicians, was noted as being "the kings seer in the words of God" [I Chron. 25:5]. These musicians not only gave to God in music, but often gave forth the word of the Lord in prophecy.

Musicians in Their Place

Something very interesting can be learned about the value of the music ministry by following the rise and fall of the nation of Israel through the book of second Chronicles. Whenever an evil king ascended the throne and held power in Israel, three negative things happened. First, the temple fell into physical disrepair. Second, the priests left the temple and began to offer sacrifices to false gods in the high places. Third, the musicians and singers left their place of worship in the temple.

Whenever a righteous king ascended the throne and held power in Israel, these three negative things were reversed. First, the temple was repaired. Second, the priests came back into the temple to offer their sacrifices to Jehovah God. Third, the musicians and singers returned to their appointed place of music and worship in the temple. Notice, for example, what happened concerning the musicians under the reforms of king Jehoiada,

> *"Also Jehoiada appointed the priests the Levites, whom David had distributed in the house of the LORD, to offer the burnt offerings of the LORD, as it is written in the law of Moses, with rejoicing and with singing, as it was ordained by David."*
>
> II Chronicles 23:18

Notice this report concerning reform under king Hezekiah after wicked Ahaz died,

> *"And he set the Levites in the house of the Lord with cymbals, with psalteries, and with harps, according to the commandment of David...And the Levites stood with the instruments of David, and the priests with the trumpets...And when the burnt offering began, the song of the LORD began also with the trumpets, and with the instruments ordained by David...And all the congregation worshiped, and the singers sang, and the trumpeters sounded... Hezekiah the king...commanded the Levites to sing praise unto the LORD with the words of David, and of Asaph the seer."*
>
> II Chronicles 29:25-28, 30; 30:21

And notice this report concerning reform under young Josiah,

"And the singers, the sons of Asaph were in their place, according to the commandment of David..."

II Chronicles 35:15

When Israel followed God under righteous leadership the temple was in order and the singers were "in their place." So it is in the New Testament. When the church is in proper spiritual order the music and the musicians will be in their proper place. If you study church history and note the seasons of spiritual renewal, you will discover that strong worship and new music has always accompanied these seasons.

God desires that His will be done on earth as it is in heaven. It is important, then, that believers who are called, placed, and graced to minister in music and lead in worship are in their place and functioning skillfully to assist the church in worship.

Worship is the First Ministry of the Church

Worship is the first ministry of the church. Every believer is a priest unto God [Rev. 1:5] and together believers are a royal priesthood [I Pet. 2:9]. The church is a spiritual house built of living stones for the purpose of offering up spiritual sacrifices to God [I Pet. 2:5; Rev. 1:6]. In the New Testament, believer-priests are called to bring a spiritual sacrifice, the sacrifice of praise, which is the fruit of lips, or words [Heb. 13:15].

In Revelation two, Jesus corrected the church in Ephesus because they had left their first love and their first works of worshipping Him. According to Jesus, they had fallen from a high place. Jesus instructed this church to repent and to return to their first works [Rev. 2:4-5].

The Old Testament and Jesus agree that to love God with all the heart, soul, mind, and strength is the first and great commandment. Music is a beautiful vehicle for the presentation of words, thoughts, and the passionate heart of worship to God. Worship is a primary ministry of the church and music is central in worship. The music ministry, therefore, is important.

In order for the worship of the church to be excellent, musicians and singers must give themselves to their ministries, become naturally and spiritually skilled, find their places in local churches, and lead the royal priesthood in its ministry of bringing spiritual sacrifices. If those called and graced for the music ministry under-esteem their ministry and do not give themselves wholly to it, the intensity, depth, and excellence of the priestly ministry of the church will be diminished.

Section Six

Getting from Called To Effective

If a man therefore purge himself
He shall be a vessel unto honour
Sanctified and meet for the Master's use
And prepared unto every good work

44

Personal Preparation

There are things which pertain to the life of Christian service that God alone is responsible for. Believers cannot call themselves to service, design their own commissions, assign themselves places in the body of Christ, or endow themselves with gifts of grace. Calling, placing, and endowing believers for service is the sole province of God.

There are things which pertain to the life of Christian service, however, that God is not totally responsible for. One of those things is the spiritual work of preparing for service. Although God will work in and work with believers as they prepare themselves, He does not do the work of preparation for them.

Believers are responsible to prepare themselves. They must assess their lives and then prepare and become fit for the Master's use. They must put away old thoughts and ways, establish themselves in the scriptures, and develop in wisdom and knowledge. They must grow in spiritual strength, increase in the fruit of the Spirit, and fashion their lives to be a "vessel unto honour, sanctified, and meet for the master's use, and prepared unto every good work" [II Tim. 2:21].

Often believers pray, "God, please use me as I am." This prayer is un-Biblical and foolish. Paul's challenge to Timothy to become "fit for the Master's use" implies that a believer might not, in fact, be fit for the Master's use. A more Biblical prayer would be, "Lord, as I discipline my life and strive toward Your high calling, continue to work in me by Your Word and Your Spirit to help me become fit for Your purposes."

Perhaps you are acquainted with the saying, "God doesn't need your ability; He needs your availability." This saying is cute and catchy, but it is untrue. Some believers are available, but incapable; willing, but not able. In this condition, they are not useful to the Lord at all. Catchy Christian sayings often do nothing more than establish believers in wrong thinking and mollify the nagging thoughts of those who do, in fact, have a sense that they need to prepare more in order to become useful to God, but choose not to make the effort.

Unfortunately, the element of preparation has been significantly undervalued by the church. If, however, believers do not take the time and make the effort to prepare themselves, they will never fulfill the ministries God has assigned them. They may be minor blessings and help a few people, but they will never fully accomplish their heavenly assignments. In order for believers to be competent carriers and effective ministers of the grace-gifts stewarded to them, they must prepare.

Preparing for Noble Work

In his second letter to Timothy, Paul penned these challenging words concerning preparation,

> "But in a great house there are not only vessels of gold and of silver, but also of wood and of earth; and some to honour [noble work], and some to dishonour [ignoble work]. If a man therefore purge himself from these, he shall be a vessel unto honour, sanctified, and meet for the master's use, and prepared unto every good work."
>
> II Timothy 2:20-21

In this scripture the "great house" is the church and the "vessels" are believers. In the church there are many kinds of vessels which perform many kinds of service. There are vessels of gold and silver — vessels which may shine more brilliantly and be more visible — and there are vessels of clay and wood — vessels which may do more practical, less visible service.

The critical truth Paul delivered in this scripture is that every vessel in the house, no matter what it is made of or what it is made to do, has the option of doing honorable or dishonorable service. A vessel which chooses to remain tarnished with dishonorable things like unrenewed thinking, ungodly attitudes, impure motivations, unbridled emotions, and fleshly passions will not become a vessel unto honor and will not perform excellent ministry. A vessel, on the other hand, which chooses to purge itself of ungodly thoughts, bridle its emotions, put to death the deeds of the flesh, renew its mind in God's Word, and develop godly qualities can be a vessel unto honor, fit for the Master's use, and prepared for every good work. Whether called, placed, and graced vessels do honorable or dishonorable service is very much dependent upon what they do with themselves.

Paul said four things about vessels which choose to exercise personal diligence and prepare themselves. First, he said that the prepared vessel would be a "vessel unto honour." In other words, it will do honorable and excellent service in the role it is called to. The NIV Bible says it will "be an instrument for noble purposes." The word "dishonour" Paul used to refer to the kind of service vessels will do who have not prepared themselves comes from the Greek *atimia* which means, "vile, shame, or disgrace." A vessel that will not prepare itself may do far worse than nothing; it may actually be a disgrace to the kingdom of God.

Second, Paul said that the prepared vessel would be "sanctified." To be sanctified means, "to be set apart from and set apart unto." A sanctified vessel is a believer who has, through diligent self-governance, set himself apart from sin, fleshly lusts, old thoughts and ways, and worthless distractions, and has set himself apart unto God's calling, purpose, and grace.

Third, Paul said that the prepared vessel would be "meet for the master's use." The word "meet" comes from the Greek *euchrestos* and means, "easy to make use of." Just as a master craftsman becomes frustrated if he has to work with fragile or flawed tools, so God becomes frustrated when He endeavors to perform His wonderful works through unprepared vessels. And just as it is a pleasure for a master craftsman to work with strong, sharp, and excellent tools to bring forth his masterpieces, so it is a pleasure for God to work through well prepared vessels to bring forth His will.

Finally, Paul said that the vessel which purged itself would be "prepared unto every good work." The word "prepared" comes from the Greek *hetoimazo*. This word referred to the oriental custom of sending fore-runners ahead of traveling kings to level rough and pitted roads, making them passable. Personal preparation is a critical forerunning activity which enables believers, at a future time, to swiftly and safely travel the roads of God's will, laboring fruitfully in their unique ministries.

If vessels prepare themselves, they will be effective and do honorable work for the Lord. If vessels do not prepare themselves, they will do dishonorable work or no work at all. If vessels prepare themselves, the Master will be able to use them. If vessels do not prepare themselves, it will be hard for the Master to use them; they may even be useless. If vessels prepare themselves, they make sure paths for themselves, will finish their races and will accomplish their ministries. If vessels do not prepare themselves, their way will be hard, they will be slowed and maybe halted, and they will not complete their ministries. Whether a vessel is graced to be an apostle, a helper, a prophet, an administrator, a pastor, a worker of miracles, a shower of mercy, a ruler, a giver of money, a teacher, or an exhorter, he must be basically prepared in order to be useful and effective!

God Needs Mature, Prepared Believers

Throughout the King James version of the New Testament the English word "perfect" is used to describe God's standard for believers concerning both their personal maturity and their readiness for service. The single word "perfect" is used to translate two different Greek words; *telios* and *artios*.

The word *telios* does not mean to be perfect, but signifies, "to be complete, to reach full maturity, to come to full age." Something is *telios* when it has reached the end for which it was begun. A fruit tree is *telios* when it has deep roots, a strong trunk, many branches, and is yielding a full and consistent harvest. A believer is *telios* when he is established in the faith, is strong and wise, is displaying the fruit of the Spirit, has found his place in the body, and is bearing much fruit for God. An intensive form of *telios*, *epiteleo*, found in Philippians 1:6, means, "to fully and intensively be made complete."

It is God's will that believers grow unto a perfect [*telios*] man and reach the full stature that Jesus attained [Eph. 4:13]. Paul declared that his purpose for teaching was so that he could present every believer perfect [*telios*] in Christ [Col. 1:28]. According to the writer of Hebrews, believers who partake of strong meat are those who have reached full age [*telios*] [Heb. 5:14]. Paul informed the Philippians that God was working in them to "perform [*epiteleo*] it until the day of Jesus Christ" [Phil. 1:6].

To become "perfect" — to reach full spiritual age — means to have comprehensive knowledge of God's will, to be skilled in the scriptures, to be strong in spirit, to be holy in life, to be developed in love and the other fruits of the Spirit, to be steadfast in faith, to be resistant to temptation, to be sensitive to the Holy Spirit, and to be effective in prayer. *Telios* is God's will for every believer and is absolutely essential for effective Christian service.

The other Greek word translated to the English "perfect" is *artios*. Other related words are *katartismos*, *katartizo*, and *exartizo*. *Artios* means, "to arrange, to put in proper order, or to put in good condition for service." It indicates a relationship between character and destiny and signifies a path of progress.

The related word *katartismos* that Paul used in Ephesians 4:12 in the phrase, "for the perfecting of the saints," literally means, "complete furnishing or equipping." Becoming *katartismos* is the process of becoming prepared for service. Just as limbs in the human body must be healthy and trained in order to maximize their unique abilities, so the members of the body of Christ must be healthy and prepared in order to maximize their God-given abilities and contribute to the ministry of the body of Christ. If members of the body are not *katartismos*, they will be little more than dead weight. They will not contribute to the body's fitness or its capacity to serve God.

The writer of Hebrews used the word *katartizo* in the benediction of his epistle. He wrote,

> *"Now the God of peace...Make you perfect [katartizo] in every good*
> *work to do his will, working in you that which is wellpleasing in*
> *his sight...."*
>
> *Hebrews 13:20-21*

Notice how the Amplified Bible renders this scripture,

> *"Now may the God of peace...Strengthen (complete, perfect) and*
> *make you what you ought to be and equip you with everything good*
> *that you may carry out His will; [while He Himself] works in you*
> *and accomplishes that which is pleasing in His sight..."*
>
> *Hebrews 13:20-21 Amp*

This scripture highlights the significant relationship between being *katartizo* and fulfilling good works. When believers allow God to work in them as He pleases, they will become what they ought to be and be equipped with everything good. When believers are *katartizo*, they will be able to "carry out His will." They will accomplish the works they are called to and please God with their service.

Another scripture that clearly links *artios* with effective ministry comes from Paul's second letter to Timothy. He wrote,

> *"All scripture is given by inspiration of God, and is profitable for*
> *doctrine, for reproof, for correction, for instruction in righteous-*
> *ness: That the man of God may be perfect [katartizo], thoroughly*
> *furnished [exartizo] unto all good works."*
>
> *II Timothy 3:16-17*

Paul informed Timothy that the scriptures were able to *katartizo* and *exartizo* the man of God. *Exartizo* is an intensified form of *artios*. The man of God can be fully completed, fully arranged, fully ordered, and fully fitted for service. According to Paul, the believer who is *katartizo* and *exartizo* is completely furnished for every good work!

Basic Training

In his second letter to Timothy, Paul exhorted him with these words,

"Thou therefore endure hardness, as a good soldier of Jesus Christ."
II Timothy 2:3

Paul identified Timothy as a soldier of Jesus Christ and exhorted him to "endure hardness." The hardness Timothy must endure was not only the tests and trials he would experience from the outside as he lived his Christian life and fulfilled his ministry. He must also endure the self-imposed internal regiment of training which would bring him to readiness for spiritual service.

After young people are called into or enlist in the armed services, they are sent to basic training. In basic training, young soldiers learn to shine their shoes, press their clothes, make their beds, and stand at attention. They get in good physical shape, gain entry-level skills, and learn to obey orders from those in authority. Long before a young soldier is issued a weapon, selected for an assignment, or sent on his first mission, he undergoes strict and intense basic training. No recruit is sent directly from the enlistment office to the front lines.

Why is basic training so important for the life of Christian service? First, basic training is important because it measures mettle, commitment, and character. Basic training does not measure the gift a person possesses; it measures the person who possesses the gift. In the spiritual life, as in the natural life, basic training thins the ranks, separating those who are gifted, but unwilling to prepare from those who are gifted and willing to prepare.

Second, basic training is important because God does not want believers to die while serving. If wonderfully gifted believers are unprepared, the enemy, circumstances, people, or even their own issues will destroy them; perhaps on their first mission. Spiritual talents, though absolutely necessary for fruitful service, are not effective in overcoming temptation, dealing with people, resisting the devil, or standing firm in times of adversity.

Third, basic training is important because it lays the foundation for future mastery in specific areas of service. No one can become a specialist without first being schooled in basic skills. Just as no fine fighting unit is composed of unskilled, unprepared, and incompetent soldiers, so an effective body of Christ is not composed of members who have not even been basically trained.

Nothing is more critical to effective Christian service than basic training. As all military personnel start their careers with basic training, so all believers must start their life of service with basic training. Although different members of the body will become proficient in different ministries, no member can bypass the critical element of basic training and be effective in service for God.

If believers diligently prepare themselves, they will be able to accomplish their God-given assignments and make God's goodness, love, and power a reality in earth. If believers do not diligently prepare themselves, their God-given assignments will never be anything more than sketches on the heavenly drawing board.

45

Jesus – A Prepared Vessel

Jesus is the most significant pattern and most important standard for New Testament ministry. Above any other person or system, believers are to look to Him as an example. Jesus said, "If any man serve me, let him follow me" [Jn. 12:26]. The word "follow" comes from the Greek *akolouthro* and means, "to follow one who precedes, or to join one as a disciple." To serve Jesus effectively, believers must "follow" Him. This includes following Him as the pattern and prototype in preparation for service.

Jesus was effectual in His ministry; powerful in preaching, teaching, and works. He did the perfect will of the Father. Jesus was not only effectual in His ministry, however. He also finished His ministry. In His High Priestly prayer, He said to the Father, "I have finished the work which thou gavest me to do" [Jn. 17:4]. He was referring, of course, to the work of His earth ministry.

To what do we attribute Jesus' effectual ministry? Certainly, He was effectual because God had called and anointed Him with the Holy Ghost and power. By the anointing of divine ability, He was able to preach, teach, heal, and minister. The fact that Jesus was anointed with the Holy Spirit was only one factor, however, in the total picture of why He was effectual.

Another absolutely essential factor that enabled Jesus to be effectual in ministry was His personal preparation. This fact is seldom taught and often completely overlooked. It is a Bible fact, however, that Jesus spent the first thirty years of His life preparing. In those years, He did no ministry. He healed no sick, raised no dead, cast out no devils, and preached no messages. Amazingly, however, at the conclusion of His preparation time and immediately prior to being anointed for service, the Father spoke these words to Him,

> *"Thou art my beloved Son; in thee I am well pleased."*
>
> Luke 3:22

The Father said He was very pleased with Jesus. But how could God have been pleased with Him? Jesus hadn't done anything! He hadn't healed anyone. He hadn't preached or taught. He hadn't worked any miracles. He hadn't cast out any devils or set any captives free. What did Jesus do in the first thirty years of His life that caused the Father to say that He was "well pleased" with Him? The answer is that Jesus prepared Himself!

Prepared to Serve

Concerning His early years, the scriptures teach that Jesus "increased in wisdom and stature, and in favor with God and man" [Lk. 2:52]. He continued to learn as He advanced in age. He increased in stature; not only physically, but also in internally. He grew in favor with God.

How did Jesus grow in favor with God? Did He stop sinning? No, Jesus was without sin. Did He quit rebelling and finally yield to His Father's will? No, Jesus was never rebellious against God. How, then, did God's pleasure in Jesus increase? God's pleasure in Jesus increased because Jesus increased and became ever more ready to serve. He matured not only in physical, mental, and emotional stature, but also in spiritual stature.

Jesus learned the Word of God and became skilled in the scriptures. By the age of twelve, He was able to ask important questions and answer difficult questions [Lk. 2:46-47]. On the occasion when He remained in Jerusalem and Joseph and Mary had to return to find Him, He was in the temple learning. His response to his parents' question about what He was doing is enlightening. He said, "I must be about my Father's business" [Lk. 2:49]. Jesus was learning the Father's business and preparing Himself to do the Father's business long before He engaged in the Father's business.

Because Jesus knew the scriptures, He had an answer for every question, a solution for every problem, and a defense against every attack. He answered the devil's temptations with, "It is written" and answered those who questioned Him with, "Have you not read?"

Jesus learned to know the voice of the Father through times of prayer. His fellowship with the Father enabled Him to go to the right places at the right times and helped Him choose the proper fellow laborers in His vision. He knew how to call upon the Father for help in times of difficulty through prayer and supplication [Heb. 5:7].

Jesus developed inner strength. At twelve years of age, He "waxed strong in spirit" [Lk. 2:40]. His inner strength enabled Him to resist the devil, withstand temptation, deal with all manner of people, and stand alone with God. His inner fortitude helped Him to set His face like flint and proceed on a direct course to His own sure death [Is. 50:7; Lk. 9:51]. His inner strength enabled Him to wrestle with the will of God in Gethsamane and overcome the temptation to draw back. Although He struggled to the point of sweating blood as He faced the ultimate sacrifice, He did not yield, but committed Himself to the will of God.

In the many difficult and potentially devastating situations Jesus faced during His years of ministry, it was not His calling or anointing that carried Him through, but His personal preparation. The force of His strong character, His knowledge of scripture, and His personal relationship with God enabled Him to pursue His course, accomplish His mission, and fulfill His destiny.

46

Seven Prepared Men in Jerusalem

A very pertinent example of the importance of preparation comes from the early church in Jerusalem. There was an occasion in that young church when the Grecian widows were being neglected in the daily distribution of food. The apostles, taking their place of leadership, instructed the church to choose seven men to perform the ministry of serving tables [Acts 6:1-7].

For someone in the Jerusalem church to be considered for this ministry, they had to meet certain basic requirements in character and spiritual development. Relating these requirements to the whole congregation, the apostles said,

> *"Wherefore, brethren, look ye out among you seven men of honest report, full of the Holy Ghost and wisdom, whom we may appoint over this business...and they chose Stephen, a man full of faith and of the Holy Ghost..."*
>
> Acts 6:3, 5

In order to be considered for the ministry of serving tables in the Jerusalem church a believer had to be a disciple — a learner and a disciplined follower of Jesus [Acts 6:1]. He could not be a recent convert, but had to come from the body of the already established. There is a substantial difference between a new convert and a disciple in terms of spiritual development.

To be considered for the ministry of serving tables, the disciple had to have an honest report among the rest of the congregation, being an example in integrity and purity. The Greek word for "honest" is *martureo*. This word indicated someone who had learned something themselves, had personal experience, and could testify of it. This person had to have their own relationship with God, be living it, and be able to testify of it.

To be considered for the ministry of serving tables, the disciple had to be full of the Holy Ghost. This meant much more than that he spoke in other tongues. He had to be Spirit-filled, Spirit-led, Spirit-inspired, and Spirit-taught. He also had to be developed in the fruit of the Spirit. He could not be a beginner in spiritual things or unfamiliar with the Holy Spirit; he had to be "full of the Holy Ghost."

To be considered for the ministry of serving food, the disciple had to be full of wisdom. He could not be ignorant or foolish. He could not be a babe or carnal in his thinking. He had to be accurate in doctrine, know God's ways, and be filled with the wisdom which comes from above. He had to be a living example of Paul's instructions to the Ephesian believers to, "be ye not unwise, but understanding what the will of the Lord is." He had to be "filled with the knowledge of [God's] will in all wisdom and spiritual understanding [Eph. 5:18; Col. 1:9].

To be considered for the ministry of serving tables, the disciple had to be full of faith. He had to know God, be fully persuaded of His Word, know how to stand upon His promises, know how to hold fast in the midst of difficult circumstances, and be steadfast against the devil's onslaught. He could not be doubtful or unstable like the double-minded man James referred to in his epistle.

Seven men who met these basic requirements were selected to serve the Grecian widows. Even though their ministry would not be a church leading or world impacting ministry, it was mandatory that they be basically prepared and have a level of spiritual maturity in order to be considered. The early church had very high standards for ministry; even for the ministry of practical service.

Two of the men chosen to be deacons went on to greater levels of effectual ministry. Philip developed a reputation for winning the lost and working miracles and was the only man designated in the New Testament as an evangelist [Acts 21:8]. Concerning Stephen, we know less because he was cut off early in his ministry, earning a martyr's crown. We know, however, that he was irresistible in preaching and teaching and did "great wonders and miracles among the people" [Acts 6:8].

Notice the excellent report about what was happening in Jerusalem because of the church there,

> *"...the word of God increased; and the number of the disciples multiplied in Jerusalem greatly; and a great company of the priests were obedient to the faith."*
>
> *Acts 6:7*

The word of God increased. The number of disciples multiplied greatly. Even a great company of the priests were obedient to the faith. Why was the church in Jerusalem able to make such a significant impact in their world? A primary reason was that their members were required to be personally prepared before they were allowed to publicly perform. It is no coincidence that the report about the impact of the Jerusalem church follows immediately after the information about their requirements of personal preparation for service.

Paul confirmed the high standard of the early church for serving when he informed Timothy that those being considered for the ministry of deacon could not be novices, but must "first be proved" [I Tim. 3:10]. To be "proved" meant to be tested, examined, and scrutinized. Believers in the early church were required to be developed in godly character and mature in spiritual life in order to be considered for the ministry of practical service.

Paul also affirmed the important element of personal preparation in his caution to Timothy to "lay hands on no man suddenly" [I Tim. 5:21]. His words are rendered this way in the Amplified Bible,

> *"Do not be in a hurry in the laying on of hands [giving the sanction of the church too hastily in reinstating expelled offenders or in ordination in questionable cases]..."*
>
> *I Timothy 5:22 Amp*

One of the purposes for the laying on of hands is to publicly acknowledge the separation of believers into recognized service to God. No one was to be hastily sanctioned for service, said Paul. Especially those who were questionable in terms of their personal spiritual development.

The early church was not in a rush to give believers ministry responsibilities; even if the ministries they were going to engage in were practical service ministries. Many problems and much trouble could be avoided if the church of our generation would learn and emulate this basic, but very essential ministry principle exemplified by the early church.

47

Timothy – A Vessel in Preparation

The apostle Paul, himself a seasoned veteran of New Testament life and ministry, understood the significant connection between personal preparation and ministry effectiveness. In order to help his young protege Timothy become effective in ministry and bear good and consistent fruit, Paul thoroughly schooled him in the concept of preparation.

In his first letter to Timothy, Paul wrote,

"Till I come, give attendance to reading, to exhortation, to doctrine. Neglect not the gift that is in thee...Meditate upon these things; give thyself wholly to them; that thy profiting may appear to all."
I Timothy 4:13-15

It is interesting, especially in light of some modern day teaching about ministry, that Paul said nothing to Timothy in about "getting out there in the Spirit" or "flowing in the anointing" or "getting out of the way so God can move." Paul never told Timothy to decrease so that Jesus could increase. He didn't encourage Timothy to open his mouth and God would fill it. He didn't tell him, "Just do your best," or, "God will use you if you are willing."

Paul did instruct Timothy, however, to "give attendance to reading...to doctrine." The words "give attendance" come from the Greek *prosecho* and mean, "to devote thought and effort." Timothy was to devote effort to reading and devote attention to his study of doctrine.

These efforts would help him develop personally and would, in turn, enhance his ministry.

Paul exhorted Timothy to "Meditate upon [or practice] these things." The NIV Bible says, "Be diligent in these matters." Timothy was to read the scriptures and meditate upon its many teachings. He was to become established in sound doctrine. He was also to think seriously about, develop, and "neglect not" the gift that had been stewarded to him.

Paul also exhorted Timothy to, "give thyself wholly to them." The words "give wholly" come from the Greek *isthi* which means, "to live in." The Darby version of the Bible says,

> *"Occupy thyself with these things; be wholly in them..."*
> *I Timothy 4:15 Darby*

Timothy's commitment to doctrine, his diligence in personal development, and his cultivation of the grace-gift entrusted to him were to be major themes in his life. By developing his personal life and cultivating his ministry gift, Timothy would enhance his effectiveness and ensure long-term fruitfulness. According to Paul, his progress and his profiting would be evident to all [I Tim. 4:15].

Pay Attention to Yourself and Doctrine

Paul continued his exhortation to Timothy with these words,

> *"Take heed unto thyself, and unto the doctrine; continue in them...."*
> *I Timothy 4:16*

Timothy was to, "Take heed unto thyself." In other words, he was to pay attention to himself. He was to take personal inventory and determine if his life was in order. Were his priorities right? Were his attitudes godly? Was he walking accurately as a wise believer or was he being a fool? Were his emotions in ascendancy and leading him down profitless paths or were they under the control of his will? Was he dominating his flesh or was his body leading the way? Timothy was to pay attention to his "self" and make sure his personal life was a good setting for his heavenly grace-gift.

Timothy was also to "take heed unto...doctrine." By so doing, he would become filled with the wisdom of God and able to bear fruit in every good work [Col. 1:9-10]. He would learn God's thoughts and ways [Is. 55:8-11]. He would have a light upon his path [Ps. 119:105]. He would be able to run and not stumble [Prov. 4:12]. Like Jesus, he would have answers for questions and a strong defense against temptation [Lk. 4:4-12].

Timothy was to "continue" in these things. The word "continue" comes from the Greek *epimeno* which means, "to abide or to tarry in." Timothy was to get into and stay in a lifestyle of consistent personal self-development, self-governance, and self-learning.

Save Yourself and Others

Finally, Paul appraised Timothy of the outcome of his self discipline, his diligent study, and his personal preparation with these words,

> *"...for in doing this thou shalt both save thyself, and them that hear thee."*
>
> *I Timothy 4:16*

"Doing" is a verb. There were things Timothy must "do" with himself in order to be able to "do" the work God had entrusted to him. If Timothy watched diligently over his own life, developed in sound doctrine, and cultivated his grace-gift, he would save both himself and those who heard him. If, on the other hand, Timothy did not watch over his life, did not develop in sound doctrine, and did not cultivate his grace-gift, his own life and the lives of those who followed him would be at risk.

48

Purge Your Vessel

In order to be consistently fruitful in service there are things believers must eliminate from their lives. Paul referred to this critical aspect of personal preparation with these words,

"If a man therefore purge himself from these, he shall be a vessel unto honour, sanctified, and meet for the master's use, and prepared unto every good work."

II Timothy 2:21

Paul said that "if" a man purged himself, he would be a vessel of honor, fit for the Master's use, and prepared for every good work. The obvious corollary is that if a man did not purge himself, he would not be a vessel of honor, would not be fit for the Master's use, and would not be prepared to do the works he was called to.

The word "purge" comes from the Greek verb *ekkathairo*. This verb is a compound of the preposition *ek* which means, "out of," and the verb *kathairo* which means, "make clean." *Ekkathairo* means, "to clean out or to clean thoroughly." To purge one's self from dishonorable things means to eliminate from one's life all things that are not of God, not of truth, not of love, not of righteousness, not of holiness, and not of sound thinking.

In his letter to Titus, Paul wrote that Jesus desired to "purify unto himself a peculiar people, zealous of good works" [Tit. 2:14]. The word "purify" he used is the Greek *katharizo*. It means, "to cleanse, or to free from defilements and sins." The word "good," which describes the kind of works Jesus wants believers to perform, means, "excellent, precious, approved, and praise-worthy." When believers are cleansed and purified, they will be able to do the excellent and praise-worthy works God has called and graced them to do.

Believers must realize that the primary responsibility for purging dross from their vessel is theirs. Only by strong decisions, diligent personal governance, the grace of God, and the help of the Holy Spirit can believers accomplish this difficult task.

Driving Out Dross

The book of Proverbs offers these succinct words concerning the purging of a natural vessel,

> *"Take away the dross from the silver, and there shall come forth a vessel for the finer."*
>
> *Proverbs 25:4*

The Hebrew word for "vessel" in this scripture could also be translated weapon, tool, instrument, or equipment. The word "dross" refers to impure, unclean things.

In order to produce vessels fit for excellent service and long term use, a finer would "take away the dross from the silver." This was the process of refining vessels by the use of fire to drive out impurities. By this process, a fit vessel would "come forth." The Hebrew word for "come forth" means, "to come out of, to proceed from, to go forth with a purpose." The purging out of dross ensured that vessels, weapons, and tools would be useful in fulfilling their tasks and not come apart while being used. Out from the hot and intense refining process would come forth fit vessels ready to go forth and fulfill their purpose.

Some believers are weak, unstable, and unfit for service. These unfit vessels do not have to be disregarded or thrown away, however. They can be put into the refining furnace of self-discipline, training, teaching and the inworking of God and have the dross purged out. Out of the spiritual refining fire can come forth vessels fit for service and ready to fulfill the purposes of God!

Fleshly Ways

Note these exhortations from the apostle Paul concerning the purging of sins and fleshly ways,

> *"...put off concerning the former conversation the old man...Where-fore putting away lying...Let all bitterness, and wrath, and anger, and clamour, and evil speaking, be put away from you, with all malice..."*
>
> *Ephesians 4:22, 25, 31*

> *"...put off all these; anger, wrath, malice, blasphemy, filthy commu-nication out of your mouth."*
>
> *Colossians 3:8*

The words "put off" Paul used in these scriptures come from the Greek *apotithemi* and mean, "to put aside, to cast off, to put away." Notice that Paul did not tell believers in Ephesus or Colosse to pray and believe that God would "set them free" from personal problems, addictions, or weaknesses. He did not advise them to attend a "break-through" or "cleansing" or "anointing" meeting. He did not tell them that "in His own timing" God would do something in them. Paul made it perfectly clear that the responsibility for getting rid of issues, addic-tions, bad behavior, sin, and anything else that could be considered "dross" was the responsibility of each believer.

Wrong thinking, fleshly activities, unrestrained emotions, and filthy communications are impurities in believers which make them weak and cause them to crumble under pressure, to be distracted by the world, to break when buffeted by Satan, and to fall apart under sustained use. These weaknesses undermine believers' confidence in themselves, taint their reputations, cause them to lose their credibility, and make it difficult for others to receive them as heavenly gifts. Not purged vessels are not only at risk themselves; they also put the grace-gifts they carry and the plans of God has assigned them at risk.

Sins and Weights

After offering a list of Old Testament men and women who pleased God and received a good report because of their obedience and steadfast faith, the writer of Hebrews exhorted New Testament believers with these words,

> *"Wherefore seeing we also are compassed about with so great a cloud of witnesses, let us lay aside every weight, and the sin which doth so easily beset us, and let us run with patience the race that is set before us..."*

> *Hebrews 12:1*

Like Old Testament heroes of faith, each believer has a unique race to run. Unfortunately, believers sometimes enter their races with sins and weights attached. According to W. E. Vine, the phrase, "the sin which doth so easily beset us," means that the sin which is not put away can easily prevail against the one who is running. In order to run swiftly and steadily and to finish well, believers must put away whatever impedes them. At the minimum, habitual sin will hinder a believer's progress. It is possible, however, that retained sin will completely ruin a believer's race.

It is not only sin that hinders believers, however. Weights can also slow them down. Unlike sins which are clearly defined by the Word of God, weights may be different things to different people. They can include bad habits, consuming hobbies, unhealthy relationships, or unprofitable personal activities. Anything that consumes a believer's time and energy or draws his attention away from his calling could be considered a weight.

Because I travel often, I understand how nice it is to take favorite extra things along on a trip. I have learned, however, that the extras can also be a curse. So it is in the long journey of spiritual life and ministry. You will soon be very sorry if you are carrying extra weight. It is a serious challenge to run the race God assigns you even if you are not carrying extra weight. So rethink your load. Purge out the sin that is impeding your progress. Put away weights and lighten up. If you do this, you will be able to run at a much better pace and will increase the possibility of finishing your race in time and intact!

Spiritual Fault Lines

Several years ago, I was invited to speak to the leadership of a certain ministry. One thing the Lord inspired in my heart for that meeting was to deal with "spiritual fault lines."

Perhaps you know that the surface of earth rests upon different underground plates. These underground plates migrate very slowly beneath the earth's surface; often in different directions and at different speeds. When these plates bump against each other, they often cause earthquakes. The places where underground plates meet and where earthquakes occur are called fault lines.

It is interesting that the surface area of the state of California rests upon more than one of these underground plates. From the surface, California looks very stable. Just beneath the surface, however, is potential disaster. If the underground plates shift too much a part of California could disappear into the ocean. What was once so beautiful and looked so secure on the surface could be gone.

Some believers are like California. Everything looks fine on the surface, but their foundations are faulty. Some parts of their life are established on the Rock of God's Word, but other parts rest on other foundations — emotions, approval from others, personal ambitions, desire for financial gain, unhealthy spiritual passions. Under pressure the fault-ridden believer's foundation will be shaken and he could lose everything.

It is imperative that fault lines be dealt with. If you have ungodly, hidden areas of sin in your life, repent and get established in obedience to God. If you have impure thinking, get a grip on your thought life and change your mind. If you have bitterness or anger toward others, get rid of it. If you have a competitive spirit, repent and move toward more pure motivations. If you covet spectacular spiritual experiences and can't do without emotional ecstasy, get back to the Scriptures and rebuild your life on the Rock. By dealing with fault lines, you will not only save yourself; you will also ensure that in the future you will impact the lives of the people you are called to and graced for.

White-Washed Walls

In the Old Testament, God spoke these stern words to a people who had built a wall that appeared strong and secure, but was weak,

> "...one built up a wall, and, lo, others daubed it with untempered [morter]: Say unto them which daub it with untempered morter, that it shall fall: there shall be an overflowing shower; and ye, O great hailstones, shall fall; and a stormy wind shall rend it...So will I break down the wall that ye have daubed with untempered [morter], and bring it down to the ground, so that the foundation thereof shall be discovered, and it shall fall...The wall is no more, neither they that daubed it..."
>
> Ezekiel 13:10-15

God chastised these people who had covered their unstable wall with untempered mortar. He told them that rain, hailstones, and strong winds would "rend" their wall. To "rend" means, "to break into or to break down." God also said He would "break down the wall" and "bring it to the ground." He said, "it shall fall." By breaking down the false wall, said God, the "foundation thereof shall be discovered." The word "discovered" means, "uncovered or revealed."

Like the white-washed wall in Ezekiel, some believers appear secure, strong, and established when, in reality, they are weak and without sound foundations. In the gentle weather of the average Christian life, they stand and may even seem to shine. In the storms of temptation, difficult circumstances, spiritual attack, and full hearted service, however, they will be exposed as walls without foundations.

Believers must engage themselves in the significant effort of properly building their "walls." Time spent in God-led construction is never wasted, but prepares believers for the storms of life, for the certain onslaught of the enemy, and for the rigors of Christian life and service.

Gaps in the Armor

The story of David and Goliath is familiar to almost every believer. In this story, David felled Goliath with a sling and a stone and cut off his head. When we consider this story, we usually rejoice in the victory of David and are encouraged to go in the name of the Lord and achieve great victories ourselves. There is, however, another very important lesson that can be gleaned from this story.

The Bible reveals that Goliath was a skilled warrior. He had fought many battles and won many victories. No one had been able to get past his large shield or escape his swift sword. But Goliath had a small opening in the headpiece of his armor. There was a weakness in his defense. He was vulnerable. Unfortunately for him and for the whole Philistine army, the small stone of a skilled slinger discovered and exploited his weakness. Goliath had only a small gap in his armor, but it cost him his life and scattered an army!

Believers must examine themselves to make sure there are no gaps in their armor. Many called and wonderfully gifted believers have fallen, not because they were of a wrong spirit, were blatantly uncommitted, or were grossly sinful, but because of a small gap in their armor.

49

Do Something With Your Self

A few years ago the Holy Spirit spoke something to my heart that immediately sobered me and has lived with me since that moment. He said, "If you fail in self-governance, you fail in the primary responsibility of your life." These words, clearly in harmony with the Word of God, are some of the most challenging I have ever received.

Whether or not believers properly govern their own lives has serious implications, not only in personal life, but also in the life of Christian service. In order to be good stewards of grace and effective ministers in the body of Christ believers must diligently and skillfully manage their Self.

Precious Stones and Proper Settings

The book of Proverbs says,

"A gift is as a precious stone...whithersoever it turneth, it prospereth."

Proverbs 17:8

Believers' grace-gifts can be likened to precious stones and their personal lives likened to the settings for precious stones. In the natural realm, the setting for a precious stone must satisfy two requirements. First, it must be strong enough to hold the stone securely and keep it from being lost. Second, it must beautifully display the stone. Believers' personal lives must satisfy these same two requirements. First, their lives must be developed enough to carry their grace-gifts and keep them from being lost. Second, their lives must complement and beautifully display their unique grace-gifts.

Precious stones are most safe and shine most brilliantly when they are set in well crafted, strong, and complementary settings. Those who observe a precious stone in a proper setting see the stone at its best and marvel at its beauty. Precious stones that are set in poorly crafted, weak, and uncomplimentary settings, on the other hand, have their beauty obscured and are in danger of being lost. Those who observe a precious stone in a poor setting will not enjoy its beauty and will underestimate its true value.

The grace-gift each believer possesses comes from God and is, therefore, beautiful and valuable. The setting for each grace-gift, however, is determined by the believer who possesses the gift. Depending upon the life-setting a believer develops, the effect of their grace-gift will either be enhanced or diminished. Because of this reality, believers must strive diligently to craft their personal lives in a manner that will both safeguard and brilliantly display their heavenly gifts.

Who you are as a person — how you think, how you speak, how you conduct your affairs — will either enhance or diminish the effect of your grace-gift. Personal maturity, self-control, proper attitudes, managed thoughts, governed emotions, ruled bodies, and well ordered natural affairs are complementary life-settings for heavenly grace-gifts. On the other hand, immaturity, carnal mindedness, ungoverned emotions, unbridled fleshly impulses, and unorganized natural affairs are poor life-settings for heavenly grace-gifts.

When heavenly grace-gifts are carried by strong, mature, self-governed believers, they will shine brightly and produce consistently for the kingdom of God. When heavenly grace-gifts are carried by weak, undeveloped, and carnal believers, they will be diminished in beauty and produce little or nothing for the kingdom of God. In a worst case scenario, a poor life-setting may cause a grace-gift to be lost.

Masterpiece Paintings and Complementary Frames

Believers' grace-gifts can also be likened to masterpiece paintings and their personal lives likened to the frames that display the paintings. Owners of masterpiece paintings seriously consider what frames they will choose for their paintings. A proper frame will protect, support, and complement the painting, enhancing its presentation. A cheap, weak frame, on the other hand, puts the painting at risk, detracts from its beauty, and will draw comments of disappointment from viewers.

Believers' lives are the frames for their heavenly grace-gifts. They must, therefore, seriously consider what kind of life they will build to frame their grace-gift. A well ordered life established in the Word of God, in the love of God, and in the wisdom of God is a strong and complementary frame for a heavenly grace-gift. A disorderly life of ignorance, immaturity, and fleshliness, on the other hand, is a weak and disagreeable frame for a heavenly grace-gift. Believers should never put the masterpieces of God's grace-gifts into weak, cheap, or ugly frames.

Lamps and Lampstands

Jesus taught His disciples something profound which helps illustrate the working together of heavenly graces and personal lives. He said,

> "Neither do men light a candle [lamp], and put it under a bushel, but on a candlestick [lampstand]; and it giveth light unto all that are in the house. Let your light so shine before men, that they may see your good works, and glorify your Father which is in heaven."
> Matthew 5:15-16

The candle Jesus referred to in this verse was a hand held oil lamp called a *luchnos*. The *luchnos* was portable and could be easily carried to whatever place needed light. A lampstand was used to elevate the *luchnos* so that its light would be broadcast effectively.

Believers' personal lives are the lampstands which support the lamps of their heavenly grace-giftings. When believers are strong in faith, established in wisdom, and developed in love, they will effectively display their heavenly grace-gifts and burn brightly in the works God has assigned them. Without the strong, tall, balanced lampstands of well-developed personal lives, however, the outreach and effect of believers' grace-gifts will be minimized.

Jesus told His disciples that no man lit a lamp and then put it under a bushel. Speaking naturally, that would be very foolish. It is also foolish, however, when believers who have been stewarded wonderful grace-gifts obscure those gifts by the bushel of immaturity, foolishness, or fleshliness.

Jesus exhorted His disciples to, "Let your light so shine." His words reveal that the responsibility for the effective shining of each light belongs to believers. One way believers can ensure that their heavenly gifts "so shine" is by fashioning strong, tall, and balanced lampstands. If they will develop their lives according to God's pattern, their measure of grace-light will travel far and influence many. The world will see their good works and glorify the Father in heaven.

Some believers' lives are like very short lampstands because they are undeveloped in spiritual stature. They are still babes that need milk. They are tossed to and fro by winds of doctrine. They barely make it from Sunday to Sunday. They are flesh dominated, carnal minded, and emotion based. These believers may not fall, but their lights will not reach much further than right where they stand.

Some believers' lives are like unbalanced lampstands. They are long and strong in certain areas, but short and weak in other areas. They may know how to pray in faith, but not know how to love their wives and children. They may worship fervently during a church service, but be depressed and angry at home. They may be strong in zeal, but weak in wisdom. They may know how to love people, but not know how to quench the fiery darts of the devil. If unbalanced believers encounter shaky ground or are bumped by the devil, they will topple. Their lamps will fall to the ground and their lights will cease shining.

Some believers have dangerous weaknesses in their lampstands because of unpurged sin. At the present time their lamps are burning brightly. It is only a matter of time, however, before their lampstands begin to crumble. When this happens, their lamps will fall to the ground, their oil will run out, and their lights will cease shining.

Some believer's personal lives are in such disarray that they are themselves the bushels that hide the light of their heavenly graces. Certainly, these believers are saved and loved by God. Certainly, they are set members in the body. Certainly, they have been stewarded gifts of grace. Unfortunately, however, their heavenly graces are obscured by the bushel of their own disorder.

Is your personal life a strong, tall, balanced lampstand or is it a weak, short, unbalanced lampstand? Does your personal life cause the grace-gift entrusted to you to be broadcast to its fullest range or does it hide, discredit, or restrict it? Is your personal life in good order or is it in such disorder that it has become a bushel over your heavenly gift? What you do with your Self in lampstand development will significantly affect what God is able to do through you in broadcasting His manifold grace to the world!

Pay Attention To Your Self

A few years ago, I was staying with a couple who had a newborn baby. One afternoon the wife was setting the dining room table for the evening meal. Because the kitchen and the dining room were not directly connected, she had to walk down a hallway to reach the dining room. In the middle of that hallway and directly in her path lay her newborn baby. This young mother stepped over and around her baby many times as she walked between the kitchen and the dining room. Several times she stepped over her baby while carrying hot food.

Each time this young mother carried something from the kitchen to the dining room, she was hindered. Each time she had to make extra effort and be extra cautious so as not to incur a disaster. Each time she put herself and her baby at risk. How much wiser, safer, and easier it would have been if she had stopped for a moment and moved her baby out of the way.

Many believers are like this woman. They are doing their tasks over and over, day after day, seeking to bless people and fulfill the plan of God. Directly in their paths, however, are obstacles that hinder them and limit their effectiveness. Like the woman, they do not take the time to clear their own paths. For years, sometimes, they are frustrated and hindered.

In his final words of instruction to the Ephesian elders concerning their ongoing ministry, Paul exhorted them,

"Take heed therefore unto yourselves."

Acts 20:28

Paul exhorted young Timothy with the same words when he told him,

"Take heed unto thyself."

Timothy 4:16

The words "take heed" from the Greek *epecho* mean, "to give attention, to check, to delay, or to stop." As they functioned in their ministries, the elders from Ephesus and Timothy were to slow down and take time to examine themselves. If their lives were not in order, they should delay or perhaps even stop their ministry work and make the necessary adjustments.

You must pay attention to your Self. If you discover that your life is out of order, you will have to do something with your Self. Certainly, it will take time and effort to put your Self in order. But you will more than make up for any lost time when your path is clear.

50

What Shall I Do
With My Self?

There are several general areas of personal life that believers must pay attention to after they are saved. Ignoring these areas will not alter their eternal destiny, but it will determine how effective they are in the ministries they are called to as graced members of the body of Christ.

Renew Your Mind

Sometimes believers suppose that they can accomplish the will of God just by passion and gifting without renewing their minds in the Word of God. They hope to be used in "present condition" and ask the Lord to use them as they are. It is not possible, however, to accomplish the will of God with an unrenewed mind. In Romans 12:2, Paul beseeched believers with these words,

> *"And be not conformed to this world: but be ye transformed by the renewing of your mind, that ye may prove what is that good, and acceptable [well-pleasing], and perfect, will of God."*
>
> *Romans 12:2*

The word "that" in the above scripture connects renewing one's mind with performing God's will. Instead of "that" we could use the words "so that." Believers must renew their minds and be transformed "so that" they will be able to "prove" — discern, recognize, approve, and do — the good, well-pleasing, and perfect will of God. Renewing one's mind in the Word of God is the beginning place for doing the Will of God.

Paul taught that the carnal mind — the unrenewed mind — is "enmity against God" [Rom. 8:7]. It is contrary to the will of God. An unrenewed mind cannot cooperate with heavenly graces. It is a travesty when right-hearted, passionate, grace-endowed believers have minds that are contrary to the will of God.

Paul exhorted the Ephesian believers with these words,

> *"See then that ye walk circumspectly [accurately], not as fools, but as wise, Redeeming the time, because the days are evil. Wherefore be ye not unwise, but understanding what the will of the Lord is."*
>
> *Ephesians 5:15-17*

The Amplified Bible renders Paul's charge this way,

> *"Look carefully then how you walk! Live purposefully and worthily and accurately, not as the unwise and witless, but as wise — sensible, intelligent people; Making the most of the time — buying up each opportunity — because the days are evil. Therefore do not be vague and thoughtless and foolish, but understanding and firmly grasping what the will of the Lord is."*
>
> *Ephesians 5:15-17 Amp*

According to Paul, believers can be saved, Spirit-filled, and destined for heaven, but be "thoughtless and foolish." When believers are thoughtless and foolish, they do not make good use of their time or of their grace-gifts. Instead, time and giftings are squandered while the clock is ticking toward eternity. It is absolutely essential that believers live "worthily and accurately" and be "sensible, intelligent people."

The preacher of Ecclesiastes wrote these profound words concerning the lack of wisdom,

> *"Dead flies cause the ointment of the apothecary to send forth a stinking savour: so doth a little folly him that is in reputation for wisdom and honour."*
>
> *Ecclesiastes 10:1*

Folly is a lack of wisdom. Folly is foolish decisions and foolish actions. Folly taints, discredits, and even ruins one who has a reputation for wisdom and honor. Even the beautiful ointment of resident grace-gifts begins to stink when believers engage in foolish things.

An unrenewed mind is a hindrance to the administration of God's grace. A renewed mind, on the other hand, is a premier co-worker with ministry grace. Determine to renew your mind with the wisdom of God's Word and make it a co-worker with your ministry grace.

Govern Your Emotions

God made the human race with emotions. Emotions are good. In fact, emotions are important. They are the coloring of our lives. They are a significant aspect of who we are. But emotions cannot be in ascendency. They cannot be the governing force or the primary driver of believers' lives or ministries. The direction of believers' lives and the works of ministry they engage in must be determined, rather, by God's Word, by the leading of the Holy Spirit, and by God's specific plan for each person.

Some believers are slaves to their emotions. They are riding the roller-coaster of the emotion-controlled life. If they are feeling good, everything is wonderful. If they are feeling bad, everything is terrible. This kind of life leads to personal frustration and makes a negative impression on others. Unbridled emotions can even amend the path God has ordained for one's life.

If believers don't govern their emotions not only will their own lives be a mess; everything they minister will be an unhealthy mix of grace-gifting and emotion. An unhealthy mix can never fully accomplish the intentions of God. If pure water is served from a dirty glass, the water will, at minimum, taste bad.

Even good emotions like sympathy and happiness can improperly steer believers or modify their God-given commissions. On one occasion some disciples were trying to persuade Paul to remain with them. They touched his emotions to the level where he asked them, "Why are you breaking my heart?" Although his emotions were demanding that he stay, his decision to leave remained steadfast according to what God had spoken to him [Acts 21:12-13].

There is an interesting example of emotions from the ministry of Jesus. Matthew 9:36 tells us that when Jesus saw the multitudes who were lost and scattered without a shepherd, He was "moved with compassion on them." He did not, however, move to minister to their needs because that was not part of His assignment on that day.

Emotions don't need to be eliminated, but they must be governed. Attend to your emotions. Make sure they are submitted to your will and to the will of God. Govern your emotions and make them a servant to your heavenly grace.

Dominate Your Flesh

The body is the physical vessel which carries heavenly graces. Unlike the spirit which is instantly transformed at salvation and the mind which can be progressively renewed through God's Word, bodies cannot be saved or renewed while on earth.

Bodies have within themselves desires and appetites. There is, Paul said, a law of sin in our members [Rom. 7:21, 23]. It is true for every believer that the "flesh lusteth against the spirit, and the spirit against the flesh: and these are contrary the one to the other" [Gal. 5:17]. Because bodies cannot be renewed, they must be dominated and consecrated to God's service. This fact, no doubt, caused Paul to write,

> *"I beseech you therefore, brethren, by the mercies of God, that ye present your bodies a living sacrifice, holy, acceptable unto God, which is your reasonable service."*
>
> *Romans 12:1*

Notice that Paul beseeched [implored, begged] the brethren concerning their bodies. God had already done something with their hearts; now they needed to do something with their bodies. Paul made a strong and impassioned request that believers present their bodies to God a "living sacrifice." These believers' bodies were to be put to death in terms of self expression, but were to be naturally alive under subjection. In this state, believers and their bodies are useful to God. Bringing bodies into subjection as a living sacrifice, although difficult, is not something to be applauded, but is simply "reasonable service."

Paul wrote these strong words to the Thessalonians concerning their bodies,

> "For ye know what commandments we gave you by the Lord Jesus... For this is the will of God, even your sanctification...That every one of you should know how to possess his vessel in sanctification and honour..."
>
> I Thessalonians 4:2-4

Paul informed the Thessalonians that every one of them "should know how" to posses their own vessel. Exercising control over one's own body is a basic responsibility of Christian life. We don't do this to gain access to heaven or to procure our own salvation. We do this to please God and to make ourselves useful in His kingdom. A body-driven life will always be moving opposite of the will of God.

It is not enough to have a "good heart" and strong emotional feelings for God. A believer can have an emotional passion for God, but be body governed. This person will find it very difficult to fulfill the purposes of God. Some believers who have a burning passion to impact the world have not yet gained mastery over themselves. Proverbs says,

> "He that is slow to anger is better than the mighty; and he that ruleth his spirit than he that taketh a city."
>
> Proverbs 16:32

In our modern church world of sound bites, compelling book titles, high intensity meetings, and plans to "take our cities for God" there is little talk about the true realities of spiritual life. The truth remains constant, however, whether acknowledged or not. And it is the truth that it takes more effort to govern one's own life than to win a city.

The body with its strong passions and appetites could be likened to a strong, spirited stallion. Just as no swift, strong, and spirited stallion has ever won a race without being controlled by the sure hand of an experienced rider, so no called and wonderfully graced believer has ever fulfilled the will of God without exercising strong governance over his own body.

Have you ever wondered how many more mighty deeds Samson would have done if he had governed his body? He was called and anointed of God in an unusual, once-in-the-Bible way. Unfortunately for him, for the people of Israel, and for God, Samson's body dragged him off the scene of effectual ministry.

Even Paul, a born-again, Spirit-filled man with a profound calling, deep revelation, spiritual experiences, and a substantial grace-gift had to keep his body in subjection. Notice his words to the church at Corinth,

> *"I therefore so run, not as uncertainly; so fight I, not as one that beateth the air: But I keep under my body, and bring it into subjection: lest that by any means, when I have preached to others, I myself should be a castaway."*
>
> I Corinthians 9:26-27

Paul did not run uncertainly or fight as one that was boxing an unknown enemy. He understood his race and knew what enemies he would have to subdue to fulfill it. What Paul wrote in the above scripture reveals that he perceived his own body as a potentially formidable enemy in fulfilling the will of God.

Paul said, "I keep under my body, and bring it into subjection." The word "subjection" comes from the Greek *doulagogeo* and means, "to treat as a slave, to treat with severity, to subject to stern and rigid discipline." Paul did not pamper his body. He did not let it push him around or control him. He treated his physical appetites with severity and kept his flesh with rigid discipline. He brought his body into subjection to the will of God by the force of his own strong will.

Paul said that if he did not keep his body in subjection, he would be a castaway. The word "castaway" comes from the Greek *adokimos* and means, "rejected, not approved, or unfit." This word was often used of metals which did not pass the test and, therefore, were not fit to be used.

Unsubjected, Paul's body would have taken him places he did not want to go. Unsubjected, his body would have caused him to do things he didn't want to do. Unsubjected, his body would have dominated his calling and kept him from finishing his race. If his body was unsubjected, Paul would have become a "castaway" — a flawed and rejected vessel, not fit for the Master's use.

Subjected, however, Paul's body became an ally; a vessel through which he spoke, touched, and ministered. Subjected, his body was a fit and approved carrier of his ministry grace. Subjected, his body, though ever unwilling, was that living sacrifice by which he accomplished the will of God.

If you do not dominate your body it will dominate your spiritual life and ministry, drag you down to the lower realms of fleshliness, and make it impossible for you to accomplish the will of God. Only by exercising strong and consistent control over your body can it be made an ally with your heart and mind and assist you in ministering your heavenly grace.

Maintain Your Health

In order for believers to remain on earth, fulfill their days, and serve God in their callings, they must remain healthy. In I Corinthians, Paul wrote these significant words about the physical body,

> *"...Now the body [is] not for fornication, but for the Lord; and the Lord for the body."*
>
> *I Corinthians 6:13*

Believers' bodies are not only for themselves, but also for the Lord. The body is not only the temple of the human spirit; it is also the vessel which carries heavenly grace-gifts. Believers are to glorify God in their bodies [I Cor. 6:13, 20]. In order to do this, they must remain healthy.

Just as dilapidated machines cannot accomplish much work, so sick bodies cannot fulfill heavenly callings. If believers do not take care of their bodies, their indwelling graces may be confined to the hospital or lost to the grave. Whether or not you maintain your physical health could determine whether or not you finish your ministry race.

Jesus said, "A body you have prepared for me" [Heb. 10:5]. His physical body was not only given to Him to sacrifice at the end of His life in order to deal with sin. His body was also the tent in which He dwelt and out of which He ministered the Word of God and the power of God while He was on earth.

In order to stay healthy, you must eat a balanced and moderate diet. You cannot overeat and diet, overeat and diet, and remain in top shape. You cannot consume can after can of soda, eat fast food every day, and expect to keep running fast. You need to eat moderate amounts of meats, vegetables, fruits, and breads. And you need to drink water and juices.

You also need to exercise. I don't mean that you have to be a body builder or a marathon runner. But you must do some kind of regular exercise. This is not only necessary for the body; it is also good for the emotions. Our generation sits too much, eats too much, and exercises too little.

Rest is also important for the physical body. Resting does not just mean sleeping at night. Resting includes taking sabbaths from work. You need time to recreate. It is essential for your body, mind, and emotions.

Early in my ministry the Holy Spirit spoke this simple word of wisdom to me: "Don't preach hard, don't pray hard." God knew that I would be traveling extensively throughout the world and ministering often. It is not unusual for me to minister 4-5 hours each day, sometimes for more than a week. Rather than wear out, I have been able to run steadily in the plans of God.

You also need to be careful about your emotions. Excessive worry is bad for the body. Every modern doctor will confirm this fact. Strong and persistent negative emotions like fear, anger, and anxiety release things into your body's system that are unhealthy.

Put Your Natural Affairs in Order

Some believers with excellent graces are limited in effectiveness because their natural affairs are out of order. They are frustrated and sometimes face seemingly insurmountable problems. If the disorder in their lives continues too long or progresses too far, it can become difficult for them to continue in effective service. Believers who do not properly manage their natural affairs may burn bright for a season, but they will not burn bright for very long. I often wondered how much more effective some believers would be if they simply made adjustments in their natural affairs.

Here are two things the Holy Spirit spoke through me several years ago at a minister's conference concerning natural affairs:

"If ministers are burning out, they are either under the wrong yoke, are not doing what they know to do in terms of prayer, study, worship, and waiting upon the Lord, or their natural affairs are out of order to the place where their minds, emotions, and bodies are exhausted."

"Purposes are accomplished by yoking the what with the how and when. The how definitely includes natural affairs. Ministry is not just by the Spirit. If natural affairs are not properly ordered, it can ruin the execution of a vision."

Did you notice the last line of the second prophecy? It says, "If natural affairs are not properly ordered, it can ruin the execution of a vision." Managing natural affairs contributes greatly to effective ministry. It will enhance the expression of grace-giftings, keeping the rivers flowing and the lights burning.

If you are always losing things, forgetting things, missing appointments, and running late, your life is out of order. If it seems that you never accomplish what you planned to accomplish, there is little doubt that you need to develop a greater measure of personal discipline. Understand that you can have the greatest vision, the most profound calling, the richest gifting, and the best of intentions, but come undone in the middle of your performance if you do not manage your affairs.

Sometimes homes are in disarray. Dirty clothes are on the floor. Kitchens are unkempt. Mail is strewn everywhere. Stairs are full of toys, shoes, and other things. If you descend toy-laden stairs, trip, fall, and break your leg, you will have a difficult time bringing your grace to someone that day. And it won't be the devil's fault or anyone else's fault. It will be your own fault.

Keep your desk in order. Clean your office. Keep your financial affairs in order. Find a way to pay your bills on time. Change the oil in your car. Clean your car. Develop reasonable eating habits and sleeping habits. Pick up your clothes. Get your affairs in order. Don't ask God to bless you any more until you do.

Examine Your Self and Adjust

Let me ask you some questions. How is your mind? Is it a clutter of activity? Can you start a thought and carry it to a logical conclusion? What about your emotions? Are they the coloring of your life and a reflection of your personality or do they dominate you? What about your body? Is it a servant to your calling or are you a servant to your body; a slave to every fleshly impulse? How are your relationships? Is your marriage sound? Do you have good friendships?

If your personal life is out of order, stop! Take a break from your task of serving and engage in the task of putting your life in order. Deal with your thought life. Get your body under control. Get your emotions settled down and in their proper place. Take time to invest in your marriage. Put your financial affairs in order. Develop meaningful relationships. Make sure that whatever should be a priority in your life is a priority. Determine what matters most, what matters some, and what does not matter at all and adjust your life accordingly.

51

God Will Help You Prepare

Although the primary responsibility for personal development lies with each believer, God will assist those who are committed to this essential endeavor. Let's examine the three primary means by which God helps believers prepare themselves.

God Works by His Word

In his second letter to Timothy, Paul emphasized the ability of the scriptures to thoroughly prepare believers for service. He wrote,

> *"But continue thou in the things which thou hast learned...from a child thou has known the holy scriptures, which are able to make thee wise unto salvation...All scripture is given by inspiration of God, and is profitable for doctrine, for reproof, for correction, for instruction in righteousness: That the man of God may be perfect, thoroughly furnished unto all good works."*
>
> *II Timothy 3:14-17*

The scriptures, said Paul, were able to make Timothy "wise unto salvation." What a strange thing for Paul to write. Wasn't Timothy already saved? And if he was not saved, what was he doing in a place of spiritual leadership? Obviously, Paul was not referring to becoming a Christian when he told Timothy that the scriptures would make him "wise unto salvation." What, then, did Paul mean?

By being made "wise unto salvation" by "the holy scriptures" Paul meant that from the scriptures Timothy could gain the wisdom he needed to walk in God's salvation in every area of his life. He could avoid foolish errors. He could remain accurate in doctrine. He could be steadfast in the faith. He could be ready for every attack of Satan. He could learn how to control the desires of his flesh. He could learn how to walk in love and wisdom in all his relationships. He could walk in physical health. The result of Timothy's development in wisdom through the scriptures would be that he would attain and maintain his walk in the salvation of God; he would be safe and sound.

Paul said that the scriptures were able to make Timothy "perfect, thoroughly furnished unto all good works." His use of both "perfect" and "thoroughly furnished" is very strong. "Perfect" comes from the Greek *artios*. It means, "useful, capable, suited for a task, or brought into perfect working order for the performing of a task." The words, "thoroughly furnished" come from a strengthened form of *artios* — the Greek *exartismenos* — and mean, "finished, completely furnished, or fully equipped." By continuing in the scriptures, Timothy could reach a place where he was useful, capable, completely furnished, fully equipped, thoroughly prepared, and in perfect working order for whatever good works he was graced to do!

Paul also referred to the effectual inworking of the scriptures in his first letter to the Thessalonians when he wrote,

> "...when ye received the word of God which ye heard of us, ye received it not as the word of men, but as it is in truth, the word of God, which effectually worketh also in you that believe."
>
> I Thessalonians 2:13

The words "effectually worketh" in the above scripture come from the Greek *energeo* and mean, "to be operative, to be at work in, to put forth power." When believers receive God's Word, God's Word works in them! James confirmed this reality about the inworking, saving power of the Word of God when he exhorted believers with these words,

> "...receive with meekness the engrafted word, which is able to save your souls."
>
> James 1:21

The word "able" James used is the Greek *dunamis* which means, "the power to perform anything." God's Word is alive and powerful [Heb. 4:12]. When believers receive the Word, it becomes operative in them and brings revelation, transformation, and preparation. When believers "let the word of Christ dwell in [them] richly in all wisdom [Col. 3:16] it changes their thinking, their attitudes, their emotions, their daily life, and the quality of their service.

In Romans 12:2, Paul exhorted believers with these words,

"And be not conformed to this world: but be ye transformed by the renewing of your mind, that ye may prove what is that good, and acceptable, and perfect, will of God."

Romans 12:2

The word "transformed" Paul used is the Greek *metamorphoo*. This word means, "to change into another form," and denotes the process of changing inwardly from one thing into something else. As believers renew their minds with the Word of God, they literally change into the person God desires them to be. This transformation enables them to live out the "good, and acceptable, and perfect, will of God." Can you fathom this reality? If you renew your mind and are transformed, you can do the perfect will of God!

In His High Priestly prayer, Jesus confirmed the essential role of God's Word in preparing believers for service. He asked the Father to do something for the men He chose as apostles and had already spent three years training when He prayed,

"Sanctify them through thy truth: thy word is truth."

John 17:17

To be sanctified means, "to be set apart from and set apart unto." As believers spend time in God's Word, the Truth will work in them, freeing them from sin, from weights, from fears, from ignorance, from people, and from self. At the same time, they will develop in righteousness, in faith, in knowledge, in wisdom, and in godly character. They will become sanctified; set apart for the Master's use.

God Works by His Spirit

God also works in believers to fit them for service by the means of His indwelling Holy Spirit. Paul revealed this inworking of God in his letter to the Philippians when he wrote,

"Being confident of this very thing, that he which hath begun a good work in you will perform [it] until the day of Jesus Christ..."

Philippians 1:6

God does not just do an initial work in sinners when He saves them. He continues to work in believers by His Spirit to bring them to full spiritual age. Paul said that God will "perform." This word, *epiteleo* — from *epi* which means "intensive" and *teleo* which means "to carry something out to the full" — signifies "an intensive and fully accomplished work."

In this same letter, Paul wrote,

"For it is God which worketh in you both to will and to do of his good pleasure."

Philippians 2:13

According to Paul, God's inworking can be so effectual that believers both want to and will do His good pleasure!

Jesus taught His disciples that the Holy Spirit would indwell them and "teach you all things" [Jn. 14:26]. He also said that the Holy Spirit would "guide you into all truth" [Jn. 16:13]. In II Corinthians 3:18, Paul taught that the Spirit of God works in believers to transform them from glory to glory into the very image of Christ. He wrote,

"But we all, with open face beholding as in a glass the glory of the Lord, are changed into the same image from glory to glory, even as by the Spirit of the Lord."

II Corinthians 3:18

The word "changed" in this verse is the same Greek word *metamorphoo* Paul used in Romans 12:2. This word signifies that process of changing from the inside. As believers look diligently into the mirror of God's Word, the Holy Spirit works in them, changing them from glory to glory, from faith to faith, from love to love, from strength to strength, from maturity to maturity, and from effective to more effective!

The writer of Hebrews penned these significant words concerning the inworking of God,

> *"The God of peace...Make you perfect in every good work to do his will, working in you that which is wellpleasing in his sight through Jesus Christ."*
>
> *Hebrews 13:20-21*

This scripture speaks of God working in believers, making them "perfect in every good work to do his will." The word "perfect" is the Greek *katartizo* which means, "to arrange, to put in order, or to make fit for service." Notice how the Amplified Bible renders Hebrews 13:20-21,

> *"Now may the God of peace...Strengthen (complete, perfect) and make you what you ought to be, and equip you with everything good that you may carry out His will; [while He Himself] works in you and accomplishes that which is pleasing in His sight..."*
>
> *Hebrews 13:20-21 Amp*

This Holy Spirit inspired prayer represents a strong heart desire that by working in us, God would strengthen us, complete us, perfect us, and make us what we "ought to be." When God works in believers and they become what they ought to be, they will be able to do what they ought to do! Let's paraphrase Hebrews 13:20-21 this way:

> *"May God work in you to put everything in order: your thinking, your emotions, your motives, your attitudes, your living, your speech. When He has accomplished this in you, you will be ready to accomplish His will in every good work. May God, by working in you, qualify you, enable you, and equip you for the work to which He has called you."*

God Works Through True Spiritual Leaders

In his letter to the Ephesians, Paul penned important words concerning the work of spiritual leaders. He said that they were for,

> "...the perfecting of the saints, for the work of the ministry, for the edifying of the body of Christ:"
>
> *Ephesians 4:12*

The word "perfecting" Paul used in Ephesians 4:12 is the Greek *katartismos* which means, "to arrange, to put in order, to make one a fitted limb." God has set spiritual leaders in the church for a profound purpose. They are responsible to help believers develop in stature and character, to put them in good working order, and to make them fitted limbs. When spiritual leaders fulfill their ministries, believers become mature in Christ and equipped for their unique ministries.

Paul was diligent in this work himself. In his letter to the Colossians, he said that he was,

> "...teaching every man in all wisdom; that we may present every man perfect in Christ Jesus. Whereunto I also labour, striving..."
>
> *Colossians 1:28-29*

By taking his place as a spiritual leader and teaching believers, Paul hoped to bring them to that place of maturity and preparedness called *telios* [mature, full age] so that he could present them to the Father ready for employment.

The writer of Hebrews offered these guiding words to believers concerning their relationship with spiritual leaders,

> "Obey them that have the rule over you, and submit yourselves; for they watch for your souls, as they that must give account..."
>
> *Hebrews 13:17*

Believers should submit themselves to true and skilled spiritual leaders. The word submit means, "to retire or to draw near to." A good illustration of submitting is to draw near to a fire. The closer one moves to a fire, the greater the effect of the heat. Believers should draw near to those who are truly called, graced, and developed as spiritual leaders. When they do so, they will feel the heat of God which radiates from these leaders and receive direction, correction, teaching, and strong training.

God Wants to Work in You

The heavenly Father desires to work in believers so that they will bear much fruit in His kingdom. Jesus expressed this truth when He said,

"I am the true vine, and my Father is the husbandman...every branch that beareth fruit, he purgeth it, that it may bring forth more fruit."

John 15:1-2

Those who have accepted Jesus Christ as Savior are branches grafted into the True Vine. Being attached to the True Vine makes it possible for branches to bear fruit. There is no guarantee, however, that every branch in Christ will bear much fruit. Each branch must decide whether it will bear no fruit, some fruit, or much fruit. Believers who show promise of effective ministry by bearing some fruit can be pruned by the Heavenly Husbandman and bring forth more fruit.

If you are already bearing fruit for God, remain in close fellowship with Him and allow Him to work in you. Ask Him to make you what you ought to be. Ask Him to prune from your life the things that are drawing your energy, but producing nothing. Open His Word and listen and learn. Take time to wait upon Him so that He can speak to you and work in you.

As you continue to mature, you will discover that not all of God's inworking is pleasant. Some is a deep and painful purging of old ways, old thoughts, old desires, and old self. This pruning of unproductive or minimally productive areas of life can be painful. The discipline of the Father can be, for a season, unpleasant [Heb. 12:6-11]. But God's desperate need for strong and productive fruitbearing sons and daughters requires it. Allow the Heavenly Husbandman to work in you so that you can become who you need to be and do what you are called and graced to do!

Section Seven

Locating Cultivating and Administering Your Grace

As every man has received the gift
Even so minister the same one to another
As good stewards of the manifold grace of God

52

Discovering Your Grace

At times you may wonder if God has a special place for you in His plans and whether a unique grace for service has been stewarded to you. Perhaps you never had an experience where the Lord directed you in a spectacular way. Perhaps you never had a vision or been given a word of prophecy. Perhaps you have never sensed a strong calling to serve a particular people or go to a particular place.

It is important to understand that when God acts to accomplish something spiritual there is not always a physical or emotional manifestation. When a sinner is saved, for example, there may be no physical experience or emotional sensation. That does not mean, however, that nothing has transpired. Something powerful has, in fact, transpired. Sins have been remitted, the sin nature has been circumcised, a translation from darkness to light has occurred, a new heart and a new Spirit has been given.

When God stewards ministry graces, nothing physical or emotional may be experienced. However, just as the new birth radically effects one's spiritual condition and is soon obvious to others, so the stewarding of a ministry graces will effect those who have received them and will soon be noticed by others. Unless a believer lacks knowledge or completely ignores their grace-gifts, those gifts will manifest through their lives and begin to produce some fruit.

Know Who You Are, Know What To Do

In order to function effectively in your place and grace in the body of Christ, you must know who you are. If you know who you are, you will know what to do. If you know who you are, you can engage in the proper activities and render the proper service.

It is often true that people don't know who they are and, thus, fail to function effectively. Some men, for example, don't realize that when they marry, they become husbands. Ignorant of that reality, they continue to think of themselves as men. When husbands think of themselves as men and act like men it has a negative impact on their marriages. If men realize that when they marry, they become husbands, they will search out what that means and live appropriately.

Likewise, many married men with children fail to realize they are fathers. They say, "It's not a man's job to change diapers, rock babies, read to children, and teach spiritual things." And they are right. These things are not a man's job. But these things are a father's job! Fathers are responsible to nurture and admonish their children; bringing them up in the Lord [Eph. 6:4]. Fathers are the ones who are truly called to the "children's ministry." Why, then, do so many fathers fail in their responsibilities? Often it is because they don't know who they are.

There is a significant connection between knowing who you are as a member of the body of Christ and fulfilling your ministry. If you don't know who you are, you will not know what to do. When you discover who you are, however, you can prepare yourself, become effective, and do your work.

John the Baptist knew who he was not and knew who he was. He admitted that he was not the Christ or Elijah, but confessed, "I am the voice of one crying in the wilderness" [Jn. 1:23]. John knew his "I am." Knowing himself in his calling was critical to the fulfillment of his ministry [Acts 13:25].

The apostles in Jerusalem knew who they were. When faced with an opportunity to leave their ministry of praying and preaching in order to meet the physical needs of widows, they declared,

> *"It is not reason [right] that we should leave the word of God, and serve tables...but we will give ourselves continually to prayer, and to the ministry of the word."*
>
> *Acts 6:2, 4*

The Message Bible renders the apostles' words this way: "We'll stick to our assigned tasks."

Paul also knew who he was. In his epistles, he often declared that he was an apostle to the Gentiles [Eph. 3:1; Rom. 15:16]. Because he knew who he was, he knew what to do. Sure of his ministry, he was able to denote the boundaries of his commission and labor effectively in his field [II Cor. 10:12-15].

In the early years of my ministry, when people would ask me, "What are you called to be in ministry?" I would tell them, "I'm just a blessing." I thought I was being spiritual and humble. Actually, however, I was being foolish. One day the Lord said to me, "I did not call you to be a blessing. Blessing is not a New Testament ministry. I called you to the office of the teacher; you are a spiritual leader." From that day forward, the way I thought about myself and the way I talked about myself changed. When my thinking changed, my ministry began to change. When I perceived myself properly as a teacher and a spiritual leader and conducted myself as such, people received me as such. Since that time there has been an increase in my effectiveness.

If you do not know your ministry grace, you will have trouble finding your ministry place. One week you may try to teach. The next week you may think you are a pastor. Later, at a special prophetic conference, someone may prophesy to you that you are a prophet. If you don't have success in that ministry, you may assume you are called to the ministry of helps. Later, influenced by someone else's success in business, you may try to go into business yourself. Confusion will abound and you will be ineffectual and personally troubled. You must be able to judge yourself according to the grace God has dealt to you [Rom. 12:3]. After you have done so, you will be able to enter into and serve faithfully in your unique ministry.

Rate Your Ability with Sober Judgement

In Romans 12:3, Paul offered this clear exhortation about assessing ministry giftings,

> *"For I say, through the grace given unto me, to every man that is*
> *among you, not to think of himself more highly than he ought to*
> *think; but to think soberly, according as God hath dealt to every*
> *man the measure of faith."*
>
> *Romans 12:3*

The Romans were to "think soberly" about themselves. The word "think" comes from the Greek *phroneo* and means, "to have an opinion of one's self, or to judge." The word "sober" comes from the Greek *sophroneo* and means, "to be of sound mind, to be in one's right mind, to put a moderate estimate upon." In the process of locating callings and ministries, believers must judge themselves with sober, sound, and right minds.

Often believers fail to think carefully about themselves in terms of calling and gracing. Some, being carnal, don't think about these things at all. Some underestimate their giftings because they are too conscious of their sinful past and present personal shortcomings. Others are too "spiritual" and get carried away into fantasy land concerning their callings and graces. The proper way to assess callings, grace-giftings, and ministries is to think soberly. The Amplified Bible renders Paul's words this way,

> *"...I warn every one among you not to estimate and think of himself*
> *more highly than he ought [not to have an exaggerated opinion of*
> *his own importance], but to rate his ability with sober judgement,*
> *each according to the degree of faith apportioned by God to him."*
>
> *Romans 12:3 Amp*

Believers should rate their ability with sober judgement. They should not judge themselves on the basis of family background, education, personality, physical ability, or social standing. They should not judge themselves based on their past life or on a dream they have about the future. They also should not estimate themselves according to the opinions of others. Rather, they should make a sober estimation of themselves, as Paul said, according to what God has dealt to them.

Don't Overestimate Your Grace

In his exhortation about soberly estimating ministry giftings, Paul warned believers not to overestimate themselves. When believers overestimate themselves, they try to take places and do things they are not qualified for. Being overextended in terms of spiritual capacity, they labor out of their flesh, minds, and emotions or just "fake it."

Believers who overestimate themselves often cause trouble for others; especially if they assert themselves in a leadership capacity. They may introduce errant doctrine. They may prophesy out of their emotions and lead young believers onto paths of error. They may get in the way of others who are truly graced to minister in the ways they are trying to minister. No matter what specific trouble they cause, believers who overestimate themselves in terms of ministry gifting will always cause trouble.

One might suppose, for example, that because he is successful in business, he is qualified to be a spiritual leader in the church. I have watched as men who had business success entered the full time ministry thinking that if they applied business principles in their ministries, they would succeed. Some have failed and know they have failed, but don't know why. Others have failed and don't even know it. You see, a man graced to conduct business may not be graced to lead in the church.

Another believer who has been used by the Holy Spirit on certain occasions to give simple prophecies might imagine that he is a prophet called by God to speak into every situation. This person would not be thinking of himself soberly or accurately. Paul said that believers should rate themselves on the basis of what God has dealt to them, not on the basis of how the Holy Spirit worked through them on one or even a few occasions.

Another believer might think to himself, "Well, I have the same Holy Spirit as the teachers who visit our church. I know as much as they do. I should be able to teach in our church." This believer would be thinking too highly of himself if God had not dealt to him the grace to minister in the office of the teacher.

I remember visiting a certain church several years ago. When I stepped into the church, I had the impression that the man pastoring the church was not called and graced to be a pastor. I tried to put this thought down supposing it was my own mind. After being there for a couple days, however, it became clear that the man in charge was not, in fact, called to pastor. I said to myself, "This church will not be here in six months." In less than six months that church closed down and the man who was pastoring left the area and left the ministry The people who had joined themselves to that church were hurt and disillusioned.

Stay sober as you rate your grace. Do not measure yourself by your education or social standing. Do not measure yourselves against others. Do not measure yourself by the praises or opinions of people. Do not measure yourself by your dreams of what you wish you were. Do not measure yourself according to how you felt in a "powerful, anointed meeting." Lofty thoughts in the midst of emotional highs can be powerful intoxicants, but they must be tempered with more sober and accurate evaluations.

Young believers and novices in ministry must be especially careful when estimating themselves. Because they are often fresh from a personal experience with God and are excited about their visions and ministries, they can overestimate themselves and get into trouble. Do as Paul said and estimate yourself "soberly."

Don't Underestimate Your Grace

Some believers think less of themselves than they should in terms of grace-gifting. When believers underestimate what God has dealt to them, they lack confidence and do not function as fully in their ministries as they should. Consequently, the body of Christ is under-supplied and the kingdom of God is cheated.

When God called Moses, a man trained in all the wisdom of Egypt and, according to Acts thirteen, eloquent in speech, Moses said, "I cannot talk." God was not pleased with Moses' "humble" attitude [Ex. 3:1-4:17]. When it was time for Saul to be anointed king over Israel, he hid himself [I Sam. 10:17-23]. When an angel appeared to Gideon and called him a mighty man of valor, Gideon responded, "Wherewith shall I save Israel: behold, my family is poor in Manasseh, and I am the least in my father's house" [Ju. 6:15]. When the Lord informed Jeremiah that he was ordained to be a prophet to the nations, he responded, "Ah, Lord God! behold, I cannot speak: for I am a child." God corrected Jeremiah with these strong words: "Say not, I am a child" [Jer. 1:6-7].

In first Corinthians twelve, Paul addressed the problem of believers underestimating their ministries with this question,

> *"If the foot shall say, Because I am not the hand, I am not of the body; is it therefore not of the body? And if the ear shall say, Because I am not the eye, I am not of the body; is it therefore not of the body?"*
>
> *I Corinthians 12:25-26*

Might a foot suppose that because he was not the hand, he was unimportant in the body? Yes, that could happen. Would that mean, however, that the foot was not an important body member with a vital ministry? No. It would mean that the foot had underestimated himself. What if the ear supposed that because it was not the eye, it was not important in the body? Would that mean the ear was not important? No. It would mean that the ear had underestimated its importance in the body.

What if a believer who is called to serve thought, "Because I'm not a pastor or an evangelist, I am not important in the body?" Would that mean the server was not important in the body? No, it would mean that the server had underestimated himself. He should grow in knowledge, properly estimate himself, and function in his place of ministry.

Do not underestimate yourself or the special grace entrusted to you. If you do, important words will remain unspoken, necessary deeds will go undone, and some of God's plans will remain unfulfilled.

53

How to Locate Your Grace

In his first epistle, Peter instructed believers to minister with the grace-gifts they had received from the Lord. Apparently, these believers knew what God had dealt to them. Unfortunately, many modern day believers do not know how to determine their callings, grace-gifts, and ministries. In this chapter, we will discover some of the basic ways to discern what ministries and grace-gifts God has stewarded to us.

Determine Your General Area of Ministry

An important first step in determining the specific ministry you are graced for is to determine the general area of ministry you are graced for. To help you locate the general area of ministry you might be graced for, I have listed three basic categories of ministry.

Spiritual Leadership or After That?

In discovering your grace, determine first whether you are called to a spiritual leadership ministry or an "after that" ministry. If you are called to a spiritual leadership ministry, then you must be an apostle, prophet, pastor, evangelist, or teacher. If you say, "Well, I believe I am supposed to teach, but I don't think I am called to the office of the teacher," then you may be graced to teach in the way Paul presented in Romans 12:7. Start there and narrow your calling. Perhaps you are called to teach a Sunday School class in your local church. Perhaps you are called as a teaching elder. Perhaps you are called to hold Bible studies in your home or teach a cell group. Perhaps you are called to take occasional missionary trips and teach.

Those who are called and graced for a spiritual leadership offices usually have a strong inworking motivation and, sometimes, an impossible-to-deny inward compulsion to do full time ministry. This inward motivation can be difficult to describe to someone who does not have it. If you say, "Well, I enjoy teaching God's Word and am happy to do it, but I am content in my secular employment," then you are most likely not called or graced for a spiritual leadership office.

Words or Works?

In his first epistle, Peter wrote,

> *"If any man speak, let him speak as the oracles of God; if any man minister, let him do it as of the ability which God giveth..."*
>
> *I Peter 4:11*

Peter indicated that ministry can be divided into words or works. Those who are graced to speak should speak as God's mouthpiece. Those who are graced to minister [work] should do so by the ability God has given them. Paul confirmed that ministry can be categorized as words or works when he wrote,

> *"And whatsoever ye do in word or deed, do all in the name of the Lord Jesus..."*
>
> *Colossians 3:17*

There are several different grace ministries that fall under the category of words. All the spiritual leadership ministries fall under this category. That is not to say, of course, that spiritual leaders can not do works. An apostle could operate in gifts of healings. An evangelist may work miracles. A prophet may also be graced to administrate. All the spiritual leadership ministries, however, because of their responsibility to teach, train, and govern the church, come under the category of words.

Other ministries that come under the category of words are teaching, prophecy, diverse tongues, interpretation of tongues, exhortation, and the music ministry. Those graced to function in these ministries should strive to speak as the oracles of God. Even a simple word of exhortation, when spoken as an oracle of God, could save someone from despair and enable them to move forward in their life.

Grace ministries that fall under the category of works include gifts of healings, working of miracles, ruling, administrating, showing mercy, giving finances, serving, helps, and governments.

Are you called to speak or are you called to work? If you are called to speak, is it in a teaching capacity, an encouraging capacity, or in a more "inspiration of the moment" capacity like giving a tongue or prophesying? If you are called to work, is it in a capacity such as helps, administration, or showing mercy or is it in a capacity such as working of miracles or gifts of healings? If you are called to a works ministry, don't spend all your time trying to speak. If you are called to a words ministry, don't abdicate your speaking to do works.

Supernatural or Natural?

Grace ministries can also be categorized as supernatural or natural. We must be careful, however, with this categorization because believers have a tendency to over-esteem supernatural ministries like working of miracles, gifts of healings, prophecy, tongues, and interpretation of tongues and under-esteem natural ministries like helps, exhortation, showing mercy, or administration. When believers observe supernatural ministries in operation, they often think, "Wow, God is really moving!" On the other hand, when they observe someone giving a cup of cold water, straightening the chairs in church, showing deeds of mercy, or administrating, they think, "Isn't that nice how they are serving the Lord."

It is obvious from the list of grace ministries in Romans 12:6-8 that God does not esteem supernatural and natural ministries on different levels. Without making any attempt to categorize ministries as important or not important, the Holy Spirit referred to prophecy, service, teaching, showing mercy, ruling, and giving finances. These grace-gifts range from what we would term supernatural [prophecy and teaching] to what we term natural [serving, showing mercy, or giving finances].

In the list of ministries in I Corinthians twelve we find apostles, prophets, teachers, workers of miracles, helpers, interpreters of tongues, governments, and gifts of healings. Paul did not separate these ministries into the categories of Important and Unimportant. We must be careful not to establish levels of significance in ministry that God does not advocate. This would be a misunderstanding of spiritual things. Whether a ministry is supernatural or natural, it is of God and critical to His plans.

All five spiritual leadership ministries fall under the heading of supernatural. Because the church is a supernatural body with a supernatural commission, it requires supernatural leadership. Other ministries that come under the heading of supernatural are diverse tongues, interpretation of tongues, working of miracles, gifts of healings, and prophecy. These ministries are necessary to deal with circumstances, sicknesses, and other things that cannot be resolved without extraordinary power.

Ministries that would be classified as natural include helps, governments, giving, exhortation, showing mercy, serving, and ruling. It is important to realize that these ministries, although less dramatic, are also born of and enabled by the manifold grace of God.

Are you called to a supernatural ministry or a natural ministry? Are you called to work miracles or work with your hands? Are you called to teach as an oracle of God or touch with the mercy of God. Are you called to serve the supernatural food of God's Word or are you called to serve natural food? If you are called to a natural ministry, never think that your ministry is unimportant. If you are called to a supernatural ministry, never think that you are more important than others. All ministry is crucial, whether natural or supernatural.

Who Aren't You?

In discovering your ministry grace it can be very helpful to determine who you aren't. Are you an evangelist? Are you an apostle?

Are you a worker of miracles? Are you a shower of mercy? If your answer to these questions is, "No," then go on down the list. Determining who you aren't may not bring you to the final conclusion of who you are, but it will help narrow the list. As you consider each ministry, ask yourself, "Could I be that gift? Do I have that grace?" If the answer seems to be, "No," you will have moved closer to discovering your grace and place.

When the Jews asked John the Baptist who he was, he confessed, "I am not the Christ." When they asked if he was Elijah, he responded, "I am not." When they asked him who he was, he said, "I am the voice of one crying in the wilderness" [Jn. 1:19-23]. John knew who he wasn't and knew who he was.

Concerning myself, I knew at a young age that I was not an evangelist. I knew that I was not called to pastor a local church. I knew that I was not an apostle. I knew that I was not called to the helps ministry. I knew that I was not a worker of miracles. I knew that I was not called to work with children or youth.

A few times in the early days of my ministry, I did accept invitations to minister to youth and children. Unfortunately, I didn't know what to do. I was out of place. I was miserable. Afterwards, I said to myself, "This is not me." And I was right. I felt out of place and was not effective because I am not called or graced to be a youth or children's minister. These realizations of who I was not helped me narrow the list of ministries that I might be graced for.

What Has Been Dealt to You?

In the parable of the talents, three different servants were dealt three different measures of talents. Jesus said that the householder "delivered" his goods to his servants. The word "delivered" comes from the Greek *paradidomi* and means, "to give into the hands of another, to give over into one's power, or to deliver something to use and take care of." In Romans 12:3, Paul exhorted believers to think soberly about what had been dealt to them in terms of ministry ability. The word "dealt" he used comes from the Greek *merizo* and means, "to divide and distribute."

In the natural realm, people often assess their physical constitution, mental abilities, personalities, and natural giftings to determine what they should do with their lives. If they are tall, strong, and coordinated, they may consider a career in sports. If they are intelligent and have a native ability with numbers, they may consider a career in accounting. If they have creative and artistic talents, they may consider a career in music or art. A similar self examination can be done in the spiritual realm. You can assess your abilities, your motivations, and your spiritual interests and gain insight about how God has called and graced you.

One of the primary reasons I migrated toward the ministry of teaching was because I discerned within myself a capacity to learn the Word of God and effectively transmit what I had learned to others. Noting these things, I said to myself, "Hmmm, what does this ability to comprehend and deliver the Word of God tell me about myself? Perhaps it tells me that I am called to teach."

It will help you greatly if you can locate the "tools" given to you because tools and tasks are always harmonious. If you went to work for a construction company and were never told what to do, but were given a hammer, would you know what to do? Would you demand a written job description and a meeting with the boss or would you know that your task was to pound nails? Of course, you would know that your task was to pound nails. There would be no reason to try to sweep the floor, paint the walls, or clean the windows. Your tool doesn't "tell" you to sweep, paint, or clean; it tells you to pound nails. If you can identify your tools, you can determine your task.

Take inventory of what God has dealt to you. Did He give you a broom, a pencil, a hammer, or a paintbrush? Do you have a mercy grace, a prophecy grace, a grace to exhort, a grace to serve, a grace to teach, or a grace to interpret tongues? Depending upon what has been entrusted to you, determine how to serve.

Have you ever played a card game? After the dealer deals all the cards, what do you do? You pick up your cards and examine them. After examining what you have been dealt, you decide how to play that hand.

In the same way, after you determine what God has dealt to you in terms of grace-gifting, you will know how you should minister. Do you have three aces, a royal flush, or one queen? Depending upon what has been dealt to you, determine how to "play." Unlike a game of cards, in the spiritual life you cannot bluff. If you are not graced for a task, you will not be effective in that task. Therefore, make a sober estimation of what God has dealt to you and minister accordingly.

Follow Your Heart

Perhaps you have said words like these: "It is just in my heart to..." or, "I keep feeling like I should..." or, "It seems like I ought to..." Have you ever wondered why it was in your heart to do a certain thing? Have you ever wondered why you felt drawn to certain people, to a particular place, or to a certain aspect of ministry?

Very often, heart motivations are ministry graces seeking expression; seeking the need they are ordained to meet; seeking to be employed in the commission God has assigned. Notice these words Paul wrote to the church at Corinth concerning Titus,

> *"But thanks be to God, which put the same earnest care into the heart of Titus for you."*
>
> II Corinthians 8:16

God put an "earnest care" into the heart of Titus for the Corinthians. The words "earnest care" come from the Greek *spoude* which means, "to be earnest in accomplishing something or to be earnestly interested in something." The word "put" is the Greek *didomi* which means, "to bestow, to grant, or to furnish something to someone." The "earnest care" that God "put" in Titus' heart was a divine interest in, heart connection with, and ability to meet the needs of the Corinthian people.

There is an attraction between grace endowments and ministry assignments. Some believers are drawn toward battered women in Asia. Some feel motivated to minister to children in Brazil. Some feel compelled to reach out to the lost while others are drawn toward study and teaching. Some have a heart for the broken hearted while others desire to administrate.

If you have a strong heart passion for the sick, it is very possible that God has called and graced you to minister in the area of healing. If you have a strong passion to assist others, it is very possible God has called and graced you for practical service. If you have a strong passion to see believers learn and grow in the Lord, you may be called and graced to teach or you might be called and graced to be a pastor. If you have a burning passion to see the lost saved, you may be called and graced as an evangelist.

In determining your grace and ministry, don't force an over-identification. If you told me that it seemed the Lord was leading you to do missions in Asia, but you didn't know if you were a pastor, a teacher, had a gift of teaching, or were an exhorter, I would say, "Who cares! Don't worry about that. Just start doing what is in your heart and let things develop."

If you can determine what moves your heart to compassion and what stirs you to action, you have begun to discover your commission, your grace, and your ministry. Don't wait for a vision, a special word of prophecy, or a dream in the night. Just follow your heart. It is smart because a supernatural ministry grace is resident there. Following your heart is an excellent way to take your first steps in the ministry God has graced you for.

Listen to The Holy Spirit

God has always directed His people by His Spirit. When His Old Testament people inquired of Him concerning His plans, He answered by His Spirit through the prophets. When His people followed His plans, they prospered.

When Saul's father lost his donkeys, he sent Saul and a servant to look for them. Those two men scoured every hill and valley, but were unable to locate the lost donkeys. Saul's servant suggested that they find a "seer" and enquire of the Lord by him. So they searched and found the prophet Samuel. When they met him, Samuel said to Saul,

> _"...I am the seer: go up before me unto the high place; for ye shall eat with me today, and tomorrow I will let thee go, and will tell thee all that is in thine heart."_
>
> I Samuel 9:19

Samuel said he would tell Saul "all that is in thine heart." He was going to tell Saul about his future; about his calling from God, his office, and his anointing. How would Samuel do this? He would do it by the Spirit of God upon him.

Another time in the Old Testament three kings needed specific direction from the Lord. They sought out the prophet Elisha because the word of the Lord was with him. Under the influence of the Holy Spirit, Elisha brought forth the mind of the Lord for those kings, enabling them to have good success in their warfare [II Kings 3:11-27].

In the New Testament, believers have the incredible privilege of hearing directly from God by His Spirit in their own spirits. Jesus prophesied that the indwelling Holy Spirit would flow like rivers out of believers' bellies [Jn. 7:37]. He said that the Holy Spirit would show believers things to come [Jn. 16:13]. Paul taught that the Holy Spirit bears witness with believers' spirits and said that the sons of God are "led by the Spirit of God" [Gal. 4:6; Rom. 8:14-16].

In the New Testament, one of the primary responsibilities of the Holy Spirit is to guide believers in the will of God. The Holy Spirit instructed Phillip to join himself to the eunuch's chariot [Acts 8:29]. While Peter was seeking to comprehend the vision of the unclean animals, the Holy Spirit told him that he should go with the three men at his door and doubt nothing [Acts 10:19-20]. When prophets and teachers in Antioch met together, the Holy Spirit revealed that Paul and Barnabas were to be a ministry team [Acts 13:1-4]. When Paul desired to go to Asia and preach, the Holy Spirit forbid him [Acts 16:6]. When

Paul's season in Ephesus was over, he "purposed in the Spirit" where he would go next [Acts 19:21].

Being led by the Holy Spirit is not something strange or something for the "super spiritual." Being led by the Holy Spirit is part and parcel of New Testament life and service. The Holy Spirit is the Prophetic Voice of God. He will show you things to come and direct your steps as you do God's business. Because you are Spirit indwelt, divine direction for your personal life and ministry is always available.

Try it On

A few years ago, I was shopping at the Galleria Mall in Dallas, Texas. As I passed by a men's store, I noticed a beautiful Italian suit in the window. The suit looked great on the mannequin and I thought it would look good on me. I wanted to buy the suit, but decided to try it on first.

When I put the suit on, my high thoughts were quickly dashed. Not only did the suit not fit me; the olive green color looked terrible on me. I was disappointed, but very glad I didn't buy the suit without trying it on. I have an important word of advice for you concerning discovering your ministry grace: Before you buy it, try it! Some things that look beautiful on others may not fit you at all.

Jesus told His disciples, "My yoke is easy." In Bible times, yokes were custom made to fit the oxen who would wear them. A wrong yoke could seriously hurt the oxen, making it difficult for him to work. In the spiritual life, God takes care that each believer has a custom fit yoke. Like the householder in Matthew 25, He graces believers according to their various abilities. If a ministry yoke does not fit you, it is not yours. It could cause you pain and trouble if you try to "wear" it.

Consider Past Fruit

As you seek to determine your grace and calling, ask yourself, "What have I already done for the Lord that produced good fruit? If you have been successful bearing "apples," you are probably an "apple tree." If, in times past, you have grown "bananas," you may be a "banana tree." Your ministry fruit will help you identify your grace root.

I know a woman who has been a pastor in a foreign country for many years. In the beginning years of her ministry, she experienced resistance, even from other ministers, concerning her work as a pastor. When she asked me what I thought about her ministry, I told her, "Let your fruit validate your calling. It makes no difference what others think or say. If you consistently bear the fruit of the pastoral office, you are a pastor."

If you have labored in an area of ministry for a season and have been bearing good fruit, you have likely located at least one area of your calling and grace. If, however, you have labored in a ministry for a season and things don't seem to be working very well, that ministry might not be your ministry. After I ministered to children just two times, I knew I was not graced for that ministry. Certainly, I care about children and their needs. I know, however, that I do not have a grace from God for that ministry.

Properly Interpret Special Assignments

It is important to understand that being sent on special assignments or being used in certain manifestations of the Spirit are not evidences that God is directing you into a new ministry. It is not unusual for the Lord to lead believers to do things that are different than their primary grace ministries. But some believers have gotten into trouble and caused trouble for others because they interpreted a special assignment or a special manifestation of the Holy Spirit as God's calling to a new ministry.

Peter was a chief apostle called and graced to minister to the Jews. On special occasions, however, he ministered outside his general grace and commission. One day, by the means of a vision and by the direction of the Holy Spirit, God sent him on a special mission to a Gentile named Cornelius [Acts 10:9-20]. When he preached, Cornelius and his whole household were saved and filled with the Holy Spirit [Acts

10:34-38]. Peter did not try to turn this special assignment into a new ministry, however. He didn't start something new called "The Cornelius Connection." After he fulfilled his special assignment to the house of Cornelius, he returned to his primary grace ministry as chief apostle to the Jews.

Something like this might happen with you. The Spirit of God may move upon you in a special way to meet a special need. That does not mean, however, that you are supposed to function that way all the time. It doesn't mean that God is giving you a new ministry. Be careful to properly interpret special assignments and manifestations of the Spirit. Always remain open for the Holy Spirit to lead you and use you in special ways, but be careful to remain in your place and in your grace.

Commit Your Works to the Lord

If you are having trouble determining your place and your grace it can be helpful to follow the simple wisdom of Proverbs. There we read,

> *"Commit thy works unto the Lord, and thy thoughts shall be established."*
>
> Proverbs 16:3

Sometimes believers have trouble determining their calling and grace because they have personal agendas and other desires. Their own thoughts, then, are in conflict with the thoughts God is speaking to them and with the way their grace is leading them. This inner conflict can lead to confusion and frustration.

When you completely submit to the Lord, your thoughts become much more compatible with the direction He is leading. Your thinking concerning His calling becomes less wishy-washy and more established and accurate. Clear your will of your own desires and commit your works to the Lord. Tell Him, "Lord, I am yours. I commit all my works to You. I am ready to do whatever You ask of me. Just show me what You want me to do." When you position yourself properly with God by making this kind of commitment, He has permission to speak to your heart and influence your thoughts. Clarity will come concerning your calling and grace.

Consult A Spiritual Leader

Because spiritual leaders are called and graced to help prepare believers for service, they can often perceive other believers' graces and help them locate their places in the body.

When Paul went to Jerusalem to confer with the spiritual leaders there, he said they "perceived" the grace given to him. The word "perceived" comes from the Greek *ginosko* and means, "to feel, to understand, and to be acquainted with." The spiritual leaders in Jerusalem were able to confirm Paul's calling because they recognized the ministry grace stewarded to him.

I often have a sense and sometimes even a clear perception of what other believers are called and graced to do. One time a pastor said to me, "I am having trouble with my worship leader. He just doesn't seem to be able to bring people into the presence of God." I responded, "It is because he is not called to the music ministry." When I said those words, it confirmed to that pastor what he had already sensed.

Sometimes people ask me, "What do you see concerning my ministry?" If it seems to me that they are generally in the will of God, I seldom say anything except, "It seems like you are on the right path." Occasionally, however, I may suggest to someone that they consider making adjustments or even re-evaluate their calling.

If you are having difficulty locating your calling and grace-gifting, it can be helpful to permit a spiritual leader you trust to speak into your life. New Testament spiritual leaders are not, of course, like Old Testament prophets. And you do have the indwelling Holy Spirit yourself. Often, however, mature spiritual leaders can perceive things about you and your calling that will be helpful. Sometimes they can confirm what you already have some direction about.

Discovering Your Grace Will Make You Free

Paul knew his commission and knew the grace stewarded to him. He said in second Corinthians ten that he would not go beyond the limits of his commission and stretch beyond his ability. Because Paul knew his commission and grace, he was free from the opinions of others, free from being moved by needs, and free from being manipulated by the devil. Knowing his commission and grace kept him free from doing good things and helped him do excellent things in his area of calling.

When I began to recognize that I was graced for the office of the teacher, I became free. Aside from a special leading of the Spirit, I am free to not do evangelistic crusades. I am free to not work with youth. I am free to not do helps ministry. I am free to not have special healing lines unless the Holy Spirit specially urges me to do so. I am a teacher called and graced to establish believers in truth, to help pastors build strong local churches, and to prepare spiritual leaders. And that is what I happily do.

When you discover your grace, you will be free from other men's labors, free from other men's opinions, free from your own personal insecurities, and free from the taunts of the enemy. You will be free to serve in your own unique calling by your own special grace!

54

Cultivating Your Grace

In order to be effective in ministry, you must not only discover your grace; you must also cultivate it. Just as a natural talent is not enough to make one exceptional in natural things, so a spiritual talent is not enough to make one effective in ministry. Natural talents must be cultivated and refined through teaching, training, discipline, and use. So, too, grace-gifts must be cultivated and refined through teaching, training, discipline, and use.

Every grace-gift can be cultivated. Every believer can become skilled in their ministry. One believer can become skillful in prophecy. Another can become accurate in interpreting tongues. Another can become creative in exhortation, knowing how to speak a word in season to the weary. Another can become a valuable server. Another can become a dynamic and effective teacher, unveiling and explaining the mysteries of the Word of God. Another can become a skilled apostle. Another can become a gracious, liberal giver. Another can become a highly effective pastor. Another can become an excellent ruler.

Jesus, the ultimate standard, was skilled in every ministry. He was an effective preacher. He was accurate in the Spirit concerning the source of people's problems. He was able to deliver healing power to those who came in faith to be healed. He knew how to wash feet. He could speak a word in season to the weary. The people of His day said of Him, "He hath done all things well: he maketh both the deaf to hear, and the dumb to speak" [Mk. 7:37].

The apostle Paul was skillful in his ministry. He stated concerning himself, "I am a wise master builder" [I Cor. 3:10]. He did not say in a self-effacing way, "Well, I actually have no idea what I am doing, but hopefully God can use me because I am willing." He did not say, "I hope that somehow the Spirit will work through me." Paul acknowledged his grace-gift, cultivated it through study, prayer, and use, and strived for mastery till he became a wise masterbuilder.

Stephen was effective in his ministry. The book of Acts records that the religious leaders in Jerusalem could not resist the wisdom and the spirit by which he spoke [Acts 6:10]. Have you ever read his message in Acts seven? Stephen knew the whole history of God's dealings with men and was able to bring forth all the important points of what the Spirit wanted to say. By ministering in this skillful way, he was able to pierce the hearts of men. Stephen was still developing mastery in ministry when he was martyred.

God Needs Your Ability

Have you ever heard someone say, "God doesn't need your ability, He needs your availability?" That statement is cute, but completely unscriptural. The fact of the matter is that God needs believers who are both available and able. If believers are willing, but not skillful, very little will be accomplished through their efforts. This is a spiritual fact which the scriptures and church history clearly bear out.

Imagine that you were building a house for yourself and a man offered to do the electrical work. Most likely, you would ask him if he was trained as an electrician or if he had done electrical work before. If the man replied that he had no training and no experience in electrical work, you would probably ask him, "What makes you think I would use you if you have no training, experience, or skill?" If he answered, "Well, I am willing," you would tell him, "No thank you, silly man!"

It is important that the house you live in be properly built. It is necessary, then, that you hire people who are skilled in their work. Why do we think so differently about spiritual things? Why do we think that the kingdom of God can be built and the purposes of God wrought by believers who have no training, no skill, and no expertise, but are willing? The fact of the matter is that it can't! Wrong thinking in this area makes God a desperate employer.

David was an Old Testament man who prepared before he served. When Saul was looking for a skilled musician to play for him, one of his servants recommended young David with these words,

> *"I have seen a son of Jesse the Bethlehemite, that is cunning in play-ing, and a mighty valiant man, and a man of war, and prudent in matters, and a comely person, and the Lord is with him."*
>
> I Samuel 17:18

These words of testimony concerned a seventeen year old youth. David was skillful in music. He was a very courageous man and a warrior. He was prudent and wise. Before David was chosen for ser-vice and anointed by God, he had prepared himself. Even after he was called and anointed to be king, thirteen years passed before he sat on the throne and ruled. The Holy Spirit testified of David's good leader-ship with these words,

> *"So he fed them according to the integrity of his heart; and guided them by the skillfulness of his hands."*
>
> Psalm 78:72

Notice that David fulfilled his work by the integrity of his heart and the skillfulness of his hands. Integrity of heart is absolutely essen-tial in ministry. But without the skillfulness of hands, the purposes of God will not come to pass.

Many years later, Paul spoke these words concerning David,

> *"[God]...gave testimony, and said, I have found David the son of Jesse, a man after mine own heart, which shall fulfill all my will."*
>
> Acts 13:22

God Did Not Speak Through a Donkey

Sometimes believers allow their doctrinal foundations to be es-tablished on cute phrases, half scriptures, personal testimonies, or Old

Testament stories. Concerning serving the Lord, I have often heard this errant statement, "Well, if God could speak through a donkey, He can speak through me." On the basis of this statement many believers have established the standard of excellence for their own ministries.

Have you ever read the account of Balaam's donkey speaking? It is found in Numbers 22:22-34. If you read carefully, you will notice that God did not, in fact, speak through the donkey. Rather, God opened the donkey's mouth and she said what she wanted to say. Can you imagine God saying, "What have I done unto thee, that thou has smitten me these three times?" That was not God talking. The words that came out of the donkey's mouth were not God's words; they were the donkey's words.

The Old Testament story about Balaam's donkey has absolutely nothing to do with New Testament ministry. God did not speak through the donkey and you must not imagine [and it would be nothing more than a vain imagination] that if you simply open your mouth divine words from heaven will fall from your lips. It surely shall not come to pass! "Lord, speak through me like you spoke through Balaam's donkey," is an ignorant prayer the Lord will ignore.

By the Spirit

A familiar scripture that has kept some believers and ministers from cultivating their grace-gifts is Zechariah 4:6. It says,

> "...This is the word of the Lord unto Zerubbabel, saying, Not by might, nor by power, but by my spirit, saith the Lord of hosts."
>
> Zechariah 4:6

In order to understand this verse, we must know its proper context. After seventy years of captivity in Babylon, God instructed His people to go back to Jerusalem and rebuild the temple of Solomon. After the people returned to build and had completed the foundation, they began to experience serious opposition. Evil counselors were hired against them to frustrate their purpose and weaken their hands.

The conflict became so intense that they ceased doing the work God had sent them to do [Ezra 1:1-4:24].

Sixteen year after the people stopped rebuilding the temple, God sent the prophets Haggai and Zechariah to stir them up to return to their work. Along with His directive to work, God promised to be with His people and help them. One of His promises was that their work would be accomplished, not by human might or power, but by the Spirit of God [Zech. 4:6].

Who was it, however, that did the actual work of rebuilding the temple? Did the Spirit of God lay bricks? Did He mix the mortar? Did He organize the labor? No. The Holy Spirit did not rebuild the temple. The people of Israel rebuilt the temple. In what way, then, was this work "by the Spirit?" It was by the Spirit in the sense that God spoke by His Spirit to His people and inspired their hearts to do the work [Hag. 1:2-11, 14]. The Spirit spoke and the Spirit stirred up hearts, but it was skilled and committed people that did the hands-on work.

Certainly it is true that in the New Testament the Spirit of God directs and empowers for ministry. Believers must recognize, depend upon, and highly esteem His essential role. They must not, however, diminish the importance of preparation and skillfulness by tossing out phrases like, "It is just by the Spirit." I've heard some ministers go so far as to say, "We need to get out of the way so that the Spirit of God can move." If I believed such silly statements, I would remain in bed every day to stay out of the Holy Spirit's way!

Some believers say, "I just want to flow with the Spirit." Sometimes this is an indication, not that they are spiritual, but that they are lazy. If believers want to make an impact that cannot be resisted, they must be well developed in character, filled with the wisdom of God's Word, competent in their callings, and skillful in following the Holy Spirit. It is wrong if believers use the prophetic words of Zechariah as an excuse for not developing mastery in the particular ministries they are called to.

The Effectual Working of Each Part

All ministry graces proceed from Christ the Head. They are delivered to the needs of people, however, through graced members of the body of Christ. Concerning this truth, Paul wrote,

> *"...the head, even Christ: From whom the whole body fitly joined together and compacted by that which every joint supplieth, according to the effectual working in the measure of every part, maketh increase of the body unto the edifying of itself in love."*
>
> Ephesians 4:15-16

The body of Christ increases and edifies itself when each member works effectually in the measure of their part, supplying what has been stewarded to them from Christ. What determines the degree of increase in the body? Does the body grow according to the desire of God? Is it enriched according to the ability of Jesus? Does it progress according to a heavenly timetable? No. Paul clearly stated that the body grows "according to the effectual working in the measure of every part."

When believers minister skillfully by the grace-gifts measured to them the body of Christ increases and the purposes of God are wrought. When believers do not minister skillfully with the grace-gifts measured to them the body of Christ is malnourished and the purposes of God are stymied. The degree of increase in the body of Christ and its effectiveness in service depends upon how effectively each body part ministers with the grace-gift measured to them.

The body of Christ could be likened to an orchestra. When each individual musician is skilled with their instrument and submitted to the conductor, the orchestra performs in a powerful and moving way. It can thrill the heart, stir passions, and make people weep, dance, or shout. There is no such thing as an excellent orchestra composed of novice musicians. So too, there is no effective body of Christ composed of undeveloped, unskilled members.

The Amplified Bible renders Ephesians 4:15-16 this way,

"For because of Him the whole body (the church, in all its various parts closely) joined and firmly knit together by the joints and ligaments with which it is supplied, when each part [with power adapted to its need] is working properly (in all its functions), grows to full maturity, building itself up in love."

Ephesians 4:16 Amp

Notice that the body builds itself up and grows to full maturity when each part is working properly in all its functions with the power adapted to it. In order for the body of Christ to grow and fulfill its mission, it is essential that individual believers cultivate and skillfully use the grace-gifts entrusted to them.

Don't Neglect Your Charisma

In his first letter to Timothy, Paul exhorted him to not neglect his grace-gift with these words,

"Neglect not the gift that is in thee, which was given thee by prophecy, with the laying on of the hands of the presbytery. Meditate upon these things; give thyself wholly to them; that thy profiting may appear to all."

I Timothy 4:14-15

A unique grace-gift [*charisma*] had been transmitted to Timothy in a sacred moment of prophecy and the laying on of the hands of the presbytery. The fact that Timothy was gifted for ministry, however, did not guarantee that he would be effective in ministry. He must not neglect his resident grace-gift. The word "neglect" comes from the Greek *amelei* and refers to being lazy or not caring. Rather than being lazy, Timothy was to "meditate upon these things." The word "meditate" comes from the Greek *meletao* and means, "to take care of, to attend to, to practice, or to cultivate." Timothy was to attend to his heavenly gift, cultivate it, practice with it, and become skilled in his ministry.

Some things can only be learned by doing. Certainly, book training and instruction from others who are skilled is important. But practice is necessary in order to develop and hone skills. For example, a person might study about the piano for years. He could never become a skilled pianist, however, without putting his hands on the keys and playing. It takes years of diligent practice to bring beautiful and excellent music to the ears of others.

In my first year of full-time ministry the Lord said to me, "The first five years of ministry are for you. You will be a blessing, but I am giving you this time primarily as a season of training. Make good use of it." I made use of that time and was able to get a good start toward becoming an effective teacher. My goal now is to be an excellent teacher and skilled spiritual leader in the body of Christ. This is not a personal ego trip. I simply desire that the church get the very best from God through me. If I am not excellent in my ministry, the church will receive less than God's best. If the church receives less than God's best, it will be less wise, less strong, less mature, and less effective than it could be.

Because I want to be an excellent teacher, I consider what will enhance my teaching gift. What will make me more effective when I stand to minister? Study, of course, is important. I must have a comprehensive overview of the will of God and a reasonable level of knowledge in every area of truth. To get this I read, meditate upon, study, and pray over the scriptures. I also read the teachings of other knowledgeable ministers and even theologians. Prayer is also important. It keeps me sensitive to the inspiration of the Holy Spirit and to the direction I should take for each service. For me, writing is also important because it helps me solidify and sharpen what I believe. And, of course, I must teach. I must use my gift in order to become a master in my calling.

I cannot yet say that I am a wise master teacher and skilled spiritual leader. I can say, however, that I know what I am doing. I am not an expert, but I am also not a beginner. If I continue on the proper course, I will reach mastery. That will be good for God, profitable for His church, and a benefit for other believers and ministers. My skillfulness in ministry will enhance the overall execution of God's plans and purposes.

Stir Up Your Charisma

In his second letter to Timothy, Paul again referenced his grace-gift when he wrote,

"Wherefore I put thee in remembrance that thou stir up the gift of God, which is in thee by the putting on of my hands."

II Timothy 1:6

Timothy was to stir up the gift of God that was in him. The words "stir up" come from the Greek *anazopurein* which means, "to add fresh fuel or to stir." Timothy was not to light a new fire; he was to enhance the fire he already had by adding fuel to it. When his fire was larger and hotter, he would make a more substantial impact. The Amplified Bible renders Paul's exhortation this way,

"...stir up, rekindle the embers, fan the flame and keep burning - the gift of God in you by the laying on of hands."

II Timothy 1:6 Amp

In the same letter, Paul charged Timothy with these words,

"That good thing which was committed unto thee keep by the Holy Ghost which dwelleth in us."

II Timothy 1:14

The words "good thing" Paul used come from the Greek *kalos* which means, "beautiful, excellent, useful, or precious." The word "committed" is the Greek *parakatatheke* and means, "a deposit, something consigned to one's faithful keeping." The word "keep" is the Greek *phulasso* which means, "to guard, to watch over, and to not let escape."

God had entrusted to Timothy a beautiful, excellent, and useful grace-gift. Timothy was to guard and watch over that precious gift consigned to his keeping and bring increase to the kingdom of God by the skillful use of it. The wonderful indwelling Helper, the Holy Spirit, would assist him in this important endeavor.

Strive for Mastery

In his second letter to Timothy, Paul wrote,

"And if a man also strive for masteries, yet is he not crowned, except he strive lawfully."

II Timothy 2:5

In the Greek, the phrase "strive for masteries" meant, "to compete as a professional athlete." In Paul's day, the professional athletes who trained hard, competed according to the rules, and won in their specific sporting events became national heroes. Paul informed Timothy that believers could also strive toward and become "professionals" in their areas of calling. They could train hard, compete by the rules, function effectively, and one day receive rich and eternal rewards.

Paul stated in his letter to the Corinthians that a person who desires to achieve mastery must be temperate in all things [I Cor. 9:25]. Paul told Timothy that those who are called to be soldiers in God's kingdom cannot entangle themselves with the affairs of this life [II Tim. 2:4]. Believers cannot get involved with everything, whether natural or spiritual, and expect to be experts in their ministries. If they entangle themselves in other things, they will not have the time or energy needed to attain excellence in their ministries.

Just as natural athletes must come under the strong hand of discipline and training in order to perfect their talents, so those who are graced with spiritual talents must come under the strong hand of discipline, study, and preparation in order to bring their gifts to performance level. In every area of ministry, master performance level can be attained!

Sharpen the Spiritual Axe

The writer of Ecclesiastes gave us this wonderful word of wisdom,

"If the iron be blunt, and he do not whet the edge, then must he put to more strength: but wisdom is profitable to direct."

Ecclesiastes 10:10

The Amplified Bible says,

"If the axe is dull, and the man does not whet the edge, he must put forth more strength; but wisdom helps him to succeed."

Ecclesiastes 10:10 Amp

Some believers imagine that they don't have time to cultivate their grace-gifts and become masters in their ministries. They think time is too short and the needs of people too compelling. The fact of the matter is, however, that over the span of a lifetime believers will accomplish far more in ministry if they first make a significant investment in charisma-cultivation.

The time and effort you invest in sharpening your axe will save you much time and effort when you swing your axe. Some believers have to put forth much physical, emotional, and mental energy in their ministries because they have not cultivated their spiritual gifts. If they would take time to sharpen their grace-gifts, they would accomplish far more with far less human effort.

A few years ago a minister friend of mine was giving too much time to helping others and not enough time to personal development. I said to them, "If you don't take time for your own development, you will continue to function at this level of effectiveness for the rest of your life. If, on the other hand, you devote the required time to develop yourself and your gifts, your life-time impact will be much more substantial!"

Spiritual Apprenticeship

Those who desire to become skillful in a natural talent often seek out a person who is an expert and an able teacher of that skill. For example, if one desires to become a skilled violinist, he will seek out a skilled violinist who is also a good teacher. Likewise, if one desires to become skillful in the sport of golf, he will seek out a skilled golfer who is also a good instructor. If a person desires to become skilled in a particular natural vocation, they often work as an apprentice under the direction of another person skilled in that vocation.

One way to develop in a specific area of ministry is to follow the example and instruction of one who is both mature and skilled in the same area of ministry you are graced for. When believers apprentice with one who is more skilled and seasoned, they can begin to use their talents under the watchful eye of a more mature believer. Within this model, needed correction, guidance, encouragement, and the refining of skills can take place without the risk of catastrophe.

The lack of mentoring in the body of Christ is one reason that few believers reach a high degree of skillfulness in ministry. When every believer has to start from ground zero and make their own way, it can take a lifetime to reach ministry proficiency.

Take the Time, Make the Effort

No matter how strong your calling or how hot the burning fire of your vision, if you do not take time to cultivate your grace-gift, you will never minister in the richness, the strength, the excellence, or the intended divine influence of your calling. I encourage you, therefore, to follow Paul's exhortation and strive toward mastery in your ministry. Do all you can do, spiritually and naturally, to prepare a good instrument for God to play through. He will supply the wind and show you what notes to play, but you will determine, finally, whether the people you minister to experience irritating noise or heavenly music. Remember, you will never deliver exceptional performance without diligent preparation!

55

Administering Your Grace

Locating and cultivating one's grace-gifts and learning to properly manage one's self brings believers to the place where their grace-gifts are ready to be administered. When believers administer their grace-gifts the needs of people are met and the kingdom of God will be enriched and expanded.

Employ Your Grace

In order for believers to be good stewards of their grace-gifts, they must, finally, administer them. Peter referred to this when he wrote,

"As every man has received the gift, even so minister the same one to another, as good stewards of the manifold grace of God."

I Peter 4:10

The word "good" Peter used to describe stewards of grace comes from the Greek *kalos* which means, "beautiful, precious, useful, or commendable." It can also mean, "excellent in nature and character and, therefore, well adapted to its ends." Believers who minister with their grace-gifts are "good" stewards; they are excellent, precious, useful to God, and worthy to be commended. Serving God and others by employing their unique graces, they fulfill one of the primary purposes for which they were saved.

Believers who do not minister with the grace-gifts entrusted to them are, indeed, stewards of grace, but they are not good stewards. They are not useful to the Lord. And although they are loved by Him, they will not be commended by Him. By failing to serve God and others with the grace-gifts entrusted to them, they fail to fulfill one of the primary purposes for which they were saved.

The New International Version renders Peter's words this way,

> *"Each one should use whatever gift he has received to serve others, faithfully administering God's grace in its various forms."*
>
> *I Peter 4:10 NIV*

Faithfully administering God's grace in its various forms is part and parcel of every believer's calling. Peter's words are rendered this way in the Amplified Bible,

> *"As each of you has received a gift...employ it for one another..."*
>
> *I Peter 4:10 Amp*

Peter instructed every believer in every generation and in every place about what to do with their grace-gifts. He said, "Employ it." Paul confirmed Peter's instruction when he wrote,

> *"...he whose gift is practical service, let him give himself to serving, he who teaches, to his teaching...he who contributes, let him do it..."*
>
> *Romans 12:8 Amp*

Concerning the believer who is graced to serve, Paul said, "let him give himself to serving." Concerning the believer who is graced to teach, Paul said he should be occupied with his teaching. Concerning the believer who is graced to give, Paul said, "let him do it." This is as simple as it can be said. Whatever believers are graced to do, they should do it!

Referring to his own stewardship of grace, Paul wrote,

> *"Assuming that you have heard of the stewardship of God's grace... that was entrusted to me to dispense to you for your benefit..."*
>
> *Ephesians 3:2 Amp*

The grace-gift stewarded to Paul was to be administered to others for their benefit. He said that his grace "was entrusted to me to dispense to you for your benefit." What Paul wrote concerning himself is true concerning every believer. Each has been entrusted with a ministry grace that should be ministered to others for their benefit.

After instructing believers to minister with their grace-gifts, Peter stated why they should do so. He said,

> *"...that God in all things may be glorified through Jesus Christ..."*
> *I Peter 4:11*

The final result of believers ministering with their grace-gifts is that God is glorified. Whether a believer teaches, evangelizes, prophesies, serves, shows mercy, gives an interpretation of a tongue, gives finances, encourages, pastors, or does any other ministry, God will be glorified because the things accomplished will evidently be of Him and of His manifold grace.

Several years ago the Spirit of God spoke to my heart from I Peter 4:11. He said, "If you will minister in accordance with this instruction, God will be glorified, people will be edified, and you will be satisfied." To that word I said, "Amen!"

Trust Your Grace-Gift

Learn to trust the grace-gift God has stewarded to you. Know that you are sufficient for your task because of your unique endowment. Say to the Lord, "Lord, if You have called me to minister in this way, then I know I have the ability from You to do so." Don't trust primarily in your natural skills or your personality, even though they can be beneficial when they are sanctified. Trust primarily in the divine endowment God has given you. Then you will be able to testify, as did Paul, that it is not really you who labors and produces, but it is the grace of God that is with you [I Cor. 15:10].

I am confident to go anywhere in the world and teach the Word of God. Why am I confident? Is it because I saw others do it? No. Is it because I have a good education? No. Is it because I have an outgoing personality? No. Is it because a teaching anointing comes on me? No.

Why, then, am I confident to go and teach? I am confident because I know that I am called and graced to teach. I have located and cultivated my grace-gift and am confident it will produce when I employ it.

Stay Within The Limits of Your Commission

In his second letter to the church at Corinth, Paul wrote about the limits of his commission. Referring to his commission as a "measuring line" for his ministry activity, he wrote,

> *"But we will not boast of things without our measure, but according to the measure of the rule which God hath distributed to us, a measure to reach even unto you. For we stretch not ourselves beyond our measure, as though we reached not unto you: for we are come as far as to you also in preaching the gospel of Christ: Not boasting of things without our measure, that is, of other men's labours..."*
>
> II Corinthians 10:13-15

Paul was careful to not go beyond the limits of what God had assigned to him. He would not violate the boundaries of his commission, stretch beyond his measure, and intrude into other men's labors. Notice how the Amplified Bible renders his words,

> *"We...will not boast beyond our legitimate province and proper limit, but will keep within the limits [of our commission which] God has allotted us as our measuring line...For we are not overstepping the limits of our province and stretching beyond our ability to reach...We do not boast therefore, beyond our proper limit, over other men's labors..."*
>
> II Corinthians 10:13-15 Amp

Paul spoke of a "legitimate province and proper limit" which God had "allotted" to him. He referred to his commission as his "measuring line" and remarked that if he overstepped his limits, he would be stretching beyond his ability. One of Paul's ministry secrets was that he did not violate the limits of his commission.

There are times in the spiritual life, especially when young in the Lord, that believers should put their hands to the plow and do whatever needs to be done. There may also be seasons when believers labor in ministries that are not their primary commission. It is not good, however, if believers labor on and on in ministry work that God has not measured to them. There is a time believers must abandon the things they are not commissioned to do and give themselves fully to the things they are commissioned to do.

The early apostles practiced this spiritual principle of staying within their own commissions. Notice their response when practical help was needed in the church at Jerusalem,

> *"...It is not reason [right] that we should leave the word of God, and serve tables...But we will give ourselves continually to prayer, and to the ministry of the word."*
>
> *Acts 6:2-4*

The apostles understood that it would not be right for them to leave their service of teaching the Word of God in order to serve tables. They refused to let their ministry work be determined by pressing needs, but remained within their own commission of prayer and ministering the Word.

The words of the early apostles should be adopted as a theme by all maturing believers. If you adopt this principle and stay within the boundaries of your commission, one day you will be able to declare, "Mission accomplished!"

Don't Labor Beyond Your Grace

In the parable of the talents, the first two servants went and traded with "the same." This means that they worked with the talents stewarded to them. Peter confirmed their wisdom when he wrote,

> *"As every man hath received the gift, even so minister the same..."*
>
> *I Peter 4:10*

Believers should minister "the same" as they have received. In other words, ministry activities should be consistent with grace endowments. If you attempt to manifest a ministry you are not graced for, you will manifest something that is not divine. It may be your flesh, your mind, or your emotions. It may be a cheap imitation of someone else's gift.

If you have no grace-endowment for a specific ministry, it is foolish to attempt to do that ministry. It would be like a blind man trying to play basketball in the NBA. It would be like a woman with a soprano voice supposing that she could sing bass in the choir. The ministry you function in must correspond to your grace endowment.

If you are not placed and graced to be a particular body part, do not try to be that part. It will be like trying to walk on your lips. That is not what lips are made for. Not only will you destroy your lips; you will also go nowhere. It will be like trying to push open a door with your nose. That is not smart. But if you do it, your nose will surely smart. It may even break.

Recently, a pastor told me about a man who had been successful in business and very effective in one on one ministry. He had led many sinners to Jesus and many believers into the baptism of the Holy Spirit. This man decided to go to Bible school. Sometime during his Bible school training, he became convinced that he was called to the full time ministry. He abandoned his business and the ministry fruit he had while a businessman and tried to get into full time ministry.

Unfortunately, this man has not been able to get settled into full time ministry and is continually frustrated. His financial situation has deteriorated and even his outreach to the lost has diminished. It is very likely that he is outside his grace and, therefore, in the wrong place. He was a great benefit to God, to the church, and to the lost when he was in his proper place. Now he is like a misplaced body part. His situation is not the result of a lack of heart, but of a lack of spiritual understanding.

What should believers do when they realize that certain needs are not being met? Well, what did the early church do about needs that were not being met? Did they assign that responsibility to believers who were graced for and employed in other ministry? No. They looked for believers who were not employed in an area of ministry, but who were mature, prepared, and able to meet those needs.

The Holy Spirit once said to me, "Always allow the needs of people to move your heart to compassion, but don't always allow the needs of people to move your feet to action." Even Jesus, though always moved with compassion because of people's needs, did not always move to meet those needs [Mt. 9:36].

Instead of trying to give what you do not possess, get out of the way and let another who is called and graced take his place, labor in his grace, and meet that need. "But," you say, "that person is not listening to the Lord and doing their part." Well, they will have to answer to God for that. If you see needs going unmet, but know you are not graced to meet them, ask the Lord to call, grace, and thrust forth other laborers to meet those needs.

A number of years ago, it was popular in some Christian circles for believers to have every minister lay hands on them so that something of each minister's gifting would be transferred to them. Some thought that this was how to acquire various giftings. Although it is true that spiritual gifts can be transmitted through the laying on of hands, it is also true that if God has not first ordained someone to a certain ministry, no gift for that ministry will be transferred to them through the laying on of hands.

A few years ago, I was ministering in a certain church. After a morning service, one of the music ministers asked me to lay hands on him for a greater gifting in the music ministry. My first thought was to not do so, but there was an unction present from the Holy Spirit. I touched him and he went down on the floor under the power of the Holy Spirit. Within the next year, he reported to me that his song writing had been revolutionized, his ministry had increased, and he was nominated for a special award in the Christian music industry. On other occasions, when believers have asked me to lay hands on them for greater giftings in different areas of ministry, I have been restrained because I did not sense that it was the direction of the Lord to do so.

You are graced to perform a specific ministry. Stay with your grace and stay in your place. Go with the inward flow. Work out of what is at work in you. Let it carry you forward in the will of God. If you follow your heart and labor out of your grace, you will be in the right place and will fulfill your unique ministry.

Minister According to Your Proportion of Faith

After teaching in Romans 12:3-6 that believers' ministry gifts differ according to the graces given to them, Paul exhorted believers to minister according to their "proportion of faith." In the phrase "proportion of faith" the word "faith" does not refer to believing God to receive a promised blessing, but refers to that confidence to minister which is present when one has assessed what God has measured to them in terms of ability for service. After soberly rating the variety and proportion of grace entrusted, believers will be able to minister with faith.

Ministry must be in agreement with the kind of grace given and with the proportion of that grace. An English word similar to "proportion" is the word "correlation." "Correlation" suggests a relationship between two or more things. There must be a correlation between the ministry grace a believer has received from God and the ministry they attempt to do.

If, for example, a believer has been graced to prophesy, he should not attempt to stand in the office of a prophet. He must determine, though, at what measure he is graced to prophesy. Will he foretell the future? Will he prophesy unto edification, exhortation, and comfort? Will he prophesy about things that help direct other believers?

If a believer is graced to teach a Sunday School class, he should not attempt to launch an international teaching ministry. If a believer is graced to pastor a local church, he should not try to be a pastor to the world. If believers attempt to minister beyond their graces and their proportion of faith, they will make trouble for themselves and for others.

Do not attempt to minister beyond the measure of grace you are confident God has entrusted to you. Do not minister according to what you wish you were. Do not minister according to what you think you may be in the future. Do not minister according to the way others minister. Minister in that way and with that boldness which is birthed out of an accurate estimation of what God has distributed to you in terms of ministry grace.

Help Others Esteem Your Gift

How others esteem you often determines what they are willing to receive from you. Another way to say this is that people's perception of you influences their reception of you. If people perceive you as spiritually mature and heavenly graced, they will be willing to receive from you. If they perceive you as ignorant, fleshly, or immature, they may not be willing to receive from you.

The apostle Paul was committed to ordering his life in a manner that made his ministry receivable. In one place, he said,

> *"For though I be free from all men, yet have I made myself servant unto all, that I might gain the more. And unto the Jews I became as a Jew, that I might gain the Jews; to them that are under the law, as under the law, that I might gain them that are under the law; To them that are without the law, as without law...that I might gain them that are without law. To the weak became I as weak, that I might gain the weak: I am made all things to all men, that I might by all means save some. And this I do for the gospel's sake..."*
>
> I Corinthians 9:19-23

Paul ordered his life that he "might by all means save some." He did not want his ministry or his message to be rejected. In one sense, he made himself a servant to all, but in another sense, he simply made himself a servant to his own calling and grace. Whatever would enhance his ministry, he would do. Whatever would diminish his ministry, he would not do.

You might ask, "Isn't there a risk that I could compromise my convictions to please people?" Yes, there is that risk. You should never abandon your convictions or modify your ministry just to make people happy. You must stand firm in the Word of God, firm in your convictions, firm in your grace, and firm in the way the Holy Spirit is leading you. Sometimes, however, if you will slightly alter your presentation — not in content, but in style — you will afford yourself a greater possibility of being received.

Paul wrote very important words along these lines both about Timothy and to Timothy. Because Timothy was young, it was likely that people would not esteem him as qualified to minister to them. A wise man in spiritual things, Paul instructed both the carrier of the gift [Timothy] and the receivers of the gift [local churches] along these lines. For example, Paul exhorted the church at Corinth to receive Timothy with these words,

> *"Now if Timotheus come, see that he may be with you without fear: for he worketh the work of the Lord, as I also do. Let no man therefore despise him..."*
>
> I Corinthians 16:10-11

And Paul exhorted Timothy with these words,

> *"Let no man despise thy youth; but be thou an example of the believers, in word, in conversation, in charity, in spirit, in faith, in purity..."*
>
> I Timothy 4:12

Timothy bore some of the responsibility for how people perceived and received him. If he acted like a youth, people would despise his youth and not receive him as a minister. If, on the other hand, he managed his life in a mature and disciplined manner, people would perceive his maturity, overlook his age, and receive him as a ministry gift.

If you conduct yourself in inappropriate ways, you will lose your credibility with people. And when you lose your credibility, you lose your opportunity to deliver to those people what God has stewarded to you. You may say, "But Jesus acted perfectly and He was not received in His own home town." That is right. He was not received in

His own home town. He was, however, received in almost every other place. In His own home town it was the fact that people could not see past His natural lineage that kept Him from being accepted. It was not because of how He conducted Himself. If Jesus had been born in another place, the people of Nazareth would likely have received Him.

Help people to receive you by living godly and moderately. If you tell course jokes, gossip about others, or conduct yourself in questionable ways, people will have a hard time receiving you as a ministry gift. If you drive a brand new Mercedes, buy expensive clothes, live in a very large house, and wear expensive jewelry, you may disqualify yourself in people's minds as one who is in the ministry for the benefit of the kingdom of God. You can never guarantee that people will receive you, but you can certainly increase the possibility that they do by conducting yourself appropriately.

Design Your Display to Sell

Any business that sells merchandise invests time and money in designing its displays. Smart businessmen know that how merchandise is displayed often determines whether or not it will be purchased. An item that is very useful, but poorly presented, will only be purchased by the smartest buyers.

Just as natural items can be displayed in ways which show them well or in ways which show them poorly, so each person's grace-gift can be presented in a striking way, in a common way, or in an unattractive way. Packaging can be critical. You should do everything possible to beautifully display what God has given you. If your wonderful grace-gift is displayed in an unattractive way, only the well-informed and mature will receive you. Of course, if you are all display, but have no real product to deliver, people will soon catch on and quit buying.

Sometimes just being friendly and caring is enough to win people. As a spiritual leader, I do my best to be friendly to everyone. I know, however, that this is not true of all ministers. I have actually had people in local churches ask me, "Why do you talk to us?" Apparently, other ministers who visited their churches could not talk to the "crowd" because it "affected their anointing." That is spiritual hogwash! Talking with people reveals to them that you genuinely care and increases the possibility that they will receive you.

On more than one occasion in my overseas travels, missionaries have asked my opinion about how to deal with ministers who won't visit with people because it "upsets their anointing." I tell them, "If these ministers can't hold onto their anointing any better than that, they have some growing up to do. Invite them back in a few years after they have matured." Some ministers, not displaying themselves with love, true concern, and wisdom have hindered themselves and given the ministry a bad name.

Another way to increase the possibility that people receive you is to do something with what is most immediately perceptible to them; that is your outward man. Be sensitive to your physical appearance. Maintain yourself in a clean and neat fashion. Brush your teeth. Fix your hair. Take care of your clothes. People will have a difficult time esteeming you as a heavenly gift if you have a poor physical appearance.

It is true, of course, that God looks upon the heart. It is equally true, however, that man looks on the outward appearance. Even the prophet Samuel was unable to see past the outer man to discern which son of Jesse was God's choice to be king [I Sam 16:7]. Remember, you are ministering to people. And they will see your outward appearance first.

Be Mindful of Timing

Divine endowments must be administered to the proper people at the proper time in the way specified by God. It is important, therefore, that you listen carefully to the Holy Spirit. You may indeed have what another person needs. It may not be the proper time, however, to administer what you have. In the ministering of heavenly gifts, timing can be critical.

Isaiah prophesied of Jesus that He knew how to speak a word "in season" to him that was weary [Is. 50:4]. There is, indeed, a right word for the weary. There is also, however, a season in which that right word should be spoken. A right word spoken out of season is sometimes worse than no word at all.

On one occasion the apostle Paul was restricted from traveling to Asia to preach the gospel to the Gentiles by the same Lord who had called and graced him to preach the gospel to the Gentiles. The Bible says he was "forbidden of the Holy Ghost to preach the word in Asia" [Acts 16:6]. Paul went to Asia at a later time, however, and "all they that dwelt in Asia heard the word of the Lord Jesus" [Acts 19:10]. Paul went to the right place, to the right people, and at the right time.

Serve Your Grace with Excellence

The manner in which spiritual gifts are administered is very important. Always minister your grace with an excellent spirit; in a fashion worthy of your calling, your grace, and your God. If you are involved in a speaking ministry, learn how to speak the word you have. The sweetness of the lips increases learning [Prov. 16:21]. Others will learn far more from your "good word" if you speak it sweetly. Proverbs says,

"A word fitly spoken is like apples of gold in pictures of silver."
Proverbs 25:11

The right word rightly spoken is like an apple of gold on a tray of silver. A right word wrongly spoken is like an apple of gold in an old paper bag! Let your right words be seasoned with grace. When people realize that you have made an effort to minister to them with excellence, they will be more ready to receive your gift. Proverbs says,

"As an earring of gold, and an ornament of fine gold, so is a wise reprover upon an obedient ear."
Proverbs 25:12

If you are a wise reprover, your words will be like fine golden jewelry. Your wise words, wisely ministered to an obedient listener, will enhance their life. If, however, you are a foolish reprover, your words may go unreceived or unheeded. That would be a waste of words and a waste of time.

No matter what grace-gifts and what unique ministry has been entrusted to you, don't forget who you are and on Who's behalf you have been sent. You are an ambassador of God. You are a messenger from heaven. You are a grace-vessel. You are a bearer of divine gifts. Be sure that what you serve is served excellently!

56

Ministering by Grace
Manifesting the Spirit

Although ministering by one's grace-gift as a unique member of the body of Christ is the primary way believers will minister, it is not the only way believers can minister. Believers can also minister in what Paul called the manifestation of the Spirit. After informing the Corinthian believers that he did not want them to be ignorant of spirituals, he wrote,

> *"Now there are diversities of gifts, but the same Spirit...But the manifestation of the Spirit is given to every man to profit withal. For to one is given by the Spirit the word of wisdom; to another the word of knowledge by the same Spirit; To another faith by the same Spirit; to another the gifts of healing by the same Spirit; To another the working of miracles; to another prophecy; to another discerning of spirits; to another [divers] kinds of tongues; to another the interpretation of tongues: But all these worketh that one and the selfsame Spirit, dividing to every man severally as he will."*
>
> I Corinthians 12:4, 7-11

In the area of ministry called "the manifestation of the Spirit" it is the Holy Spirit who manifests through believers, speaking or acting through them in supernatural ways; beyond their natural abilities, beyond their knowledge, and even beyond their grace endowments. Paul listed nine different manifestations of the Spirit [I Cor. 12:8-10].

Paul said that, "the manifestation of the Spirit is given to every man to profit withal." The words "to profit withal" come from the Greek *sumphero* which signifies, "to bring an advantage, to be profitable, to be expedient." God has designed and incorporated this aspect of ministry so that the church, His kingdom, and all mankind will have an advantage and can profit, not only in spiritual life, but in all areas of life. Designing and entrusting this area of ministry to the church further enables God to accomplish His will in ministering both to His own and to the world.

Paul said that the manifestation of the Spirit is "given to every man." The word "given" comes from the Greek *didomi* and means, "to deliver over into one's care, to entrust, to commit something to be administered." God entrusts different manifestations of the Holy Spirit to different members of the body; to "every man." To one believer may be entrusted the manifestation of the Spirit in the word of wisdom. To another believer may be committed the manifestation of the Spirit in the gifts of healing. To another believer may be granted the manifestation of the Spirit in the discerning of spirits.

The particular manifestations of the Spirit are not resident gifts in believers as are grace-giftings. God does, however, select certain believers to use on a consistent basis in the various manifestations of the Spirit. When believers discover how God has chosen to work through them in the manifestation of the Spirit, they can cultivate a cooperative working together with the Holy Spirit in that area and become very useful to God. One believer could be used by the Holy Spirit on a consistent basis to prophesy. Another could be used regularly to interpret tongues. Another could be used by the Holy Spirit in the gifts of healing.

The diverse manifestations of the Spirit are wrought by the one Holy Spirit through different believers. Paul said,

> *"But all these worketh that one and the selfsame Spirit, dividing to every man severally as he will."*
>
> *I Corinthians 12:11*

The word "worketh" comes from the Greek *energeo*. This word means, "to show forth, to be at work, to put forth power, to display activity." In this area of ministry it is truly the Holy Spirit Who shows Himself forth, Who puts forth power, and Who displays Himself active and operative.

Paul said that the Holy Spirit divides His manifestations to every man severally as He will. The word "dividing" comes from the Greek *diaireo* and means, "to divide into parts, to cleave, to distribute." The word "severally" comes from the Greek *idios* and means, "privately, one's own, belonging to one's self." One translation says that the Holy Spirit "apportions" His manifestations to each as He decides. Every believer, then, will have "their own way" that the Holy Spirit manifests through them.

Paul did not teach that the Holy Spirit manifests as He wills, but that He divides His manifestations as He wills. This is an important distinction. The Holy Spirit chooses, according to His will, to use particular believers in certain manifestations. Believers, then, have the responsibility of permitting the Holy Spirit to use them in the way He has chosen. Of course, believers do not determine when the Holy Spirit will manifest; they must be ready at all times to yield to Him.

So What's the Difference?

Ministering by the manifestation of the Spirit is different than ministering by resident grace endowments. When believers minister by their grace endowments, the source of their ministry gifting is the internal, resident grace-gift which has been stewarded to them. Because grace-gifts are permanent, there can be a consistent expression of grace-ministry. Believers can, in a sense, minister at will out of their internal grace endowments.

When believers minister in the manifestation of the Spirit, the source of their ministry gifting is the temporarily manifesting Holy Spirit. In the manifestation of the Spirit, it is the Holy Spirit who is seen or heard and the Holy Spirit Who produces results. Because the Holy Spirit is not always manifesting Himself, ministering in the manifestation of the Spirit is not as consistent or as predictable as ministering by resident grace-giftings.

When the Spirit of God manifests through believers, it is like a puppeteer slipping his hand inside a puppet. When the puppeteer takes possession of the puppet, he endows it with actions, words, and a personality. The puppet can now say things and do things it can not say or do on its own. When the puppeteer removes his hand, the puppet becomes dormant again.

In a similar way, when believers cooperate with the Holy Spirit in the manifestation of the Spirit, they allow the Holy Spirit to express Himself through them in words, deeds, and personality. They facilitate the Spirit by offering themselves as a means by which He can express what He wants to express.

The manifestation of the Spirit in the New Testament is somewhat similar to the way the Spirit of God "came upon" men in the Old Testament. When He came upon them, they became like different men [I Sam. 10:6]. Great things, even incredible things, were wrought as the Holy Spirit possessed them and expressed Himself. When the Holy Spirit lifted from these men, they returned to "normal." The manifestation of the Spirit in the New Testament is not so different.

The Manifestation of the Spirit in the Book of Acts

Prior to His final departure from earth, Jesus informed His disciples that the Holy Spirit would come upon them, empower them, and make them effectual witnesses [Acts 1:8]. Throughout the book of Acts we see the fulfillment of that promise. In Acts chapter two, the Holy Spirit was poured out for the first time. This fulfillment of Joel's and Jesus' prophecies made believers recipients of the Holy Spirit and supernaturally empowered them to speak and to work.

Although the disciples were filled with the Holy Spirit in Acts two, the manifesting of the Holy Spirit for special service can be found several places in the book of Acts. One place, we read this: "Then Peter, filled with the Holy Ghost, said" [Acts 4:8]. These words seem to indicate that the Spirit of God manifested through Peter in an unusual manner, enabling him to speak in an extra-supernatural way at that moment. Peter could always function as an apostle because he was called and graced as an apostle. There were times in his ministry, however, when the Holy Spirit used him in special ways for special needs and special situations.

Paul also experienced this special manifesting of the Spirit. In Acts thirteen, he encountered a Jewish man named Elymas who was resisting and perverting the things of God. In a confrontation with that man, Paul was "filled with the Holy Ghost" and declared to Elymas that he would be blind for a season. Immediately, Elymas became blind. As a result a man named Sergius Paulus was converted [Acts 13:6-12]. After the temporary manifesting of the Spirit abated, Paul continued on in his apostolic ministry, laboring by the grace that was resident in him. This special manifestation of the Spirit [perhaps a gift of faith or working of miracles] was for a particular occasion to accomplish a specific thing.

Yielding to the Holy Spirit

In ministering by the manifestation of the Spirit, preparation and training are not the most essential factors. The Holy Spirit can manifest just as powerfully and accurately through the educated or the uneducated, the rich or the poor, the mature or the immature, men or women, adults or children. The most uneducated man could flow beautifully in prophesy. The quietest person could be used by the Spirit in the gift of faith or the working of miracles.

Ministering in the manifestation of the Spirit is not dependent upon education, training, preparation, or natural talent. The key, rather, to ministering in the manifestation of the Spirit is a willingness to yield. When believers are willing to yield, they can be used by the Holy Spirit in one or more manifestations of the Spirit.

Recently, a pastor told me that while teaching during a church service, he suddenly knew by the Spirit that someone had a particular pain in their body. When he spoke out that word of knowledge a woman responded and came to the front of the church. Before this pastor could even think about how he might minister, he punched the woman in the place of her pain. She was instantly healed and he was completely shocked. This pastor told me that he had never been used that way before or since. Because he had been willing to yield, however, the Holy Spirit manifested Himself and the woman was instantly healed. It seems that the Holy Spirit used him that day in the word of knowledge and in a working of miracles or a gift of healing.

Many years ago, in the early years of my ministry, I was ministering in music at an evangelistic outreach in the country of Denmark. One evening, a young man approached me, holding out his hand to shake mine. When I took his hand, I knew immediately that he had a demon. He did not look or act demon possessed, but I knew he was. I asked if I could minister to him and upon his consent I commanded the demon to come out of him. His eyes lightened up and he asked to pray with me and made a decision to make Jesus his Lord. I believe I was used by the Holy Spirit in the manifestation of discerning of spirits and, perhaps, the gift of faith. I had never been used that way before and have never been used that way since.

Ministering by Grace, Manifesting the Spirit

Ministering by grace endowments and ministering in the manifestation of the Spirit can work beautifully together. I have been in meetings when a strong manifestation of the Holy Spirit in the gifts of healings came upon a particular minister as he was teaching. The minister stepped over into that area of ministry, manifested the power of the Holy Spirit in the gifts of healings by laying hands on the sick, and had supernatural results. When the Holy Spirit finished manifesting in that special way, the minister returned to his regular grace ministry and resumed his teaching.

I have personally experienced the blending of these two general areas of ministry myself. Although my calling and grace-gifting is to teach, I am occasionally used in the manifestation of the Spirit called prophecy and sometimes used to interpret tongues. Sometimes these manifestations of the Spirit confirm what I have teaching. Most often, however, they bring specific direction to a church or to an individual.

A few years ago, I was teaching a Bible study for a group of Christian doctors and residents. Before I began to teach, I sensed a stirring of the Holy Spirit and spoke out these words of prophecy,

> *"There is a spiritual thrust to your work. And there must be spiritual preparation. There will be spiritual resistance. But you will make a spiritual impact."*

On another occasion, I was just about to begin my message in a local church when I sensed that the Holy Spirit had a specific word for the pastor. I spoke out these simple words of prophecy, "Mark carefully the boundaries of your calling."

This church was about to make a substantial financial commitment in the purchase of a radio station. Because of the simple word of prophecy I gave, they decided to pray more about that decision. After praying for a season, they felt that the Lord was telling them to postpone their purchase. Within one year, an opportunity was presented to this church to buy a much needed building and they were able to capitalize on that opportunity. The pastor told me later that if they had bought the radio station first, they would not have been able to buy the church building. The word of prophecy the Holy Spirit spoke through me was important to the direction of that church.

While ministering the Word of God in a city-wide meeting several years ago the Holy Spirit began to manifest. My attention was directed to a man sitting on the front row to my left. His hair was combed back and he was dressed in blue jeans and a T-shirt. I approached him and asked if he would be open to a word from the Holy Spirit. I had no idea at that point what I was going to say, but as soon as he said that he was open, I said to him, "I hear the Lord say that He wants to make a gentleman out of you."

After that short word, I turned to walk back to the pulpit. The Holy Spirit was not finished, however, so I turned and walked back to him and said, "The Lord wants to make a gentleman out of you because He has a woman for you. And if you don't make some adjustments, you are going to miss her." As I walked back to the pulpit, I started to panic because I wondered if the man was already married! I talked to him after the service and he told me he was not married and that the word I gave him was right on and impacted him significantly.

Very recently, this same gentleman walked up to me after one of my meetings and asked me, "Do you remember me?" I didn't recognize him, so I answered, "No, I honestly don't recognize you." He proceeded to remind me that about seven years ago I had given him a word from the Holy Spirit about God making a gentleman out of him. Instantly, I remembered and reminded him of where he was sitting that night and what he was wearing. He proceeded to tell me that he had taken heed to that word and was now married to a beautiful and Godly woman. I was so thrilled to hear that what the Holy Spirit had ministered to him had guided his life and that he had, indeed, received blessings that God had for him.

Concerning the way I am used by God in the manifestation of the Spirit, I can say, "Sometimes the Spirit of God uses me in prophecy and sometimes He uses me to interpret tongues." Concerning my ministry of teaching, however, I would not say, "Often the Holy Spirit uses me to teach." I would say, "By grace I am a teacher and, therefore, I can always teach." As I minister by my indwelling teaching grace and cooperate with the Holy Spirit in the manifestation of the Spirit, believers and local churches are edified.

Each believer should locate and cultivate their grace-gift and minister effectively as a member of the body of Christ. Each believer should also be aware, however, of the possibility of ministering in the manifestation of the Holy Spirit. Needs can be met, important things can be said, and wonderful works can be accomplished through that ministry that cannot be accomplished in any other way. God, in His wisdom, has ordained several ways of ministering to maximize the potential impact of the body of Christ in the world.

57

Fulfill Your Stewardship

Like every member of the body of Christ, you have been given a unique ministry assignment, are a unique member in the body of Christ, and are the steward of a unique ministry grace. Peter made this reality clear in his first epistle when he wrote,

"As every man has received the gift, so minister the same one to another, as good stewards of the manifold grace of God."

I Peter 4:10

Peter's words could be paraphrased this way,

"Whatever specific assignment God has entrusted to each one of you and in whatever unique way He has gifted you, minister to one another on that basis. When you minister with the unique abilities God has given, you are being a faithful steward of the many different grace-gifts God entrusts to believers."

It is a very serious matter to be called with a heavenly calling, to be strategically placed into the body of Christ, and to be stewarded a special ministry grace. Some believers, realizing the seriousness of their calling, may be tempted to turn away from it. There is no way around the "problem" of being called and graced, however. God's will cannot be altered. His plan cannot be modified. The ministry graces He has stewarded cannot be "returned to sender." In this sense, the callings and giftings of God truly are without repentance.

At times, you may want to draw back from your calling. Initially, the realization that you are called, that you have a heavenly mission, and that a unique grace-gift has been entrusted to you can be exciting. The ongoing laying down of personal desires to fulfill the will of God is not always pleasant, however, to the flesh or the soul. This unpleasantness is not something you should feel guilty about, however. We all wish, at times, to remain children with no responsibilities. We all wish, at times, to escape the burden of fulfilling a heavenly assignment. There is a price to pay to accomplish the will of God and it often seems high.

When the time arrived for Jesus to complete His mission, He besought the Father for a change of plans. He said, "Abba, Father, I know all things are possible for you." Jesus was pulling on the heart strings of the Father, hoping, perhaps, to escape the suffering, the sacrifice, and the obedience of death. Although He wrestled considerably in His soul as He faced the sacrifice of obedience, He was able to say, "Father...not as I will, but as thou wilt" [Mt. 26:39]. Jesus drank the cup, endured the pain, paid the price, laid down His life, and fulfilled God's plan.

During the years of His ministry, Jesus told His disciples, "My yoke is easy and my burden is light" [Mt. 11:30]. Notice Jesus did not say there was no burden or yoke. There is, in fact, a burden of service for you. There is a yoke you must wear as you plow the field where God has sent you. You can be confident, however, that the Lord will not give you a burden you cannot bear or a yoke that does not fit you. Just as the plowman fashions a yoke to fit each ox, so the Master will fashion a yoke that fits you. And just as the householder gave talents to each servant according to their abilities, so God will assign a ministry to you according to what you are capable of accomplishing by the merging of your spiritual and natural abilities.

There are Things Appointed for You to Do

Paul's encounter with Jesus on the road to Damascus was very dramatic. What he saw and heard that day marked him forever. It was the turning point of his life and the beginning of his service for the Lord. During that encounter, Paul asked the most important question in life when he said, "Who art thou, Lord?" Jesus responded by saying, "I am Jesus whom thou persecutest."

When Paul realized who he was speaking with, he asked the second most important question in life. He asked, "Lord, what wilt thou have me to do?" Jesus did not respond by saying, "Oh, I don't know, Paul. I just apprehended you today because I felt sorry for you; I didn't want you to go to hell. I'll talk to the Father and see if there is anything you can do for Us." Rather, when Paul asked, "Lord, what wilt thou have me to do?" Jesus responded with these words,

"Arise, and go into the city, and it shall be told thee what thou must do."

Acts 9:6

Jesus informed Paul that there were things he "must do." The word "must" is from the Greek *dei* and can mean, "a necessity established by the counsel and decree of God." Jesus' words to Paul were strong and clear. But the words He spoke were not only true concerning Paul; they are also true concerning you. There are things you must do!

Years later, Paul recounted those words Jesus spoke in a meeting with his Jewish brethren. He stated,

"...And the Lord said unto me, Arise, and go into Damascus; and there it shall be told thee of all things which are appointed for thee to do."

Acts 22:10

Jesus told Paul that there were "things which are appointed for thee to do." The word "appointed" comes from the Greek *tasso* and means, "to ordain, to pre-determine, or to arrange things in a certain order." Before Paul was saved there were works assigned to him; works pre-determined by God for him to do. This reality is also true concerning you. There are things appointed for you to do!

When God called you, He called you for a purpose. When He made you a vessel in His house it was because He already had works planned for you. You are, "[God's] workmanship, created in Christ Jesus unto good works, which God hath before ordained that [you] should walk in them" [Eph. 2:10]. You are part of the "us" in Paul's word to Timothy when he wrote,

> *"Who hath saved us, and called us with an holy calling, not according to our own works, but according to his own purpose and grace..."*
>
> *II Timothy 1:9*

Just as Paul was a chosen and graced vessel, you are a chosen and graced vessel. There is no doubt about this fact. Only one question remains, "Are you willing and prepared to do the works assigned to you?"

Fulfill Your Ministry

When Jesus concluded His earth ministry, He spoke these words to the Father,

> *"I have glorified thee on the earth: I have finished the work which thou gavest me to do."*
>
> *John 17:4*

The word "finished" Jesus used is the Greek *teleioo* which means, "to accomplish, or to carry through completely to the end." Believers must follow the example of Jesus by completing the works God assigns to them. Finishing pre-assigned works glorifies God!

The book of Acts records these words about John the Baptist,

> *"And as John fulfilled his course..."*
>
> *Acts 13:25*

The word "fulfilled" in this verse comes from the Greek *pleroo*. This word means, "to fill to the top so that nothing shall be wanting, to make complete in every particular, to carry through to the end, to accomplish, to execute." John the Baptist's ministry was very unique. It was short and distinguished by this simple message: "Repent, get ready, the Messiah is coming." Although John did no miracles, he was declared by Jesus to be the greatest prophet that ever lived [Jn. 10:41].

John prepared a group of disciples that Jesus could draw from and helped set things in motion for Jesus' three years of ministry.

The book of Acts records this testimony from God concerning David,

"...I have found David the son of Jesse, a man after mine own heart, which shall fulfill all my will."

Acts 13:22

The word "fulfill" in this scripture is the Greek *poieo*. It is most often translated "do." *Poieo* carries the idea of causing something, producing something, or being the place from which something shoots forth. After King Saul failed to do God's will, God looked for a man with a different kind of heart; a man committed to His purposes. David was the man which, God said, would "do" all His will.

When Paul knew by the Spirit that he must go up to Jerusalem and endure great trouble, he told the elders from Ephesus,

"But none of these things move me, neither count I my life dear unto myself, so that I might finish my course with joy, and the ministry, which I have received of the Lord Jesus..."

Acts 20:24

The word "finish" Paul used in this verse is the Greek *teleioo*, which means, "to accomplish or to carry through completely to the end." The realization that he had a course to finish and a ministry assignment to complete was one of the primary motivating forces in Paul's life. In his second letter to Timothy, he wrote,

"...I have finished my course."

II Timothy 4:7

The word "finished" Paul used here comes from the Greek *teleo*. *Teleo* means, "to perform, to execute, to complete, or to fulfill." It implies that the things accomplished correspond to the things assigned. Remaining conscious of the fact that he had been given a specific assignment helped Paul to complete his specific course.

In his epistle to the Colossians, Paul included a strong word for a man named Archippus. Apparently, Archippus needed some encouragement concerning his stewardship, so Paul wrote,

> *"...Say to Archippus, Take heed to the ministry which thou has received in the lord, that thou fulfill it."*
>
> Colossians 4:17

The words "take heed" come from the Greek *blepo* which means, "to discern, to perceive, or to discover." Archippus was to discover his ministry, accurately discerning what the Lord had given to him. The word "received" comes from the Greek *paralambano* and means, "to join one's self to something, or to not reject something offered." Archippus was to embrace his ministry and join himself to it, taking ownership of what God had offered him. The word "fulfill" Paul used comes from the Greek *pleroo* which means, "to fill up, to consummate, or to perform." Archippus was to discern the ministry he had been given, engage fully in it, perform it, and fulfill it. The Amplified Bible renders Paul's words for Archippus this way,

> *"And say to Archippus, See that you discharge carefully [the duties of] the ministry and fulfill the stewardship which you have received in the Lord."*
>
> Colossians 4:17 Amp

Don't Let Your Grace Be in Vain

In his first letter to the Corinthians, Paul wrote these words,

> *"...and his grace which was bestowed upon me was not in vain; but I laboured more abundantly than they all: yet not I, but the grace of God which was with me."*
>
> I Corinthians 15:10

The Amplified Bible renders his words this way,

> *"...His grace toward me was not [found to be] for nothing — fruitless and without effect. In fact, I worked harder than all of them [the*

apostles], though it was not really I, but the grace...of God which was with me."

I Corinthians 15:10 Amp

The grace bestowed upon Paul was not in vain; it was not "fruitless and without effect." It is possible, however, that ministry graces be stewarded to believers in vain. In the parable of the talents, the servant entrusted with one talent did not use his talent and made no increase for his master. The talent stewarded to him was, therefore, stewarded in vain.

In the spiritual life, the "one talent man" is often most in danger of not using what has been stewarded to him. The man with five talents knows he has been entrusted with something significant. The man with two talents knows that he has received something notable from the Lord. The man with one talent, on the other hand, may think that what has been stewarded to him is really not that significant and, therefore, fail to make use of his talent.

In his first letter, Peter declared that "every man hath received the gift" [I Pet. 4:11]. The word "received" comes from the Greek *lambano*. One meaning of *lambano* is, "to receive what is offered, to take possession of, or to lay hold of a thing in order to use it." Jesus used this word *lambano* in His parable of the talents when He said,

"And so he that had received [lambano] five talents came and brought other five..."

Matthew 25:20

The householder in the parable "gave" talents to his servants. Notice, however, that each servant had to "receive" the talents. They had to take possession of the talents given to them, use them as if they were their own, and make increase for the householder.

Like the servants who received talents, you must receive the grace-gift God has offered to you. You must take possession of it. You must lay hold of it and make it your own. You must use it as a good steward of the manifold grace of God and make increase for the Master.

Giving An Account

When Jesus comes again, every believer will give an account, not only of what they have done with their own life, but also of what they have done with the grace-gifts entrusted to them. Those who have been given much will be expected to report a substantial increase for the Master's kingdom. Those who have been entrusted with a lesser measure will be expected to report an increase proportional to what they were stewarded. Every believer will give an account to the Lord of what he has "done in the body" [II Cor. 5:10].

Those who faithfully employ what has been entrusted to them will be judged as "good stewards of the manifold grace of God" [I Pet. 4:10]. They will receive words of commendation from the Master and be entrusted with a greater realm of ministry in the future. Those who were unfaithful and failed to make use of their talents will be judged as unfit servants. What they have will be taken from them and their future could be in jeopardy.

Jesus addressed His own disciples concerning the issue of faithful service with these words,

> *"Who then is a faithful and wise servant, whom his lord hath made ruler over his household, to give them meat in due season? Blessed is that servant, whom his lord when he cometh shall find so doing."*
> *Matthew 24:45-46*

Like all other believers, you have been called to serve in the household of God. There is a "meat" you are expected to distribute in due season. Will you be faithful and wise? Will you work in your season to give what has been stewarded to you? The servant who is "so doing" when the Lord returns will be blessed. Jesus said this concerning the faithful and wise servant,

> *"Verily I say unto you, That he shall make him ruler over all his goods."*
>
> *Matthew 24:47*

Notice that Jesus began this statement with "Verily." His words are a strong statement of fact. If you are faithful in service, you will be rewarded. If, however, you are not faithful there will be no reward. In the same context, Jesus said this concerning the unfaithful servant,

> *"The lord of that servant shall come in a day when he looketh not for him, and in an hour that he is not aware of, And shall cut him asunder, and appoint him his portion with the hypocrites: there shall be weeping and gnashing of teeth."*
>
> Matthew 24:50-51

Just Do It!

According to His own will, God called you, placed you in the body of Christ, and stewarded a unique ministry grace to you. Now you must decide whether or not you will locate, cultivate, and be a good steward of that grace. I encourage you to emulate the two faithful servants in the parable of the talents. Accept the plan of God. Lay hold of the grace stewarded to you and make it your own. Prepare yourself by developing a strong, steadfast personal life. Cultivate your grace and become an expert in your ministry. Then get out in the market place of life and minister to others according to what God has stewarded to you.

As you minister faithfully and skillfully, you will bring increase to the kingdom of God, be a great blessing to others, and ensure for yourself rewards and these wonderful words from your Lord, "Well done good and faithful servant."

If you fail to minister by the grace given to you, others will be robbed of heavenly blessings and God's kingdom will suffer loss. You will be the log jam in the flow of God's gifts to His own and to the lost. Because of your failure, some people will remain broken hearted. Some will remain untaught. Some will remain sick. Some will be without direction. Some will remain discouraged. If you are not faithful to administer your grace, the body of Christ will be deficient in the area you are graced. You will also suffer personal loss in the future in terms of rewards.

Right now there are people waiting for you. Right now, God is depending upon you. Never say, "I am not equipped for this job." Never say, "I can't fulfill my calling." Rather, say of yourself, "I am a steward of grace. Something divine has been entrusted to me. I have been grace-gifted to serve the Lord effectively. I have something unique that people need. I have an assignment and I have the adequate power and supernatural sufficiency to complete it. I am going to locate my grace-gift, embrace it, manage it, cultivate it, and use it for the benefit of God and his kingdom!"

Contact Information

If you enjoyed *Grace for Effectual Ministry* and would like to know more about Guy Duininck and the work of Master's Touch Ministries, note the Contact Information below. God Bless!

Guy Duininck
Master's Touch Ministries
Box 35543
Tulsa, OK 74153

Guy Duininck @ Facebook
Master's Touch Ministries @ Facebook
www.masterstouchministries.com